ANYONE CAN SCULPT

ANYONE CAN SCULPT

REVISED EDITION

ARTHUR ZAIDENBERG

A BOOK OF ESTABLISHED AND
NEW METHODS AND TECHNIQUES
FOR AMATEURS AND STUDENTS

1817

HARPER & ROW, PUBLISHERS

NEW YORK, EVANSTON, SAN FRANCISCO, LONDON

 For information address Harper & Row, Publishers, Inc., 49 East 33rd Street, New York, N.Y. 10016. Published simultaneously in Canada by Fitzhenry & Whiteside Limited, Toronto.

STANDARD BOOK NUMBER: 06–014800–4

LIBRARY OF CONGRESS CATALOG CARD NUMBER: 76–138776

TO TOMMY

CONTENTS

FOREWORD

Since this book appeared in its original edition I have done a great deal of sculpting in many media, especially in welding iron, steel, and bronze. In the course of revising it I have added a large section on the methods of welding as well as other techniques of sculpture which I have learned in the past few years.

Because I believe profoundly that the soundest method of teaching is to instruct at the same time that one learns, I am imparting to the student who works with this book the methods I have found to work for me.

That there are other methods and certainly more experienced teachers of some of these sculpture forms I have no doubt, but it is hoped that the student will achieve a freedom of approach from those outlined here and go on to further studies, for an artist studies and learns throughout his creative life.

ACKNOWLEDGMENTS

The author wishes to acknowledge with thanks the valuable aid and advice of the Sculpture Center, Sculpture House, Segy Gallery, A. A. A. Gallery, the Rudolph Gallery (Woodstock, N. Y.), Amy Small, sculptress, and the Metropolitan Museum of Art.

The following photographs are reproduced through the courtesy of:
Sculpture House (N. Y.): pp. 20, 21, 23, 36, 37, 38, 39, 41, 42, 43, 51, 52, 55, 56, 57, 64, 65, 126, 130
Metropolitan Museum of Art (N. Y.): pp. 22, 27, 28, 29, 132, 153
Amy Small: p. 29
Jacques Heliczer: pp. 29, 142, 143, 144
Union Carbide Corporation: pp. 98, 102, 103, 104
Robert Palmer: pp. 106, 108
Jeremiah W. Russell: p. 114
Bernie Nathan: p. 118
Joseph Forman: pp. 158, 159
Segy Gallery (N. Y.): p. 160
Rudolph Gallery (Woodstock): p. 149
A. A. A. Gallery: pp. 81, 89, 140, 156
Werner Muckenhirn: pp. 165, 166

INTRODUCTION

In the past few years sculpture has reached heights of public popularity of a magnitude certainly equal to that of painting, a situation which has not existed since the Golden Age of Greece.

Innumerable galleries have sprung up devoted entirely to contemporary sculpture and a market exists for the sculptor's work as rich and thriving as that for the painter's.

Whereas practically the only source of interest in professional sculptors' output in the past was the public monument field or the commissioned "bust" of some dignitary, now the general art-loving public crowd the museums and galleries to see the wide range of exhibitions by the many brilliant and inventive sculptors of our time, and modest collectors as well as the museums follow the widely varied schools of modern sculpture with passionate attention.

The art columns of newspapers and magazines review and reproduce examples from sculpture exhibits, and book publishers print splendid editions about contemporary sculptors which are eagerly bought by a large public.

This happy renaissance of the field of sculpture may be attributed to a number of causes, not the least of which is a general awakening of intense awareness of all the arts. Specifically the great increase of interest in modern sculpture may be attributed to two additional major causes.

The first is education of the art public to new understanding of spatial values in art, introduced by the cubists and advanced by the many varieties of abstract concepts by which painters searched for new dimensions to escape the two-dimensional limits of their canvases, without recourse to eye "tricks" such as perspective and shadows. The obvious path to wider expression of spatial relationships lay in sculpture and many contemporary painters began to use both media of expression.

The second major cause of the involvement of artists with sculpture was the release from the almost exclusive use of ponderous materials which restricted their flights of fancy and demanded laborious struggles with the resistant character of those materials.

The many new technological advances placed in the hands of sculptors tools and materials which allow them to "play" creatively instead of devoting far too much physical effort to carving and chiseling "monuments."

It must not be inferred from the preceding paragraph that fine sculptors have all abandoned stone and wood carving and that these beautiful media are not valid in contemporary art expression. Use of these materials will be covered in this book and the student sculptor is strongly advised not to suppose that the "easy" medium is the one to be chosen automatically.

However, it is to the vast range of malleable metals and the innumerable synthetics, as well as the splendid tools now available to further the daring concepts of modern artists, that much of the freedom and excitement engendered in the contemporary sculptural scene must be attributed.

ANYONE CAN SCULPT

ANYONE CAN SCULPT

The title of this book is not intended to convey the idea that sculpture is easy, a craft and art to be practiced lightly and casually, one which requires no study or serious application to its inherent problems.

The use of the term "anyone" carries with it no implication of disrespect for a medium of expression in which great art has been expressed throughout the history of man. "Anyone" implies that man has potential for accomplishing things which require a high degree of dexterity and finesse, a fact which has been demonstrated in innumerable ways and among the widest range of peoples of all classes and culture. Millions learn to write script (a skill of no mean requirements), embroider, make pottery, and play musical instruments, among countless other accomplishments. All these call for a discipline which can easily be measured against that required for modeling and carving.

The impulse to practice these above-mentioned commonplace skills has always existed. They are accepted social activities, regarded as proper studies for children and as normal accomplishments of the average person of fair education.

The proficiency attained by great numbers of people is considered remarkable only by those who practice no manual art. In towns in Europe where virtually everyone, from early childhood, makes lace or embroiders highly intricate designs, the prevalent wonder is, not that they can do these things, but that others cannot.

I mentioned previously the skill of writing script. If the reader will consider for a moment, the extraordinary fact that every child in school soon becomes proficient in this truly fluent and difficult manual discipline is curiously taken for granted. I am sure that we should all be appalled at the thought of learning to write script for the first time as adults—from scratch, so to speak. We should devise a platitude similar to the one commonly groaned when learning to draw is suggested to an adult, "I can't draw a straight line." Yet, given no choice, no refusal, nor possibility of failure admissible, we all learn to contrive fairly legible script, some of us truly beautiful script, with a minimum of pain and struggle in the learning process.

I have maintained in other books that anyone can draw and paint. These generalizations were always accompanied by the repeated qualifying statements that anyone can if he really wants to apply himself with unstinting honesty, sufficient time, and rich amount of curiosity and sense of experiment.

I repeat, in all sincerity, the statement that "anyone can sculpt"—providing that he add to the above-mentioned qualifications, a love of manual labor, for, let us face it, sculpting entails a good deal of that, and it is not the least pleasurable part of it.

In this book I shall approach the sculpture process with, I hope, the freshness that necessarily comes with new discovery and an unacademic attitude. My personal view of the art of sculpture is that it is one which is least restrained by orthodoxy. The wide range of materials available, the infinite numbers of tools from which to choose and the inventive possibilities allowable in a medium which ranges from whittling to mobiles has made somewhat dated the professional sculptors' academic attitude toward materials and their use.

Unlike the painting process which is limited to the use of pigments for coloring and only varies in their application in combination with a medium (i.e., oil, egg tempera, or water), sculpture employs virtually every conceivable solid from clay to stone and metal and, in many modern conceptions, a combination of many of these substances in one work.

It would be quite impossible for any one "master" to be expert in the vast range of this medium of art expression where each material calls for its own inventive approach and contains within itself limitations.

It is true that for such time-honored sculpture processes as bronze casting the expert is essential as an instructor. But in this ever less popular medium of sculpture the professional caster has replaced the sculptor and the highly technical process is now out of the direct hand of the artist and in the technician's workshop.

For the carving of wood, the choosing of stone, or the modeling of plasteline, the expert is not required. The materials and tools have their own voices and soon impose their own discipline on the experimental student.

HOW TO USE THIS BOOK

This book does not intend to imply that it will teach you all there is to know about the techniques of sculpturing, nor does it pretend to make a sculptor of you. What it may, and I devoutly believe it can do, is to imbue you with some of the zest for the joys of modeling and carving and free you from some of the fears which beset every beginner.

When you have skimmed through the various chapters on the different sculpture processes, choose one approach that appeals to you. Special care has been taken to compile this book in such a manner as to simplify the process steps. Perhaps this has been done at the risk of oversimplification, and in some cases, a process step may have been eliminated which, if included in your work, might make for longer life to your piece or perhaps greater strength. If this has happened in a number of cases it has been a calculated risk.

I am not of the school which considers craftsmanship as its own reward. The statement, to me, is worth far more than the process, and if in eliminating time-honored steps and hoary strictures, I have eliminated boredom and barriers to creation, I have achieved my intention.

There is included in each chapter a list of materials, tools, etc., the minimum necessary to the basic approach. This minimum is listed with an eye toward economy, a supposition that there is not a well-furnished sculpture supply shop around the corner from your home, and a consideration of the nuisance value of an overabundance of tools and paraphernalia calculated to confuse and frighten the neophyte.

I remember well the shocked pity of several of my friends who are sculptors upon seeing my early efforts and noticing the few amateur tools with which I had tackled relatively ambitious projects.

I do not deny that subsequent experience (and I wish to acknowledge the value of the advice of these friends) proved to me that more professional tools and equipment helped to ease my labors. But, had I waited for the advice, arranged for the purchase and learned the use of each of these tools and paraphernalia, I should have delayed my happy plunge into a lively project.

Item: Hold on to your happy innocence. It will lead you into paths of discovery sooner than will the instruction of the best of teachers.

The above advice should not lead you to suppose that bad tools are preferable to good ones. By all means observe in these pages the repeated advice, "Keep your tools sharp."

Each tool must further your needs and not hamper them. That does not mean that a homemade one cannot often do what a store tool does, or that inventiveness in contriving ingenious modeling tools will rob you of your serious status as a sculptor.

In utilizing this book do not feel that the methods suggested are the only ones. You may have encountered others. These are suggested for you if you know no others. They have accomplished their purpose for me and may well do so for you, but your choice should be free and critical.

Plunge bravely into whichever of the processes you decide upon. The only punishment for failure is that you will have to do it over. Do not lose your purposefulness for that reason. You are sure to have innumerable failures from the most severe and critical standpoint. From the fun and progress standpoint they will all be successes if you retain your enthusiasm.

Imparting enthusiasm for the media of sculpture is one of the main themes of this book.

TIME AND SUBJECT

The sculpture process is inevitably a slow one requiring, as it does, a preparatory procedure much more elaborate than that of any of the other arts. One can approach a prepared canvas, in painting, colors already mixed in tubes, and begin painting directly in the explicit terms required to express that which one wishes to express. In writing or in music there are no mechanical delays to giving forth with ideas or sound.

Also, the poor sculptor must undergo a stern period of "working while waiting" in order that he may reach that point in his material when the actual creative process may come into full play.

If he chooses to work in the modeling materials clay, plasteline, etc., he must prepare a suitable base and armature; then, before he can really model, he must build up the mass which never again will be seen but will become the "stuffing"—the entrails and guts of his creation.

If he carves wood or stone, he must chop and whittle until he reaches that point in the resisting mass of hard substance where he may begin to express the contours and forms he seeks.

In choosing a subject for sculpture, the guiding consideration is always the material. It is obvious that stone or wood do not lend themselves to the same subject freedom as does clay. Modeling allows for expansion of gesture; carving is confined to the limits of the piece of raw wood or stone. Conception and realization, in a work of art, are difficult enough without imposing the additional struggles involved in combating the material's natural opposition.

But, it must be borne in mind that one must not let the material become the ruler. Good sculptors have achieved in carvings of stone or wood the fluidity and play usually associated with the modeling materials, and notable pieces of monumental and monolithic strength have been evolved from the soft modeling materials.

Landscape obviously is ruled out by the character of the sculpture medium. Things of contained volume, of simple bulk and outline are best for carving. Subjects of more fluidity may be approached in clay, but always unity and simplicity are desirable features. In the really free form sculpture, and in mobiles and stabiles, the subject choice is as free as the imagination.

DRAWING FOR SCULPTURE

PAINTERS often take to sculpture in order that they may, through working in large masses, profit by the discipline and transfer qualities of solidity to their painting.

In a similar way, the sculptor should make drawings of his projected sculpture, primarily, as sketches from which to work out his plan since one cannot sketch in clay or stone, and also as line and form studies to guide structure.

Because drawing for sculpture is not an end in itself, a good deal of the self-consciousness which plagues the draftsman is noticeably lacking in drawings by sculptors. They tend to be freer at the same time as they have good solidity. Drawings by sculptors are usually very honest. The sculptor looks at the figure to be drawn for sculpture purposes much as a navigator scans the sea, not for superficial enjoyment of its surface beauties, but in order to judge by its character the course he must chart.

The sculptor's drawing is generally basic and simple.

A few generalizations may be learned in preparation for drawing the figure or forms of any kind. Here we shall briefly cover these generalizations in a manner which, to my best belief, is adequate to the simple direct approach.

WORKING FROM A MODEL

If you can find a model to pose for you, I would suggest that you do so. There is much to be learned from observing solid form, motionless for your study and emulation in clay. We all "know" the human figure from casual observation, in movement or in repose, but the opportunity to really study it will reveal to the student a unity and flow of structure from head to foot which must be transferred to the clay if your figure is to be sculptural in quality.

Liberties may be taken with anatomical truths; exaggerations are permissible and often desirable, but the essential architecture of the human figure is good. (I use the word "good" in its best sense, not to mean pretty or chic, or graceful, but rather to mean earthy, real, and satisfying.) That essential architecture, if transmitted to your study, will be good sculpture.

This essence lies in simplicity and can only be arrived at by disciplined elimination of the irrelevant and stress of the forms which are pertinent to the structure and flow.

If your town boasts an art school, there is a life class (unfortunately few small art schools have sculpture classes, but a corner of the life class will suffice for your modeling stand and a few pounds of clay). If there is no professional model available, you can persuade some friend to pose, if not nude, then in a bathing suit. You are not interested in skin tones, but in form. Have your model assume a simple, solid pose, one he or she can hold easily and naturally. Extravagant gestures may be left to your inventions without the model when you are not concerned chiefly with the study of the basic human form.

When you have arranged a satisfactory pose, study its meaning. What is the intention of the pose? Follow its flow until you arrive at a conclusion which may be expressed in two or three main lines of direction. These lines of direction should be interpreted in your armature.

The armature is not to be a complete skeleton, but rather a simple scaffold, firm but not so firm that your figure will be crucified on it. It should be sufficiently pliable so that it may be manipulated into positions that will never obtrude on your work, and yet support the inert masses of clay adequately.

Here are some figures and suggested armatures for figures about 15 inches in height—a size neither too small for solid form nor too large for quick study.

When you have constructed the most suitable armature for the pose, pause before you begin applying clay.

Study the main masses of form. Which masses are basic and which are relatively secondary? Where is the balance and which masses support the others?

Roll sausages of clay (see clay) and begin to apply them to your armature, the main supporting masses first, so as actually to face the architectural truths of the structure, the secondary forms to follow. Pack the clay well around the supporting armature, making the sausages of clay join together by pinching and merging one with another. Try to avoid air pockets or too thin connections.

As you build your figure, avoid stopping for small anatomical forms like fingers or toes. Your concern should be with the large forms and these, too, should be kept as simple as you can, avoiding the surface detail which is not relevant to the movement and structure.

When you come to smaller forms such as feet and hands, make them "sculpturesque"—i.e., sturdy supporting and functioning forms, not dainty appendages, weak and useless.

Do not "scratch draw" fingers and toes. Model the essential shape of the whole range of five fingers or five toes.

Form is a verb as well as a noun, and in making form, stress the verbal action.

An understanding of drawing is good for sculpture, but you are not using the drawing medium. Good line should be kept, but bear in mind that you are working in three dimensions, not simulating, but actually building those dimensions. The front, back, and sides of your work must be done in unison and not one at a time independent of the other.

When you have achieved a simple solid version of the model, don't, at this stage, attempt a portrait. Facial features and distinctive small details of hair, nails, special anatomical attributes of the particular model are less important to you than is the general human form.

Put some damp cloths around your figure, change the model's pose, or better still, shift your position to a different viewpoint and begin again.

ANATOMY FOR THE SCULPTOR

Human anatomy is extremely complex. Medical students will tell you that their anatomy course is one of the most heart-and-brain-breaking among the courses they must take.

Until relatively recent years, art students, both painters and sculptors, were required to study anatomy almost as thoroughly as medical students. My own sad waste of time at such studies in the Beaux Arts in Paris and in the National Academy in New York required an almost equal length of time devoted to forgetting what I had learned before I was able to feel free in drawing the figure as I saw it instead of as I knew it.

Study of internal anatomy is a little like the study of botany before attempting to paint flowers or geology before painting rocks. It is nice to know, but virtually superfluous to your needs as an art student unless you intend to do academic studies of an extremely realistic nature.

For most purposes, an observant eye, coupled with a general understanding of the main masses of form and their relation to each other is all you require for modeling or drawing the human figure in its essential character.

SKETCH FOR A FIGURE

Your first drawing sketch should be made with the concept in mind rather than as a working drawing for the mechanics of sculpture.

At this point you are still unencumbered by the resistance of the material. You are giving free rein to your flight of creative fancy and it should be unrestricted. Having conceived your theme and its freest expression, you must now decide which material of sculpture would be most suited to the execution of your concept. Does it call for the spontaneity and relative freedom of gesture possible in clay modeling, or does it need the monumental weight of stone to give it proper expression? Would it perhaps be best expressed in the uninhibiting medium of the mobile—in wire and glass, twine and what have you?

Having made your decision go back to sketching.

Your second sketch should be a "working drawing," i.e., a blueprint for the translation into terms of three dimensional sculpture your two dimensional drawing. This is the point at which the sketch for sculpture differs most from that which is made as a preliminary for painting.

It would be profitable for the student to see drawings made by sculptors and to notice how there invariably enters into the character of the drawing a concept of solidity, a three dimensional vista unusual in drawings by painters. Such drawings are available in reproduction and should be studied.

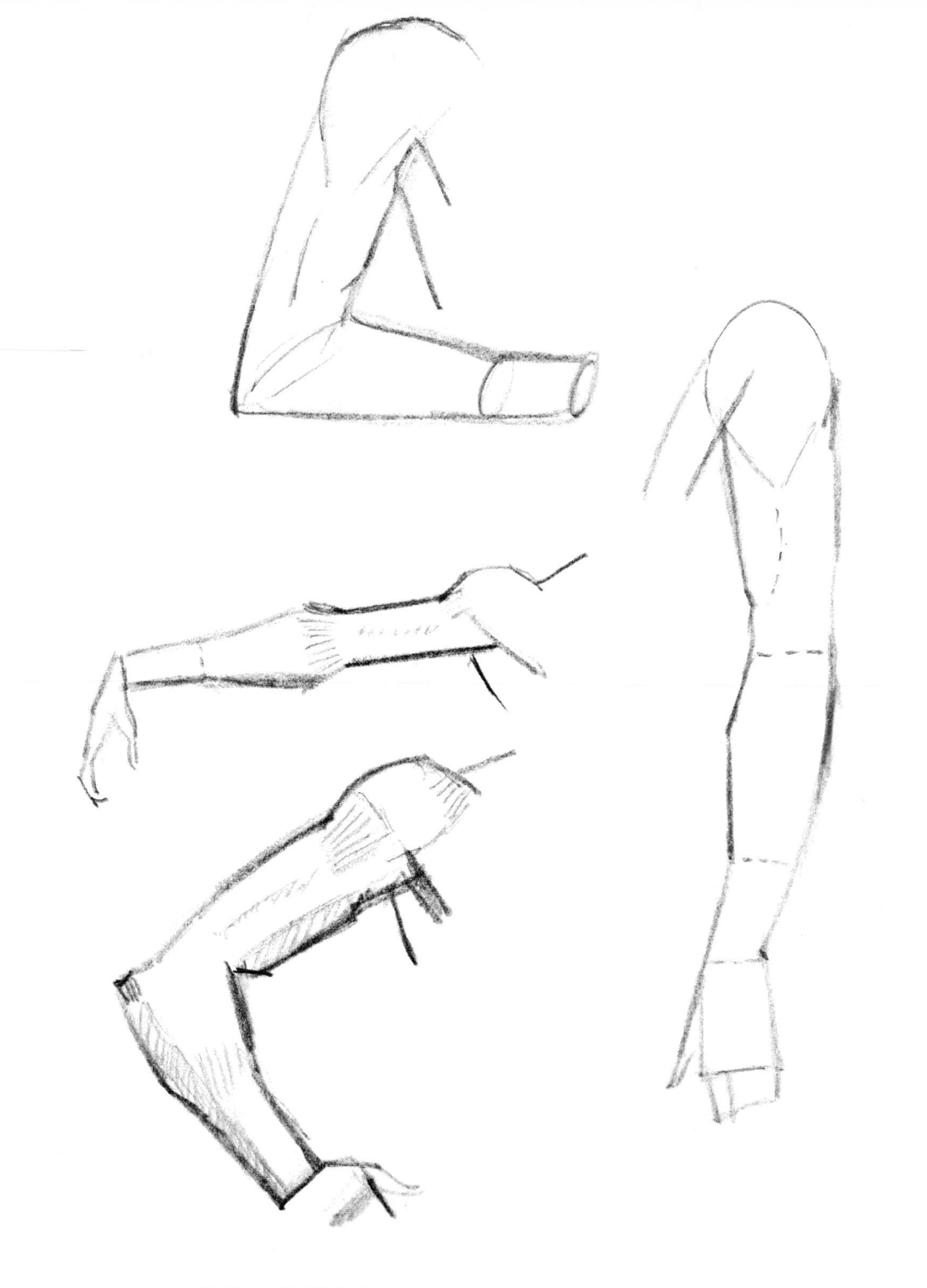

THE ARM

Boldness and strength in elimination of nonessentials and stressing or even exaggerating of component parts always results in sound drawing. It is especially true of drawing for sculpture.

These arms are reduced to the bare essentials of form.

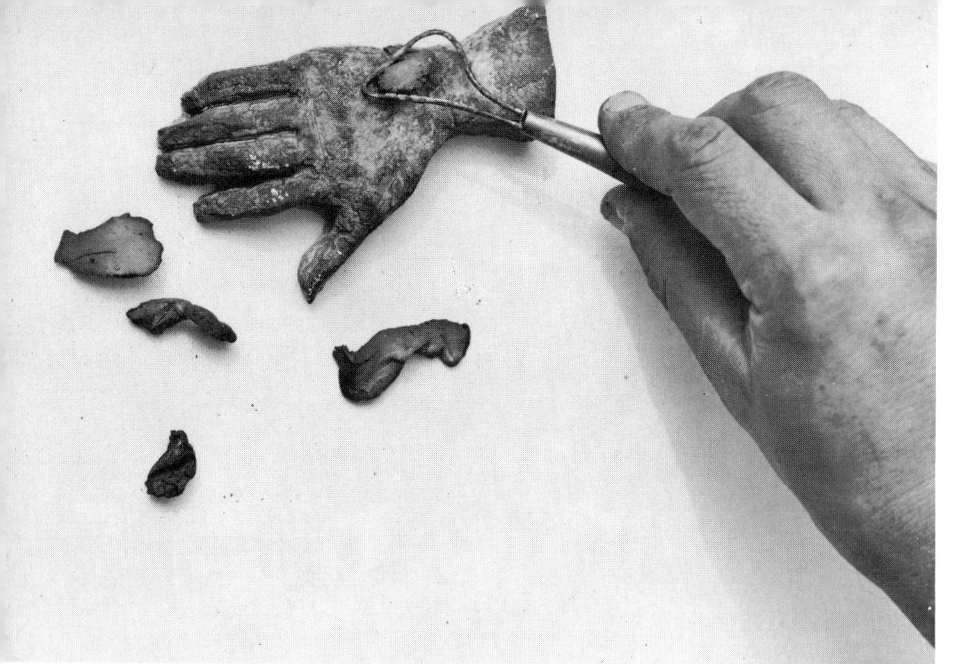

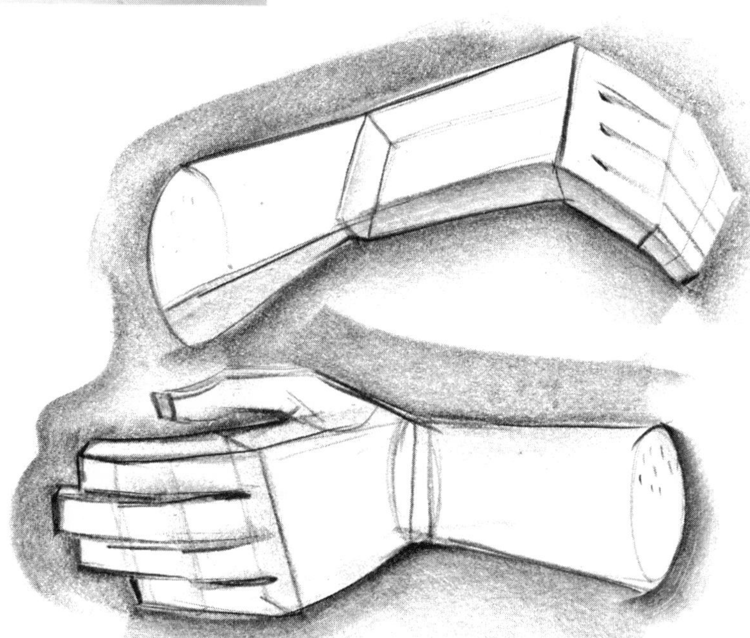

THE HAND

The wrist tube joins the oblong solid which is the back of the hand and palm at its narrow end.

The solid widens until it reaches the line of the knuckles where the range of the fingers begin.

See the fingers as tubes divided into three main parts, from the upper to the middle range of knuckles, then to the beginning of the range of small forms which are the tips.

Study the geometric simplifications of the accompanying drawings of hands.

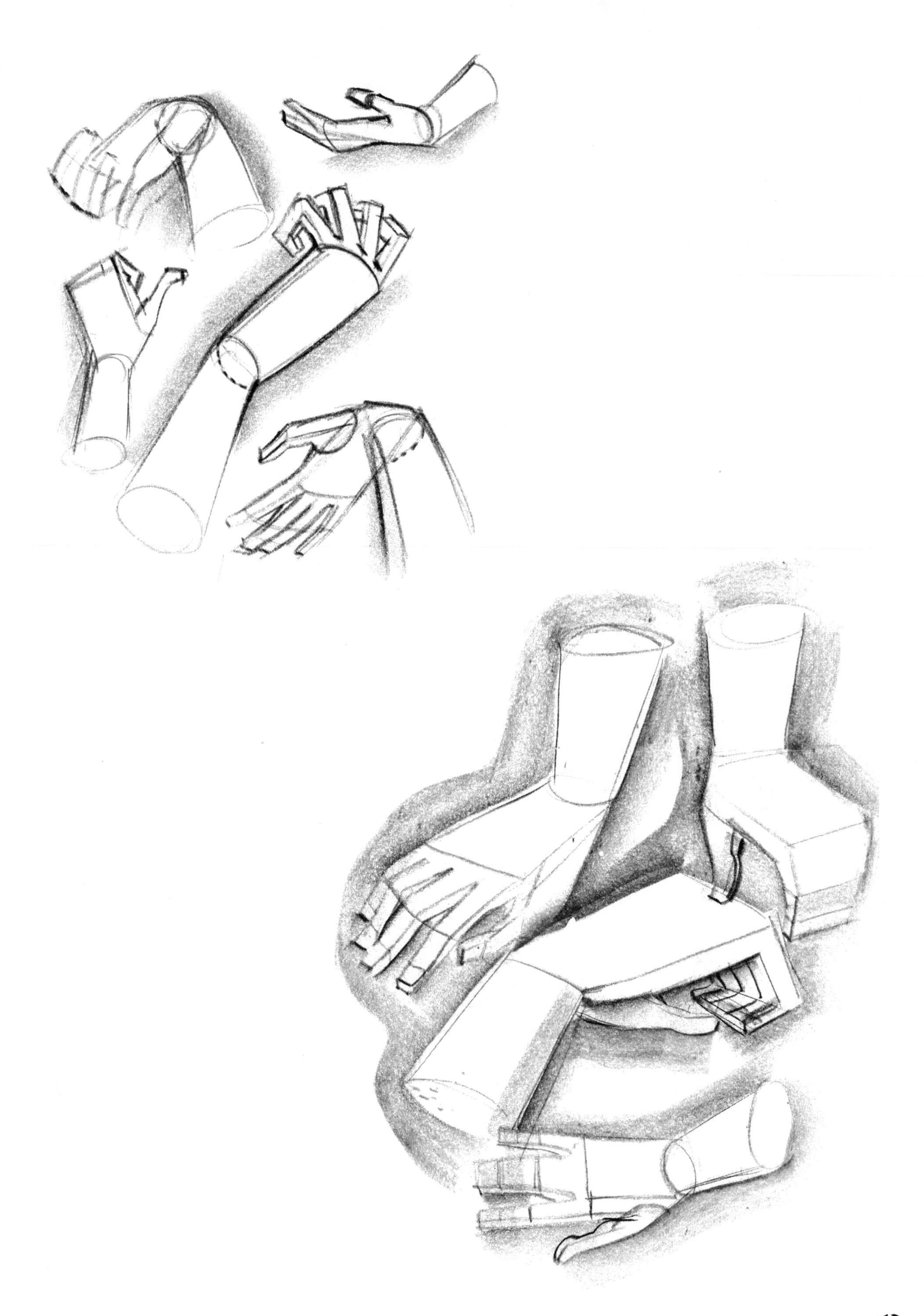

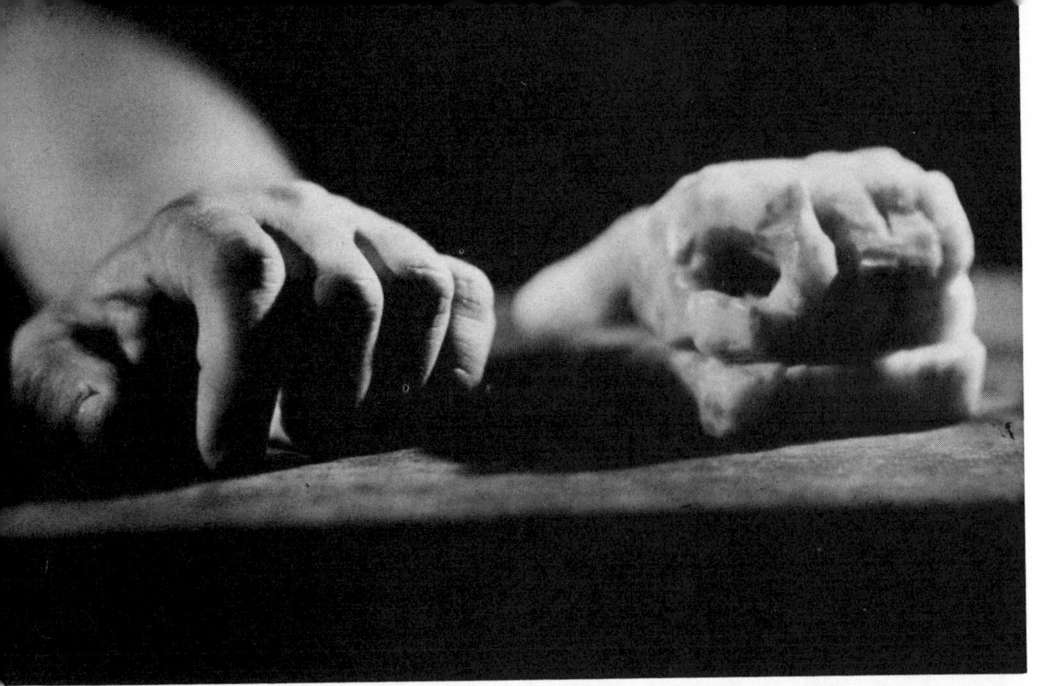

SOAP HANDS These hands are carved in soap. They serve as studies for carving in more permanent, hard material.

A small oblong cake of soap, a pocketknife or a razor blade are all you need in order to make such studies.

Make your quick pencil plan of the proposed hand, working it out in large planes with the third dimension in view.

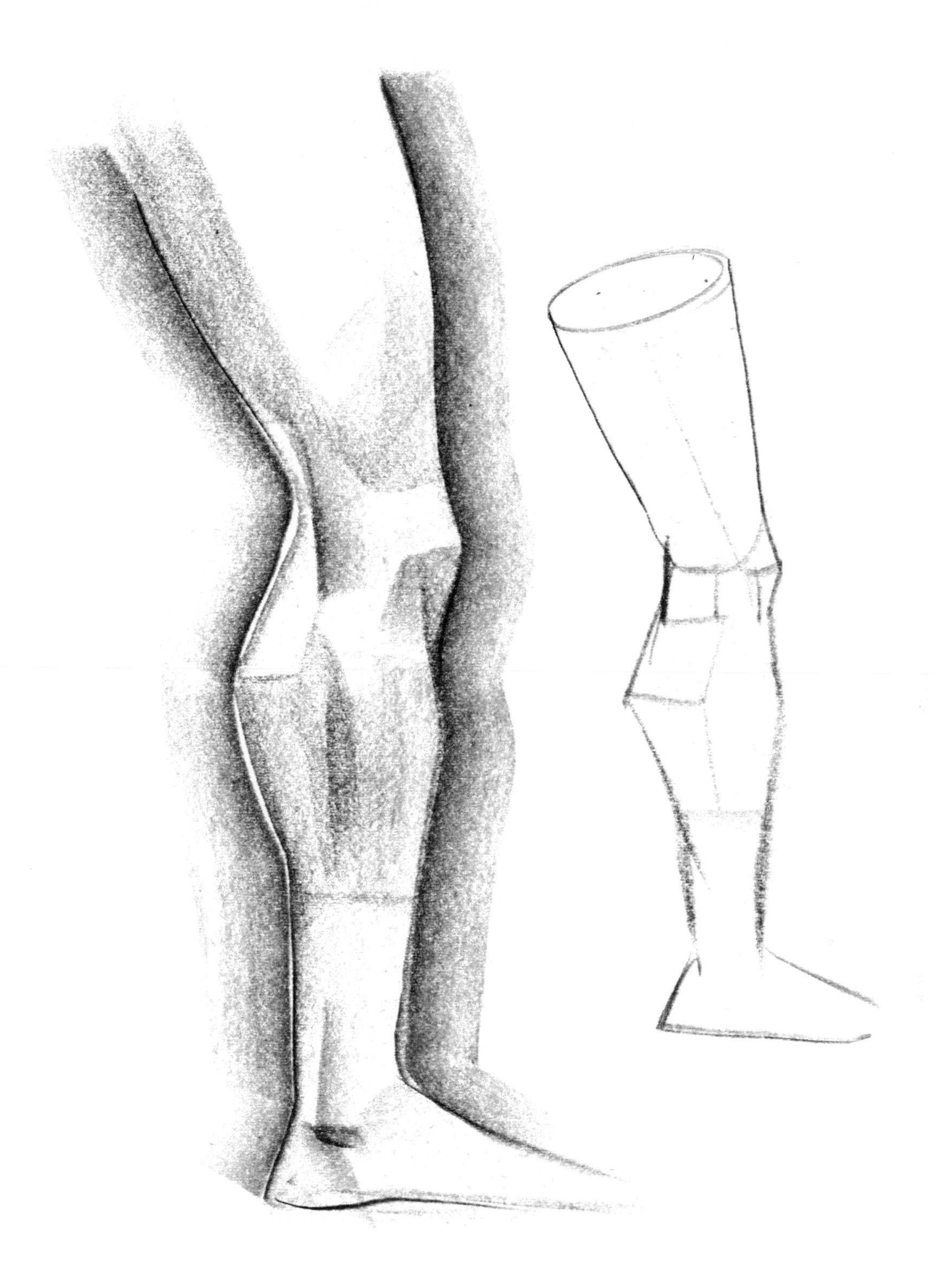

THE LEG

Legs must be viewed by the sculptor as what they in reality are—pedestals.

See the leg in terms of three main tube forms: (1) from the thigh to the knee joint, (2) from the knee to the lower end of the calf, (3) from the calf to the ankle joint at the apex of the triangle of the foot.

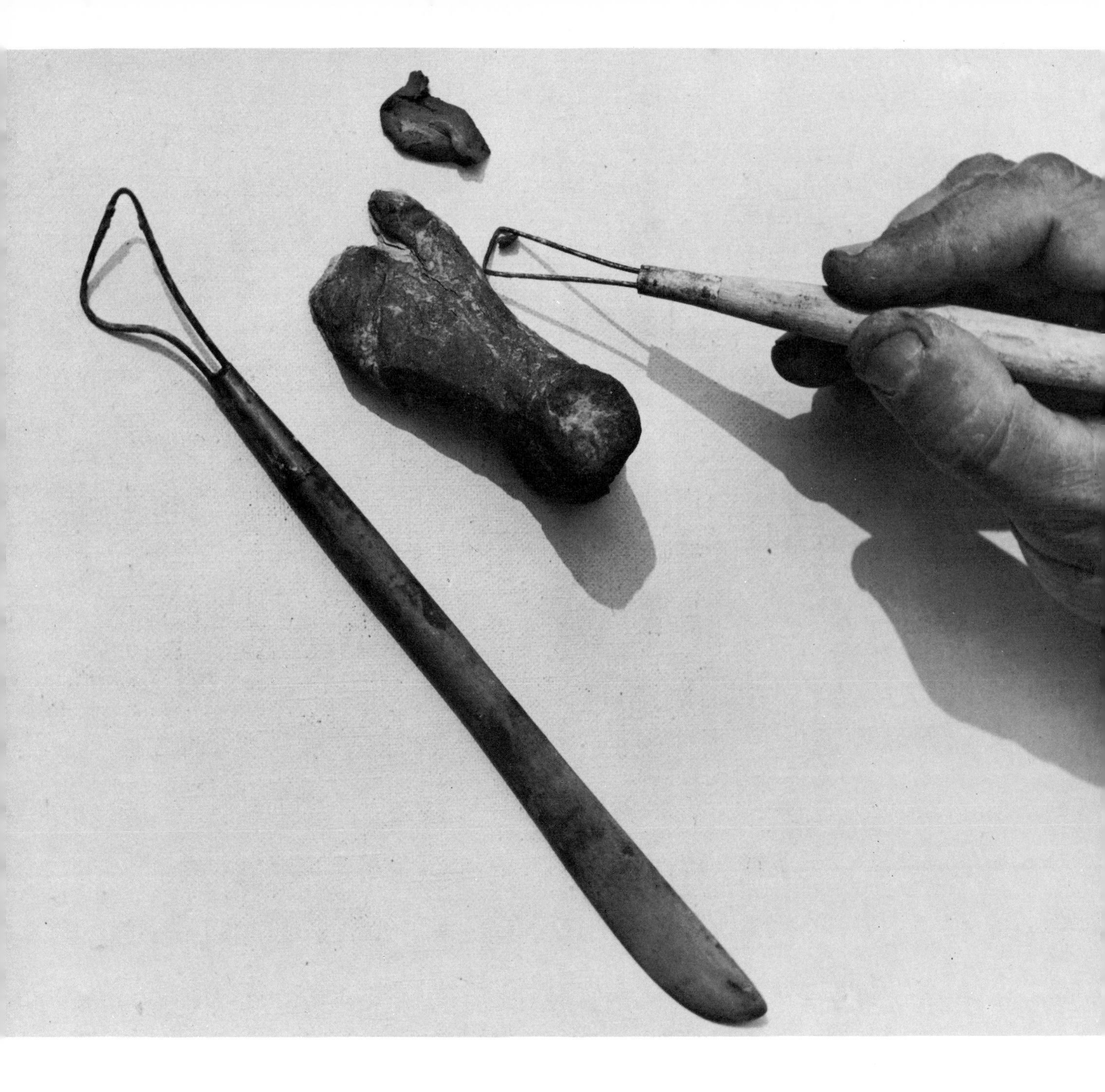

THE FOOT

Seen in profile at eye level, the foot is basically a triangle. The ankle tube descends into the apex firmly and the long gentle plane of the top of the foot descends to the range of the toes.

For sculpture purposes a drawing should not involve itself in the trivial and incidental. See the toes as a series of planes rather than as separate entities.

Notice how they are treated here.

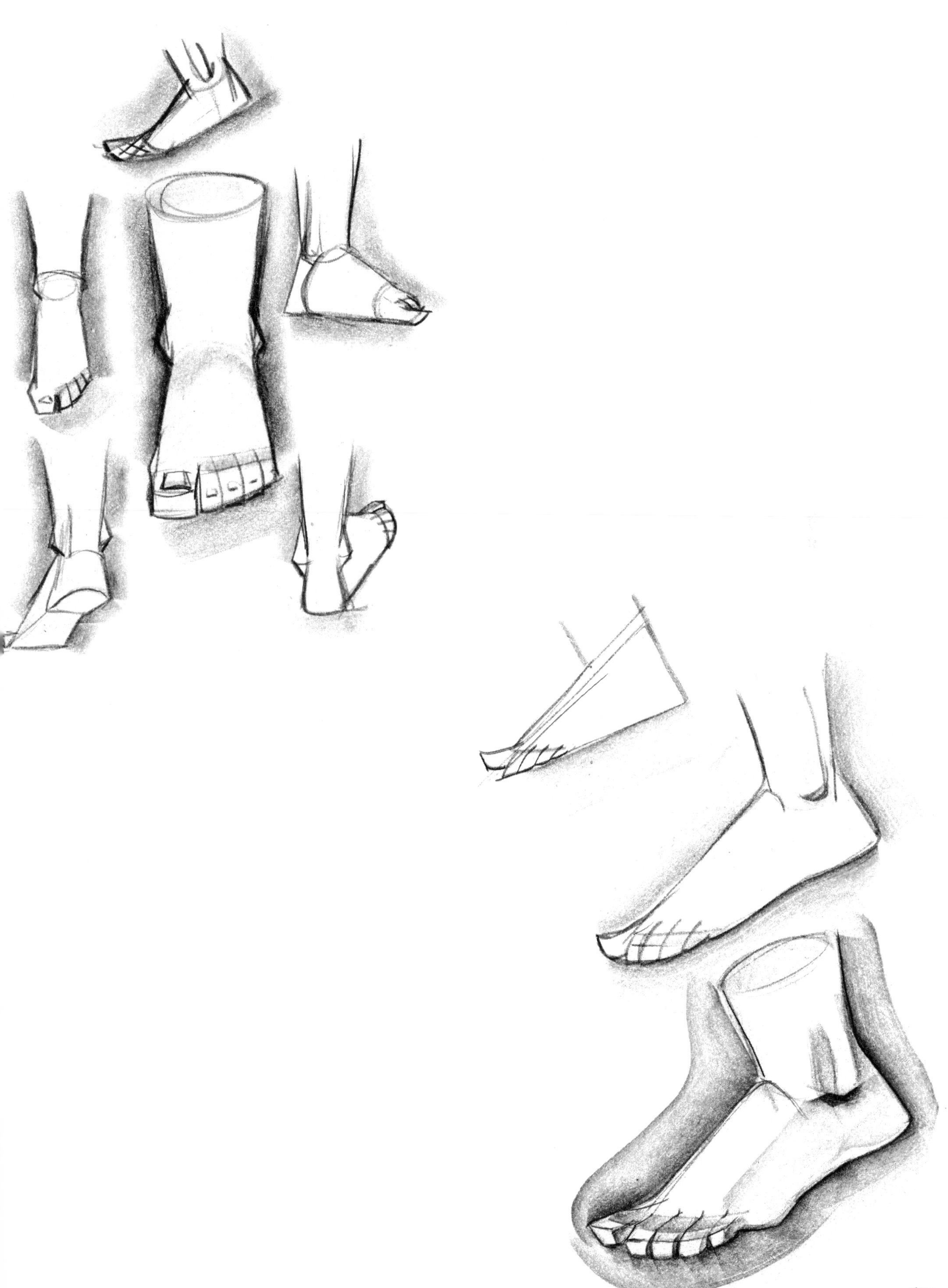

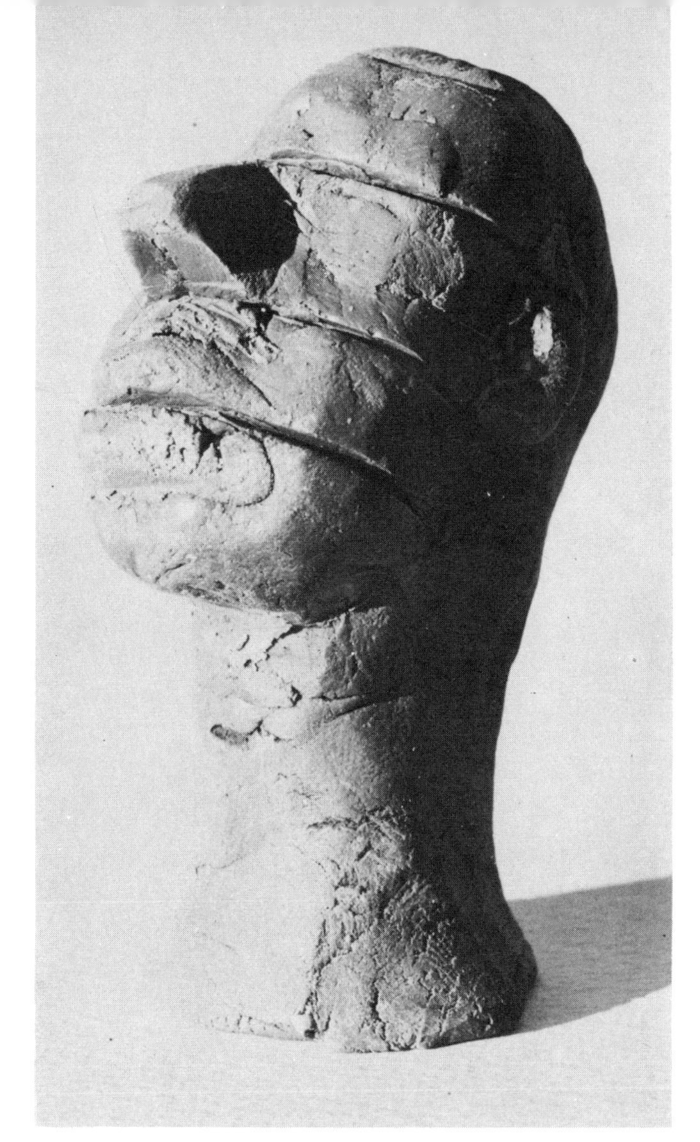
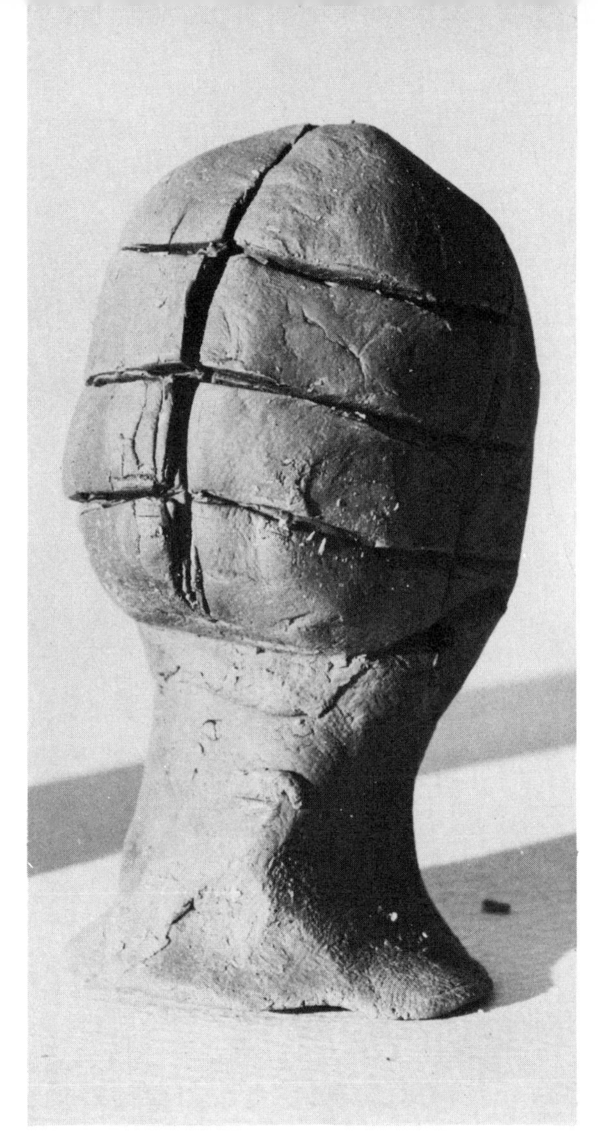

THE HEAD

In studying the head for eventual sculpture, draw its basic planes, searching out the geometric forms in which and upon which lie the secondary forms of the features.

In these studies of heads two approaches have been followed.

In one instance the heads have been treated as squared blocks exaggerating the sharpness of the plane separations in order to show the chief characteristics of these planes.

In the second plate the heads have been rounded closer to the actual but the planes are still marked.

The sculptor generally treats his modeling and carving in a somewhat similar manner, working from the rugged to the refined.

The incidentals of skin texture and coloring are not part of the sculptor's problem and he may concentrate fully on the form essence, which is the base of his sculptural interpretation of the head.

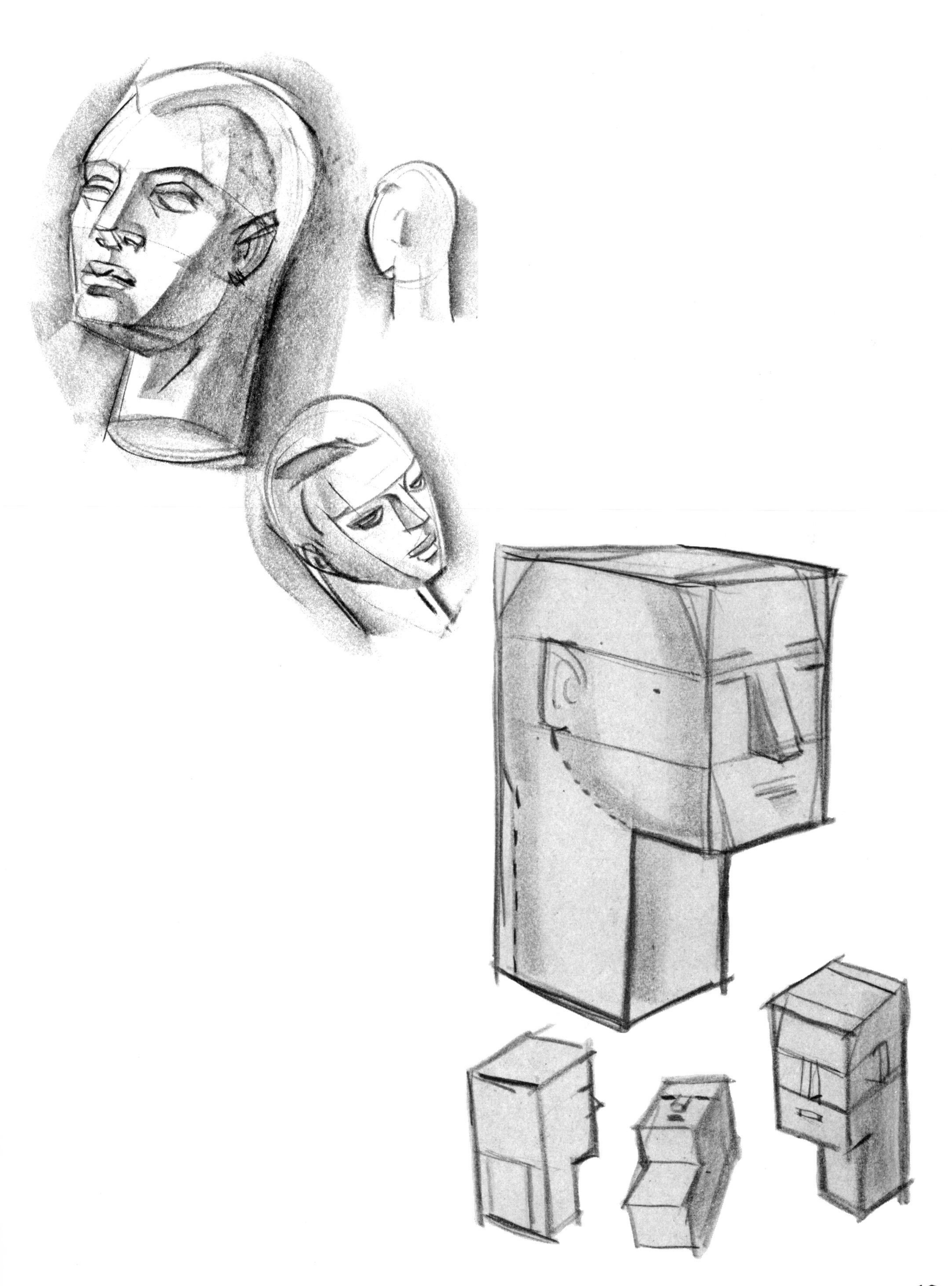

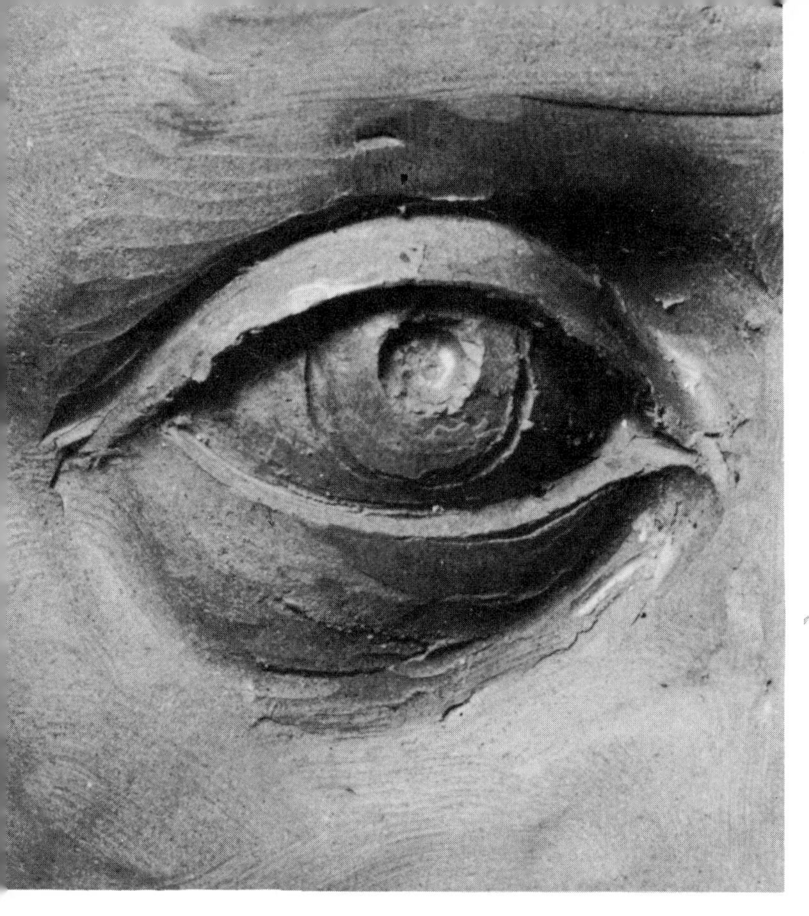

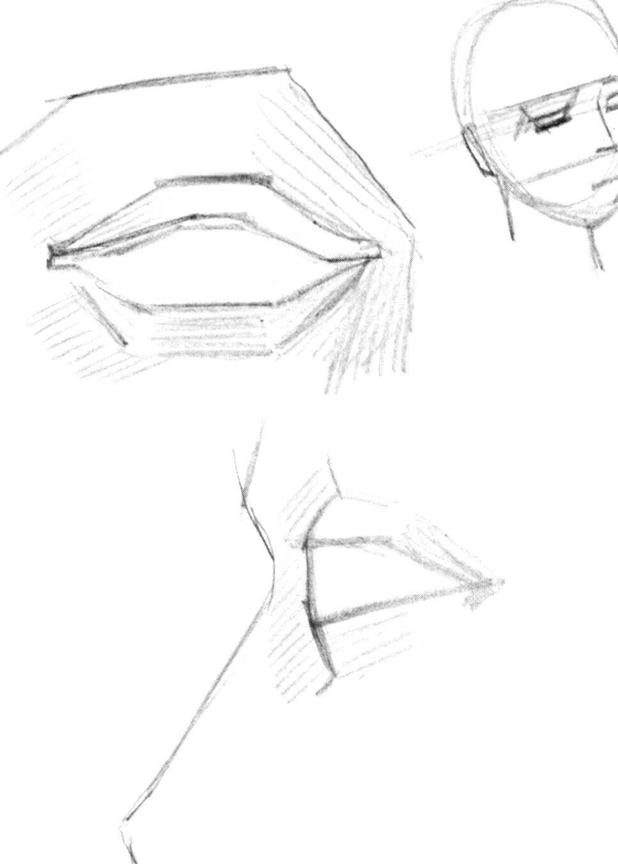

THE EYE

The usual sculpture piece, lacking color as an aid to explaining detail to the viewer, must rely on well-defined forms to indicate the character of a feature.

The eye is a thing of movement and sensitivity. To capture these characteristics is a subtle process. The tendency is to overload with scratched detail in the modeled eye.

A few well-modeled contours to suggest the planes of the eye and its firm position in the head often suggest far more than overdrawing.

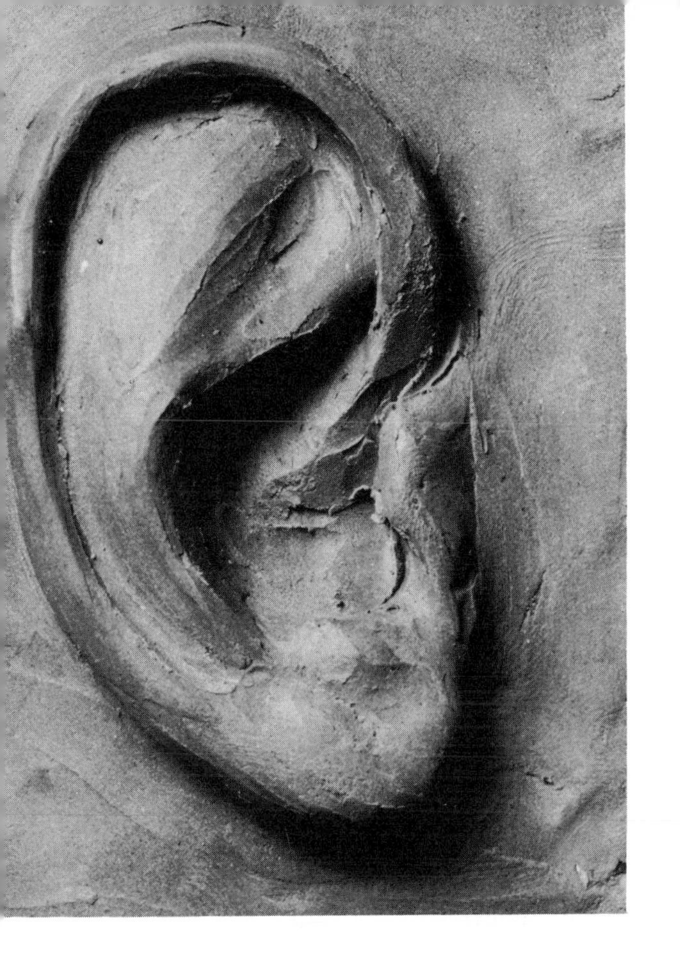

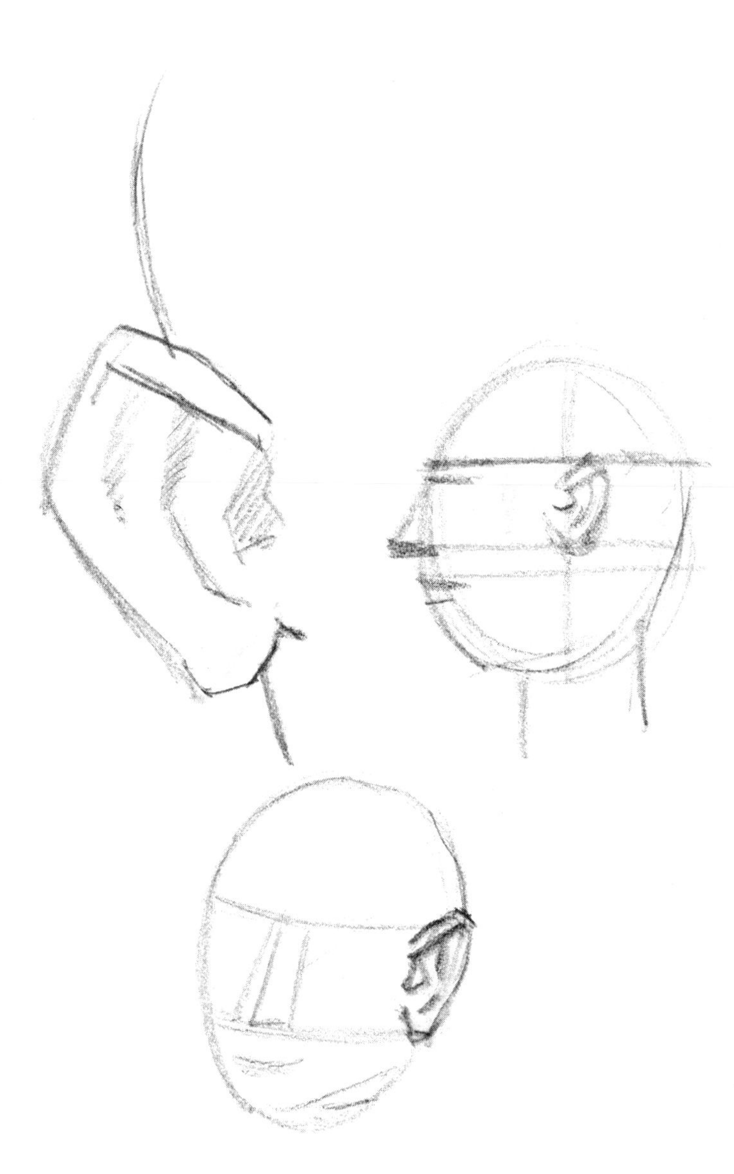

THE EAR

The ear is not a maze of directionless forms as it is so often drawn and modeled.

Study its contours so as to discover their paths and planes. In drawing the ear, simplify and search for strength.

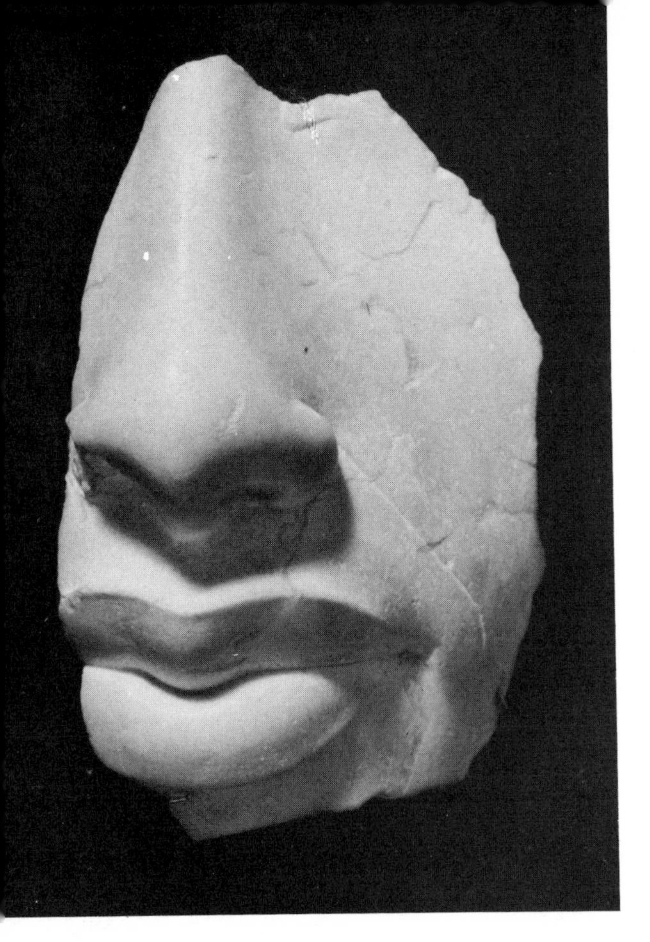

Queen Nefertiti, from el'Amarneh, 1375-1358 B.C., Egyptian.

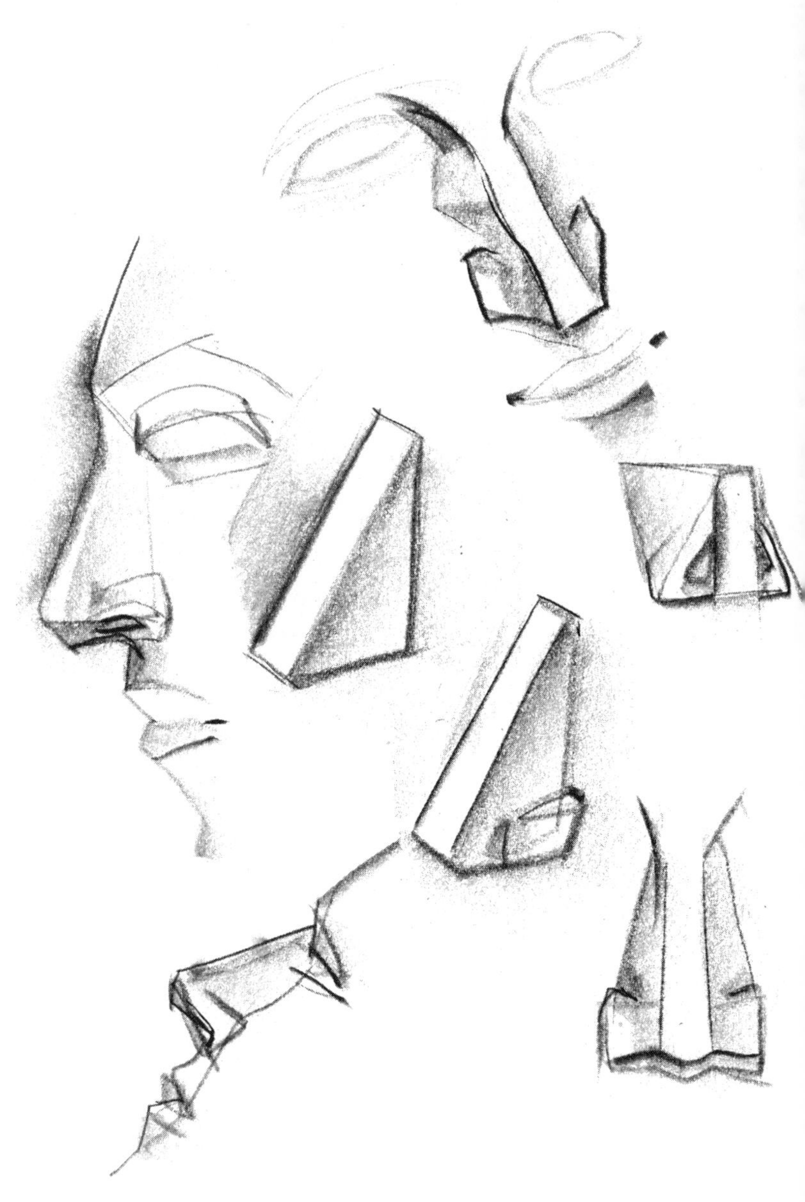

THE NOSE

In visualizing the nose for sculpture, its essential cube shape is what should be the base for your ultimate realization in three dimensional form.

In making drawing studies with such a goal in view eliminate the non-essential vagaries of various nose types and concentrate on a two dimensional study of the form.

Here are a number of basic nose shapes made with the three dimensional in view.

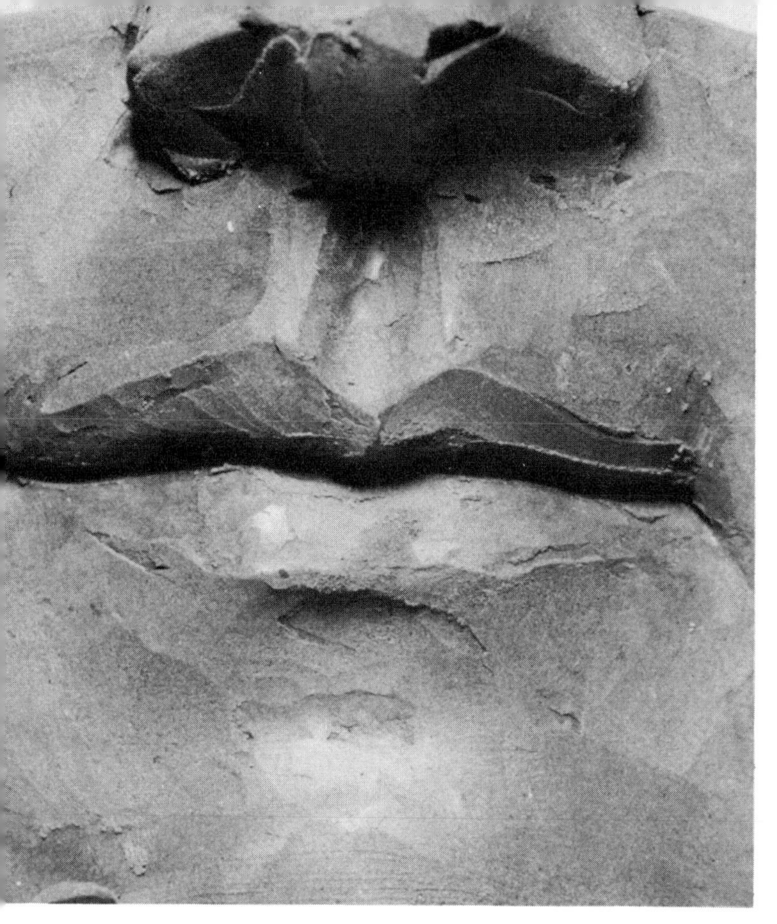

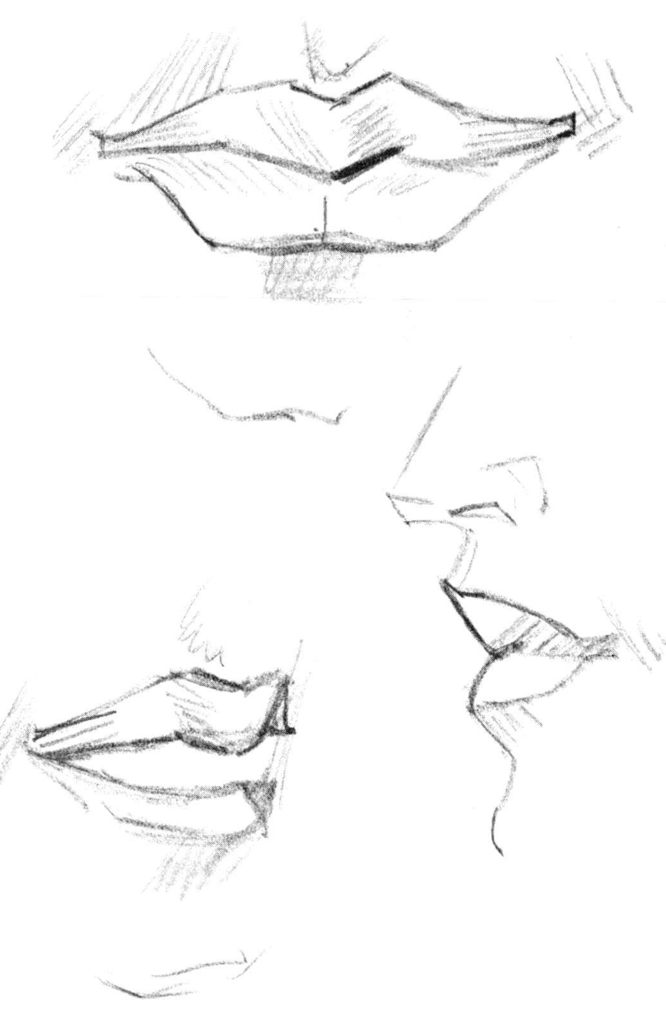

THE MOUTH

The lips and mouth area are forms of very definite modeling and should not be represented as either a rosebud or a hole in the center of the face.

Notice in the clay model of the lips how full and firm are the planes.

TWO HEADS IN SOAP This study for a strong head, eventually to be carved in stone, is still in its rugged blocked-out cuts showing the direction of the main planes and the indication, without detail, of the features.

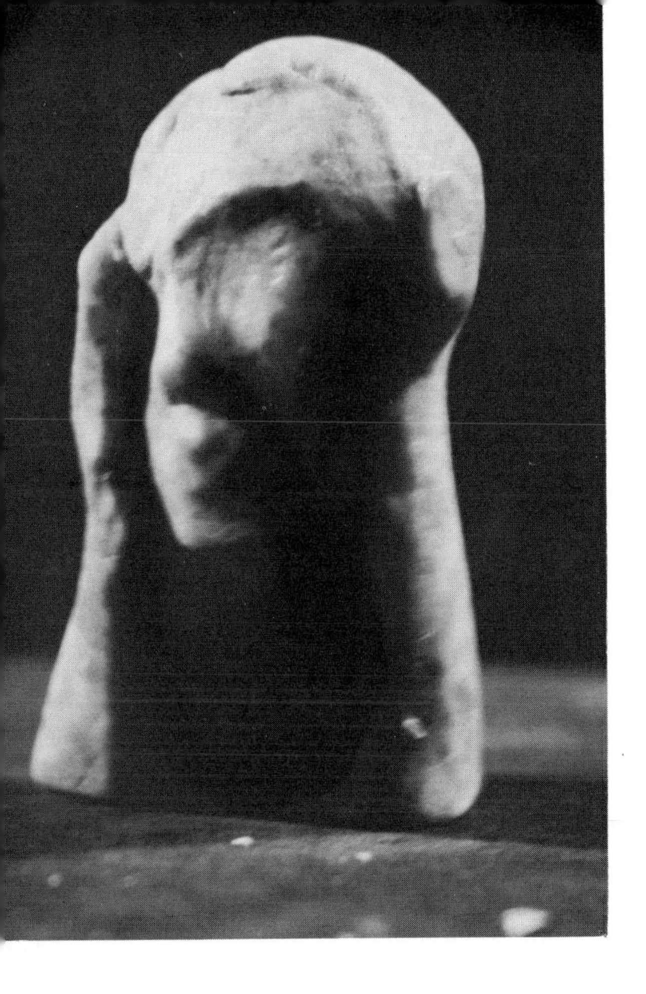

This study has been smoothed and gives the invaluable prevision of how the stone piece will look when the planes have been rounded and the stone sanded and polished.

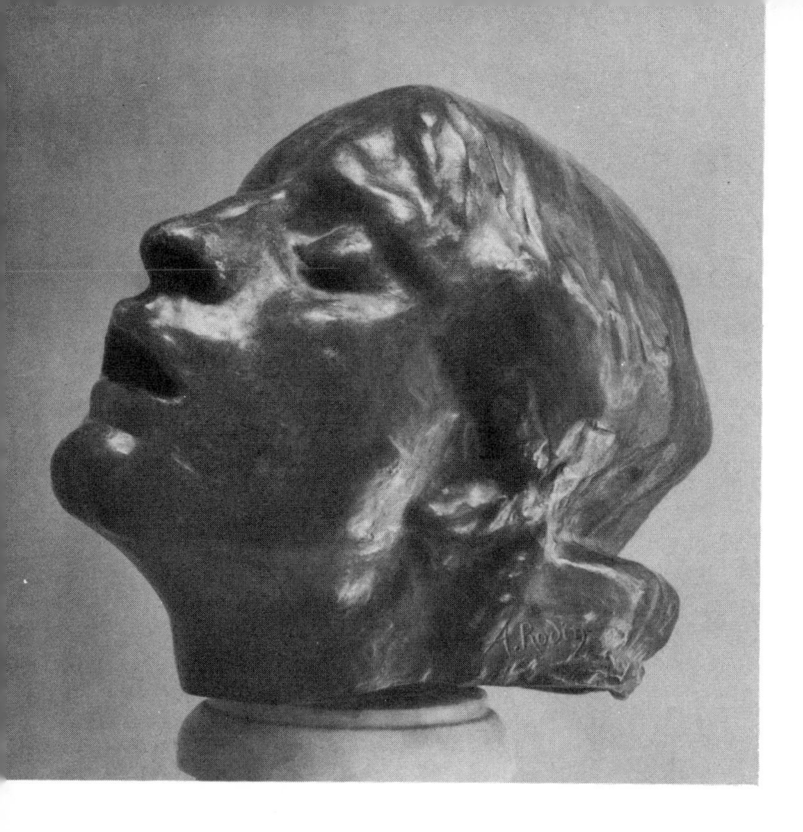

This beautiful, emotional head by Rodin makes no use of varying textures to express hair or lips, yet its subtle modeling produces the maximum of realism without sacrifice of sculptural unity.

The painter may express form through color an shading, the sculptor is restricted to masses in rel: tion to other masses as a means of interpretatio Even though he may vary texture somewhat to ai in simulating realism, an excessive use of varyir textures cheapens and weakens the large sculptur: quality to be obtained by simplicity.

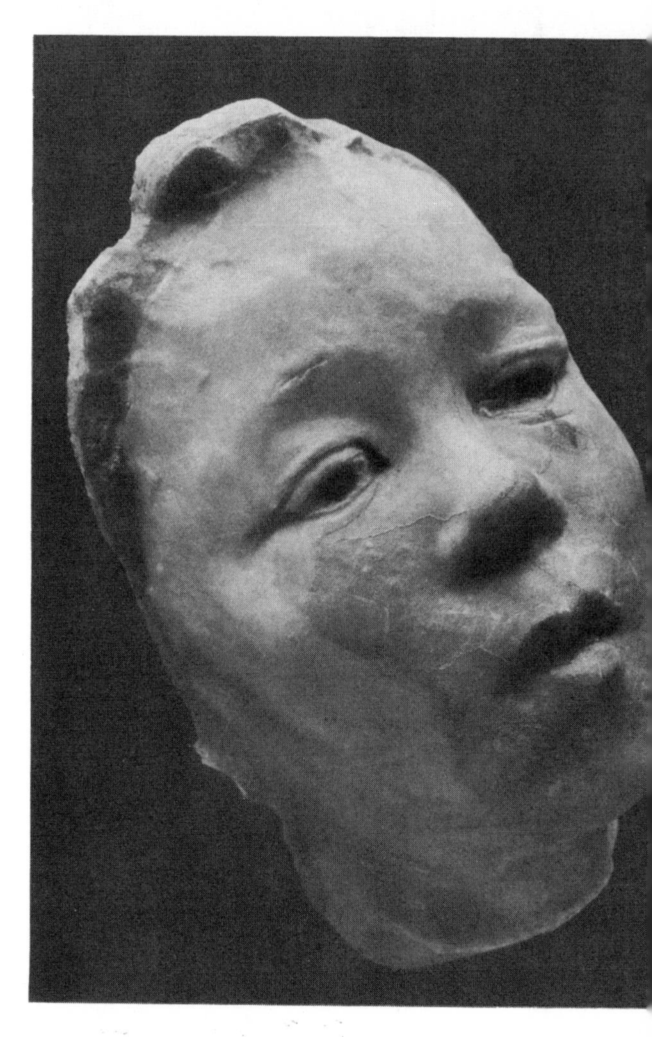

Michelangelo's powerful David. This great, simple head, like the best of the Golden Age Greek sculpture, idealizes and conventionalizes forms and features. The forms sought for are the universal rather than the transiently "real."

Greek heads.

Head of a Negro, Egyptian, seventh century B.C.

King Akh-en-Aten, from el'Amarneh, 1375-1358 B.C.

Head of an early Eighteenth Dynasty lady (about 1500 B.C.). Wife of a Theban official.

Portrait head of a courtier, Egyptian, end of Fourth Dynasty, about 2590-2560 B.C.

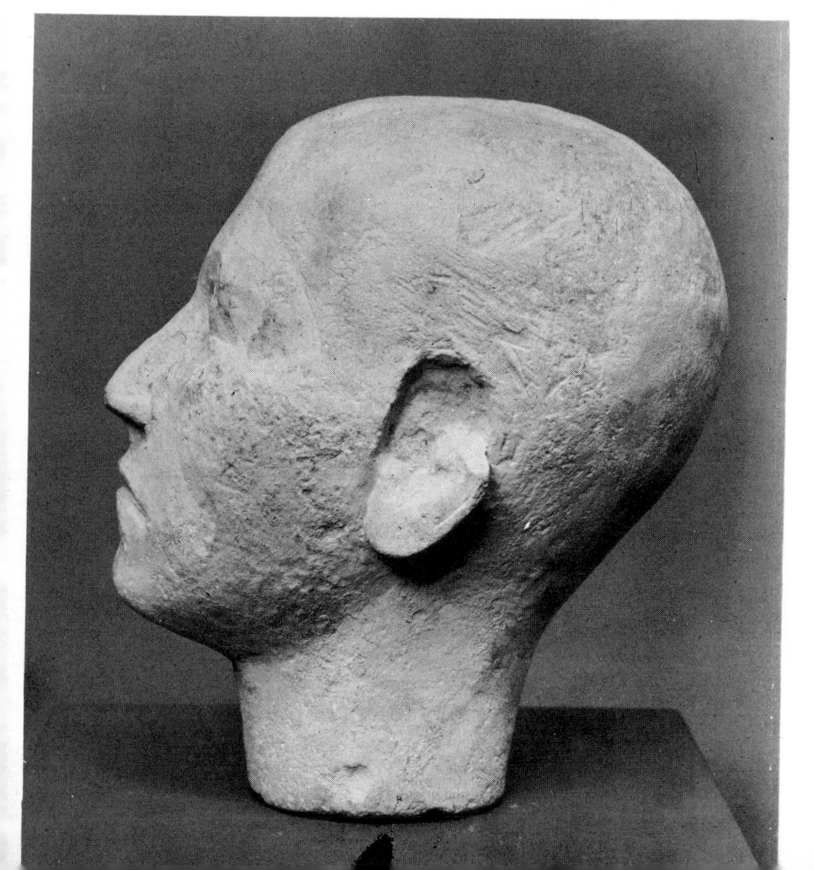

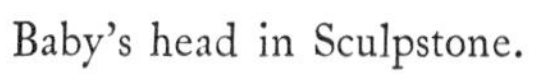
Baby's head in Sculpstone.

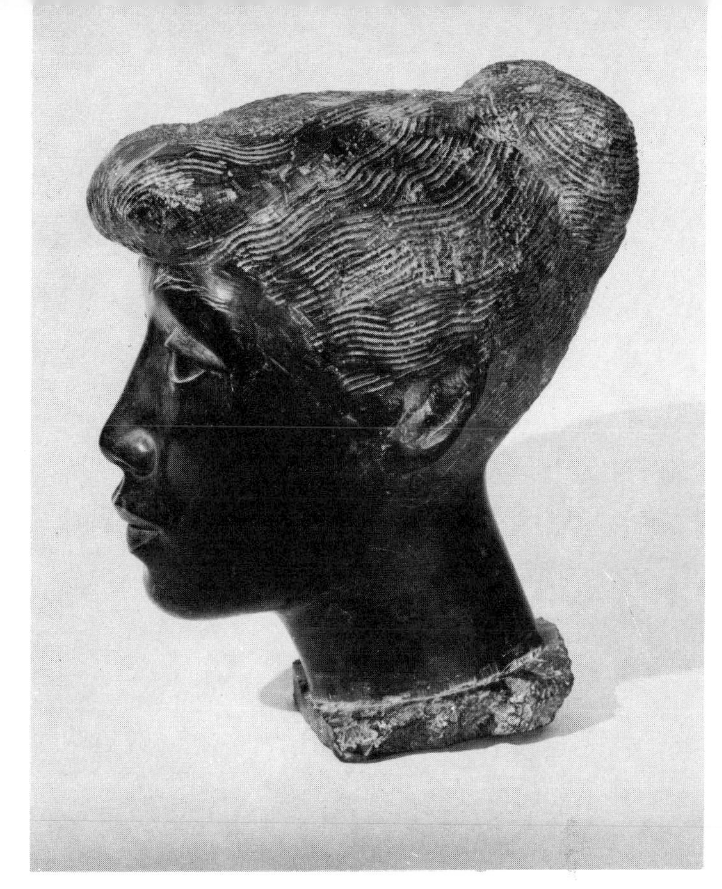

Woman's head in Sculpstone

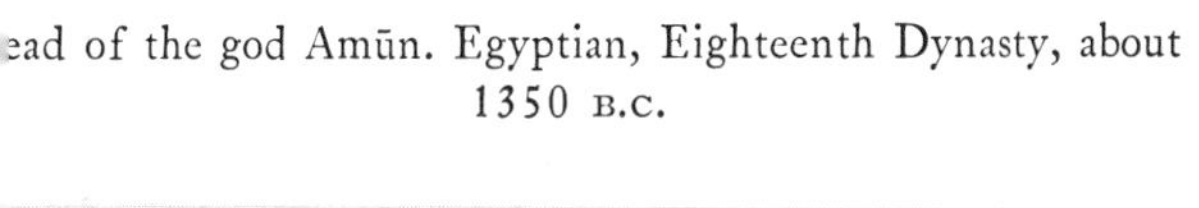
ead of the god Amūn. Egyptian, Eighteenth Dynasty, about 1350 B.C.

Beautiful use of the forms suggested by the original shape of the marble. By Amy Small.

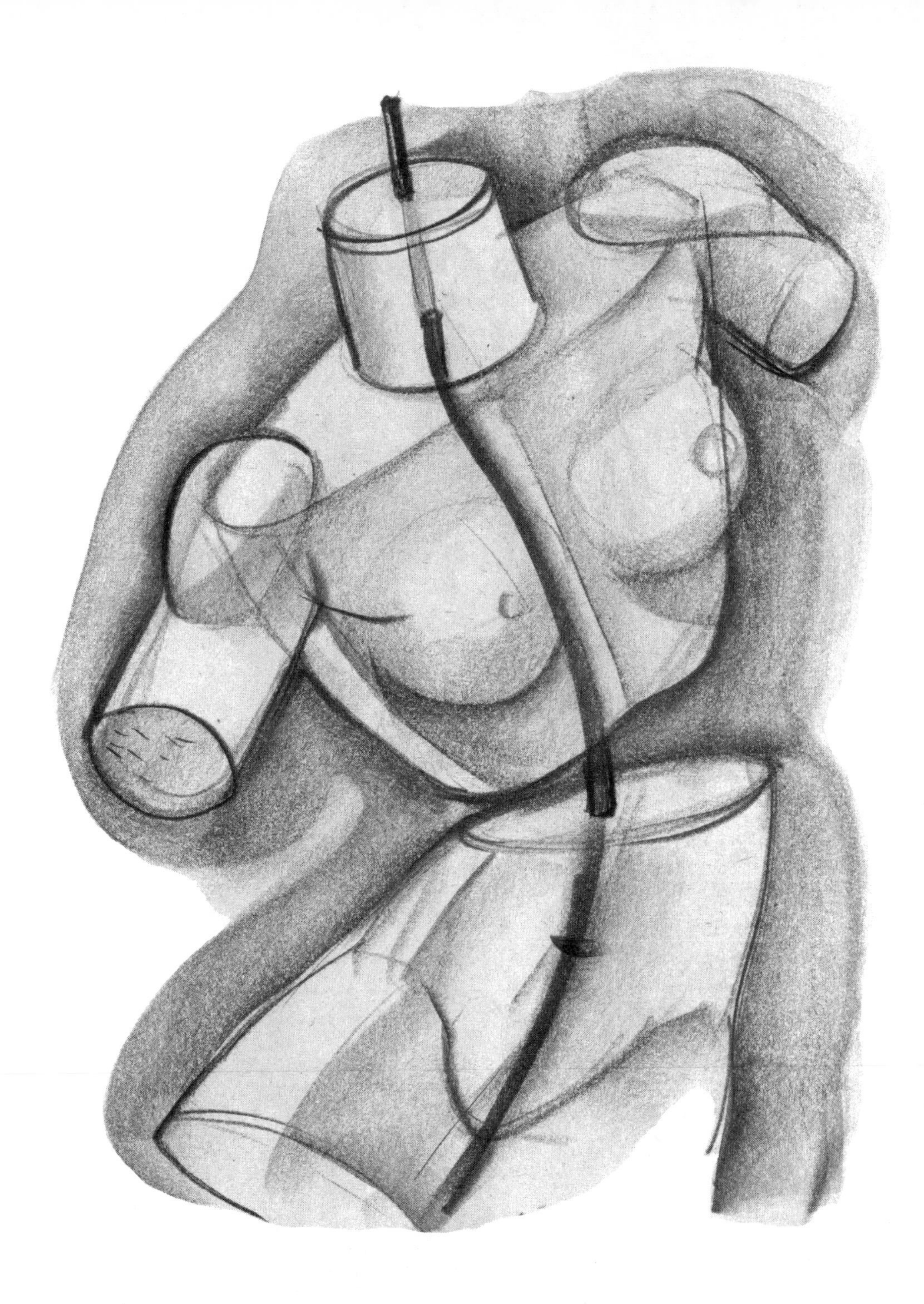

THE TORSO

Violent action does not distort the basic figure forms as much as it appears to.

This enlargement of the torso shows how it is merely the lines of direction of the shoulders, breasts, waist, and pelvis which change in relation to each other when action of this nature takes place.

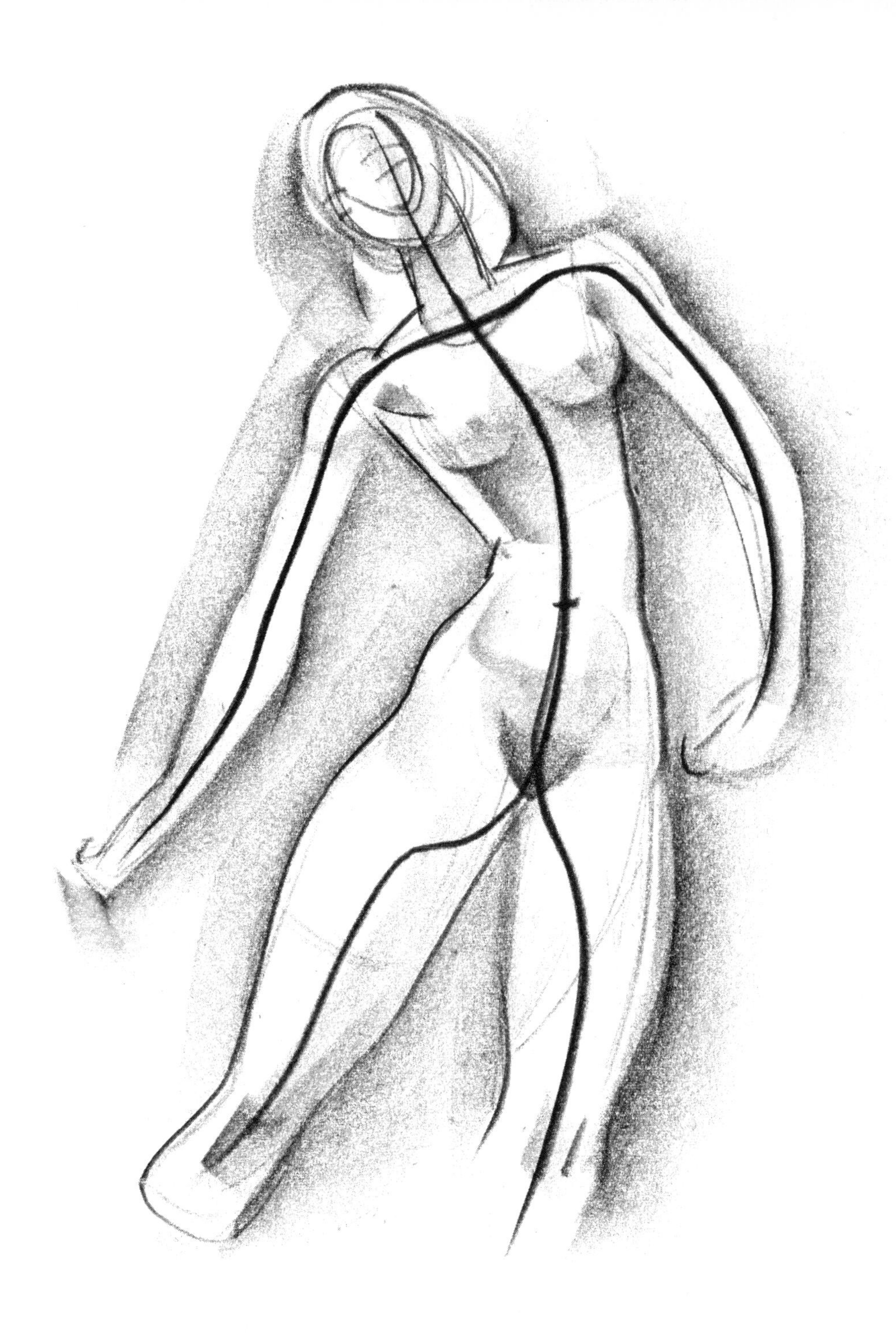

ACTION

In sculpture, as in life, action must be accompanied by a counteraction in order to attain balance.

In sculpting action figures it is better to rely on the balance of weight against weight, stress against strain—balance, rather than require your undersupport, the armature, to bear the burden of an unbalanced distribution of the masses.

TOOLS

VIRTUALLY every carpenter tool is useful to the sculptor at some time or other. The sculptor must invent and improvise during the course of his preparations for the sculpture of each work. His work base, its firm setting on the working surface, the metals and woods of the armature, the buttresses and struts to support weight masses before they set, etc. are all adventures in minor carpentry, and familiarity with hammers, wire cutters, pliers, files, etc. is a necessity. Such familiarity is acquired during the course of making a number of pieces of sculpture, acquired by the trial and error system. A student soon learns which tools best serve his needs for each particular problem and the acquiring of the tools themselves is an inevitable part of the sculptor's life. A menacing array of expensive carpenter tools is not necessary. An expensive tool chest with myriads of mysterious pieces has caused the ending of a good many careers in amateur carpentry. Do not overburden yourself with impedimenta which will get in your way physically and spiritually. For most purposes a junior tool set will suffice.

Here is a list of the virtually indispensable carpenter tools for your basic workshop:

1. Saw—a small handsaw for cutting bases, etc.
2. Shears—for cutting shims, tin, etc.
3. Pliers—twisting wire, pulling nails, etc.
4. Nails—assorted
5. Level—for balancing base, etc.
6. Calipers—for measuring proportions, etc.
7. Plumb and line—for balancing
8. Galvanized wire—18 gauge
9. Claw hammer
10. Penknife—for drawing in clay with point and the blade for sundry cutting.

No sculptor's tool has yet been devised which can replace the fingers for modeling purposes.

The carving process for this reason is perhaps less sensitive, since it severs the possibility of creating forms directly by the use of the finger tips, but must achieve its results instead with the use of sharp steel.

In modeling, whether in clay or plasteline, the fingers are in direct contact and the "feel" of material is transmitted to them at the same time as the play of the individual touch is registered on the soft material. The application of clay directly by the fingers and the working, smoothing action is as individual as a person's signature.

It is fine, of course, to be in a position to go to an artists' supply shop and order all the tools recommended in the elaborate catalogues issued by sculptors' supply companies. There have been developed beautiful stands which elevate at the turn of a wheel, turn on ball bearings, and which look like fine modern furniture.

Finely tempered chisels of every shape and size for stone, wood-cutting chisels beautifully beveled into scoops and gauges, fine wooden modeling sticks gracefully turned, and innumerable other accessories and gadgets are available and, frankly, very desirable.

But they are expensive and, fortunately, not indispensable.

Add to your sense of experimentation in the actual fashioning of figure an inventiveness in the contriving of tools and you will not only save considerable money, but you will have thought a good deal about the special needs involved in each problem, and tools and the work become one.

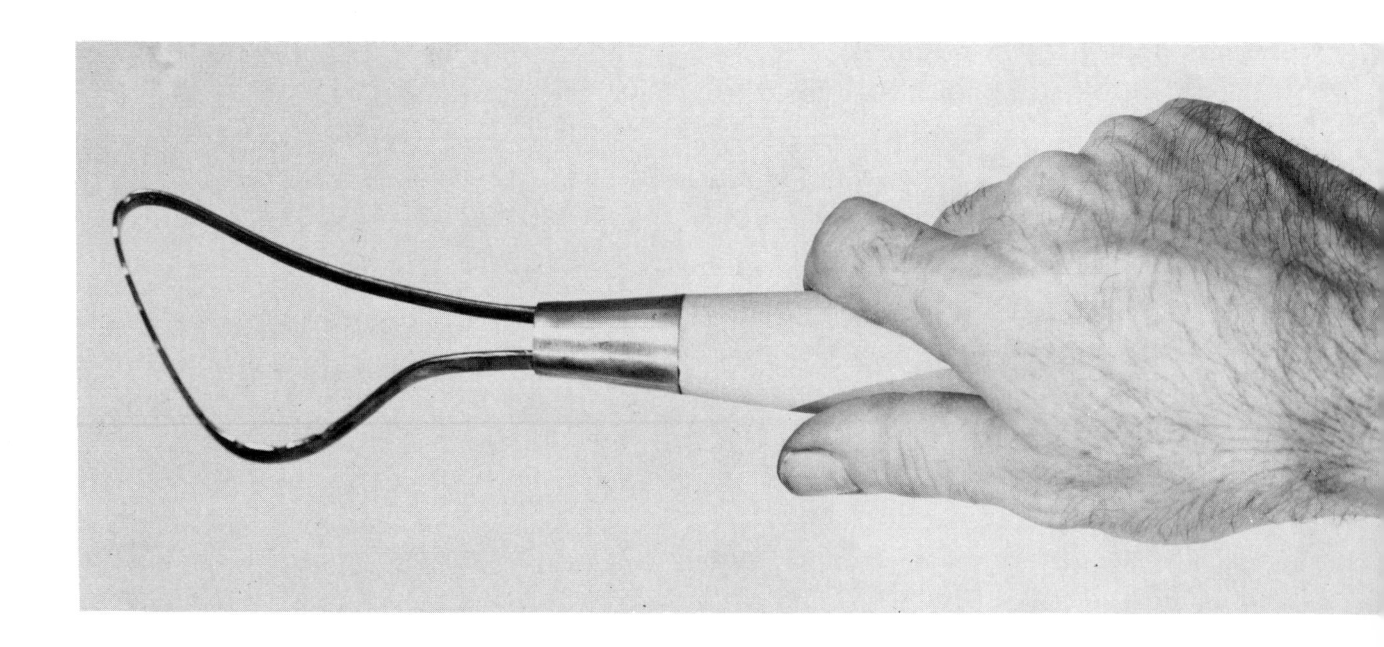

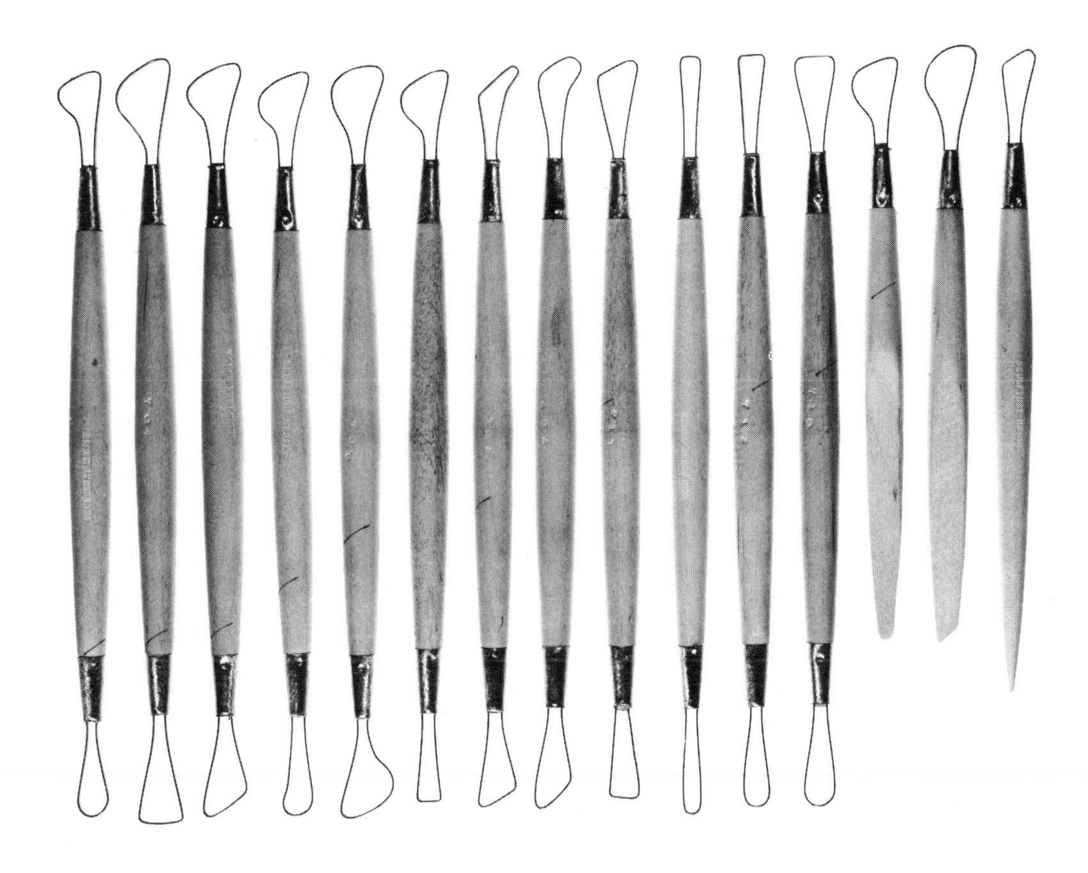

Good chisels may be bought at hardware stores and they may be shaped on an inexpensive grindstone and finally sharpened on an oil stone.

One can often pick up cheaply at country auctions a whole box of quarrymen's tools which a local grinder can transform into fine stone-carving tools for very little additional.

In place of the wooden, clay modeling tools, which are extremely expensive, one can use many varieties of five-and-ten wooden kitchen utensils, quite adequate for most purposes.

A modeling stand may be constructed at home using an old piano stool as turntable, a high bar stool as a base.

Wooden modeling tools with heavy firm wire ends twisted into various shapes for work in various sizes are commercially produced for sculptors. They are quite expensive, but since they do not wear out with use as do the chisels, it is hardly worth while spending the time in fashioning one's own.

However, with ingenuity, one can evolve quite adequate substitutes for such tools. Ordinary spoons can perform many of the offices of these tools.

Here are illustrated the standard wire-end tools. Plastic modeling tools have been devised. They are quite as effective as wooden ones and about one quarter the price.

They are more easily cleaned and are more durable than the wooden ones.

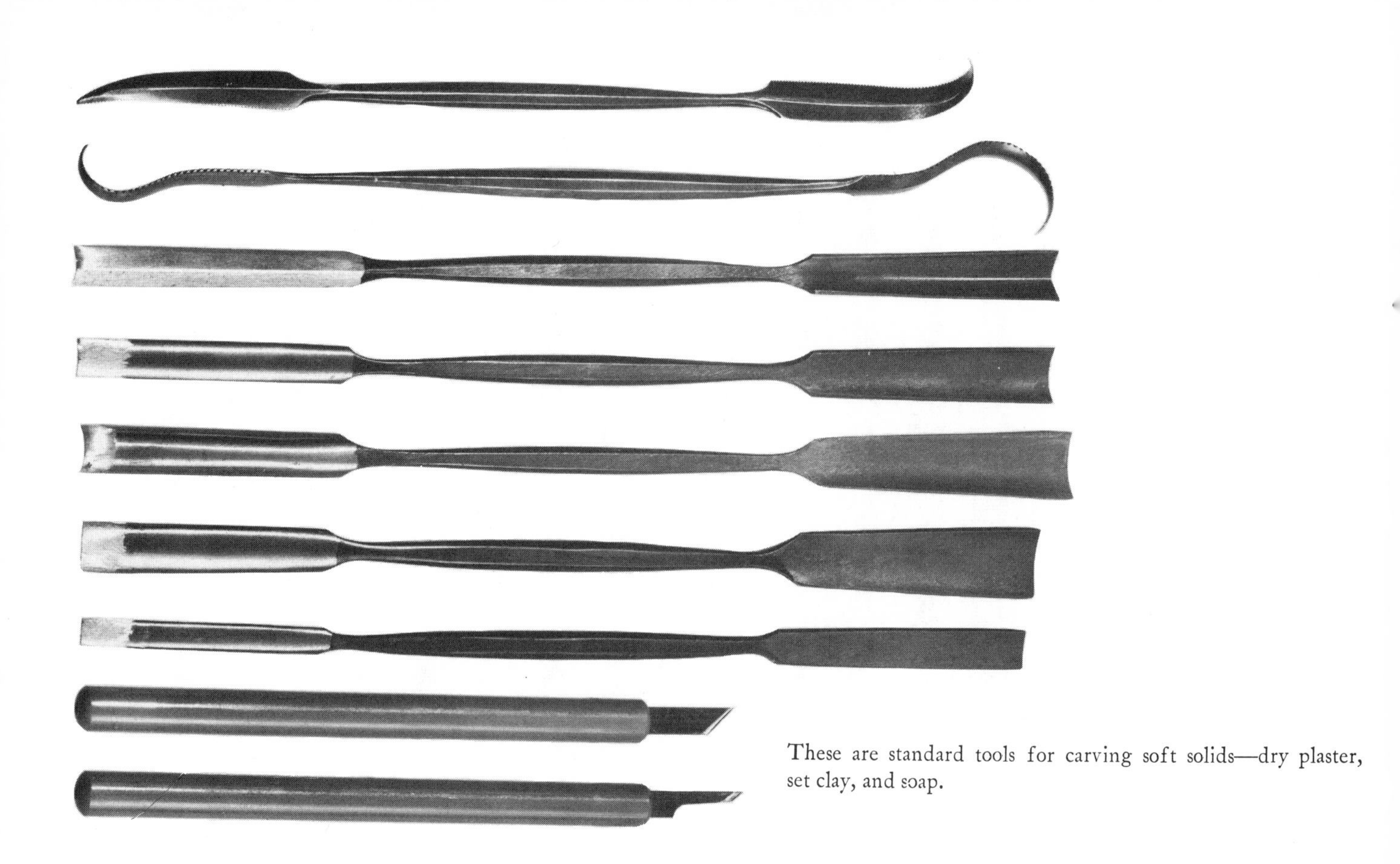

These are standard tools for carving soft solids—dry plaster, set clay, and soap.

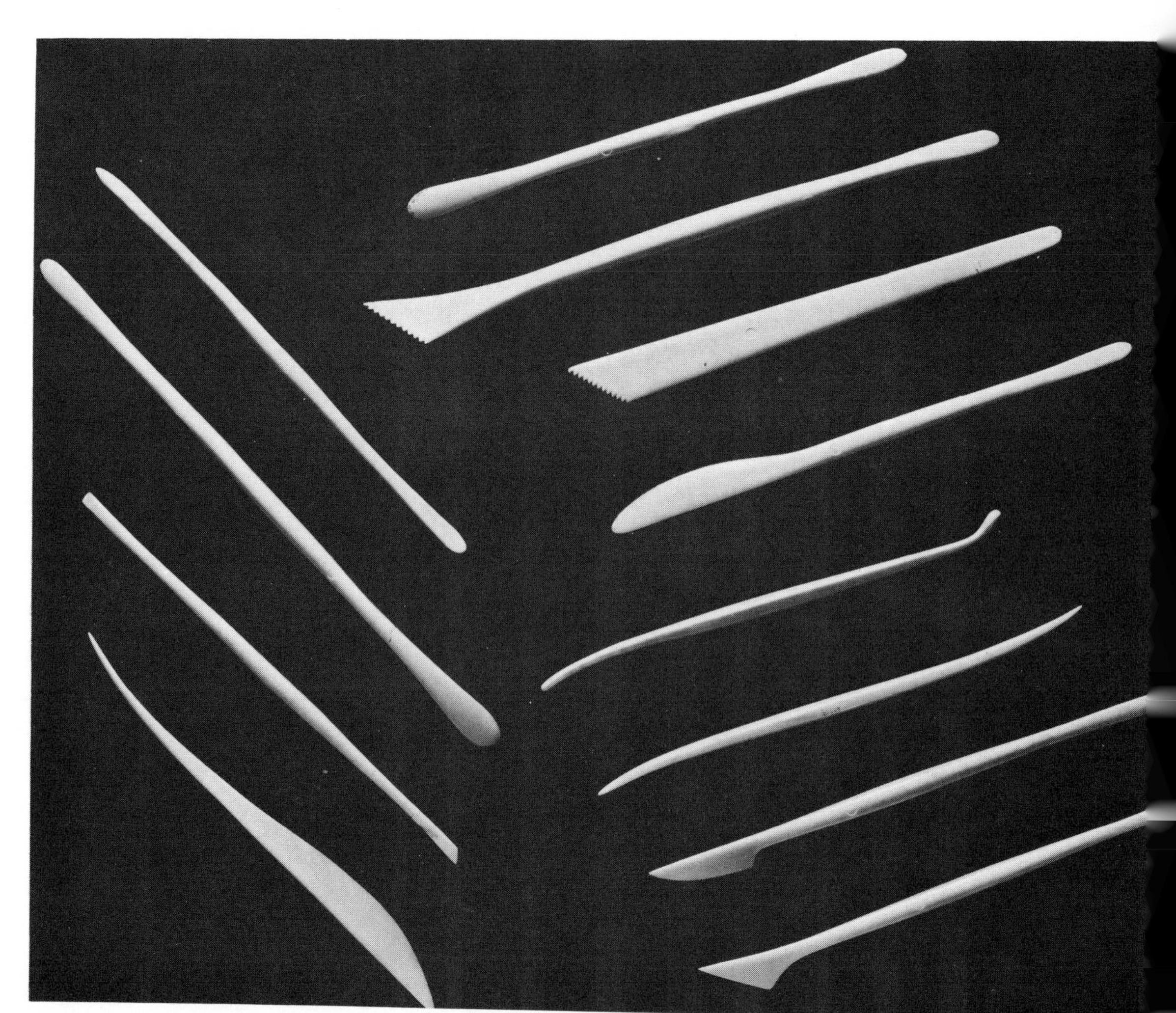

Plastic tools.

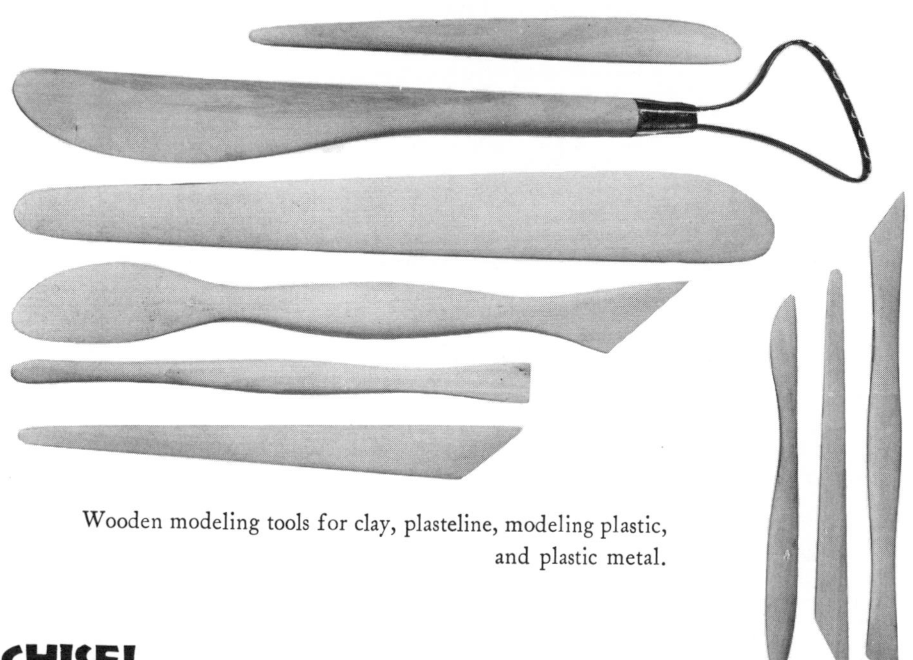

Wooden modeling tools for clay, plasteline, modeling plastic, and plastic metal.

TOOTH CHISEL

The tooth chisel should be used next in the shaping process.

Its teeth make a serrated path which rounds as it plows and clears the forms of the irregularities made by the point chisel, preparatory to the detail cutting.

The size of the tooth chisel varies with the size of the areas to be cleared. If improperly used, at too direct an angle, or inclined to one side or another the teeth may break or wear very quickly and in some cases disproportionately.

They may be filed long and sharp again, but eventually they wear out if filed too often. Give this valuable tool special care in use.

This is a good complete set of steel tools for carving limestone or marble.

Illustrating point chisel.

POINT CHISEL

This is the tool for shaping the stone into the general form preparatory to the working of finer detail. It is used to chop off large slivers and chunks of the stone.

It must be held at an angle to the stone (shown here) and one soon acquires the right amount of force with which to strike the chisel depending on the hardness and grain of the stone. Always remember, even in the first shaping process, to work around the stone, keeping all areas in equal state of advancement.

Point chisels come in various sizes and thicknesses. I have found a long chisel preferable to a short one.

The chopping process, which may well be a tedious one if the tools are dull, may also be a very pleasant one if a certain rhythm of striking is found and the sharpened tool begins to chop large pieces in a controlled, speedy manner.

Remember that, in stone or wood, one cannot add pieces, and careful thought should be given to the areas to be removed, the protuberances to be left and the cavities permissible.

Your idea should be so conceived as to utilize the greater part of the stone with which you work. Do not take a large stone and chop laboriously until you reach the small inner dimensions. Rather split the stone into the size close to your projected design and then go to work with your point chisel.

BUSHING HAMMER

Illustrated here is a bushing hammer, a particularly good tool for pulverizing the stone for rounding forms.

Obviously it cannot be used on small, narrow surfaces, but for massive rounding it is much more effective than the tooth chisels and much faster.

It has a striking surface of many teeth about 1/8 inch long which crushes the protruding stone areas, leveling and turning the stone surface to the desired evenness.

Two kinds of bush hammer.

Here a bushing chisel is being used instead of the bush hammer. Smaller surfaces are more easily approached since better control of this tool is possible.

FILES AND RASPS

One should use the pointing tooth and bushing chisels as far as possible before using files and rasps.

Files are essentially smoothing and finishing rather than carving tools. Overreliance on them for the contriving of your forms tend to make for a softness of contour and an indefiniteness of edge which take away much from the strength of your concept.

Files are to be had in various sizes, shapes, and strength of tooth, each with its special uses for smoothing surfaces.

Here is a series of different rasps:

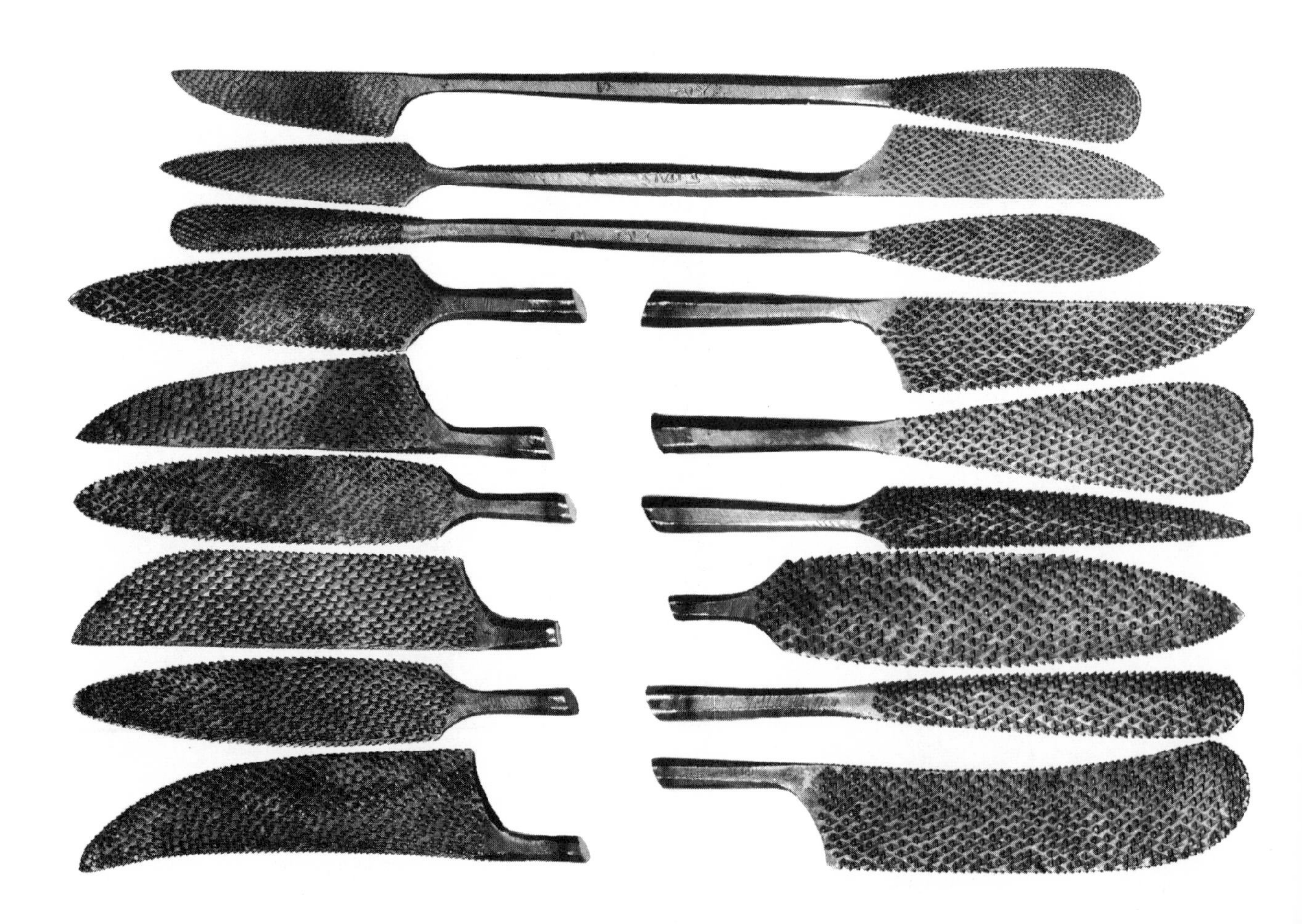

The best wood- and stone-carving tools are made from hand-forged steel.

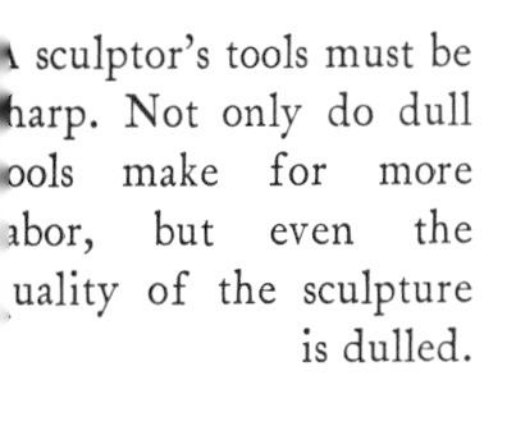

A sculptor's tools must be sharp. Not only do dull tools make for more labor, but even the quality of the sculpture is dulled.

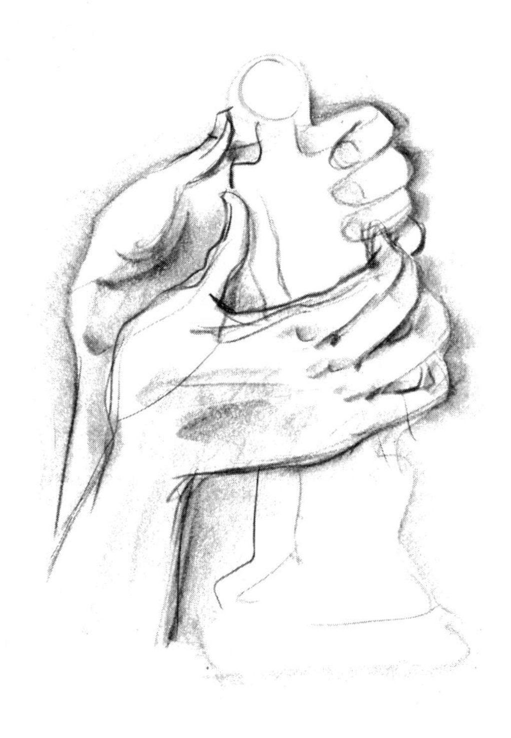

MATERIALS

CLAY is put up in two-, five-, and ten-pound cans for shipping by mail. Inexpensive and easily preserved if kept damp.

At beaches and in many country localities the natural clays are excellent for practice modeling.

Recently there have been perfected various types of clay which harden to a stonelike quality and which may be tinted to resemble granite, marble, etc. (For a list of commercial houses which mail various clays see p. 177.)

Plasteline is also sent by mail in one- and five-pound cakes. This remains permanently semisoft, may be used over and over again, and is fine for study purposes.

Plaster of Paris is obtainable in any paint or building-supply store. Its use for casting is commonly known (see "Casting"), but it also makes a fine direct carving material when cast into solid blocks (see p.127 for method).

Wood—Most common woods are available at lumberyards everywhere and almost any hard wood can be used for carving (walnut, mahogany, oak, etc.). Fine work can be done in soft wood (pine) by the whittling process with a jackknife.

Stone suitable for carving is available everywhere in the U.S.

Bluestone—New England, New York.

Limestone—New England, New York, and almost everywhere else.

Granite—New England.

Marble—Vermont and Western states.

Sandstone:—Most localities.

A soft stone similar to soapstone is being quarried in the Carolinas and is being sold commercially.

Granite is particularly hard. Because it is so resistant to happy ease in realizing one's concept, it is not desirable as an amateur's medium and pro-

---

Note to the revised edition: Some of the products used in this book are no longer available under the same trade names. Similar materials may be obtained from the supply houses listed on page 177.

fessional sculptors only use it when great durability is essential (public monuments, etc.) or when it is the only stone available.

It does not cut or chip; it must be smashed or pulverized into the desired shape. Much heavier tools and hammers are required to work in granite than, say, in marble or limestone.

The carving process in granite, essentially the same as in the softer stones, calls for an expenditure of energy and strength, so great as to make it a medium of necessity and not preference.

Alabaster—The best alabaster comes from Italy. Its translucency makes it a very interesting stone for certain pieces. It is easily cut and many fine pieces have survived through centuries, exposed to the elements.

Almost every stone in existence is potentially carvable if one has the proper tools. The variations in hardness and colors are infinite and choice is most often made on the bases of availability and what is most suitable to the special problem.

THE POTENTIAL OF THE MATERIAL

In many ways it may be said, the sculptor is separated from his medium when he works for casting.

There is no great interchangeability between two such media as clay and metal and the loss of contact between the original work material and the cast result is often very noticeable.

In many cases even where the sculptor does not cast but interchanges his medium, transferring without marked differences of approach from clay to stone, the failure to understand and exploit the true potentials of each different material shows upon and weakens the translation. A clay figure copied painstakingly in marble neither becomes good stone nor remains good clay. Something has been lost of the value of directness in stone and the original lightness of clay has been distorted.

Direct carving has gained greatly in popularity in recent years and that is all to the good.

The feel of the wood, granite, or marble has its own implications and should be awarded its own place as the direct source of inspiration.

The clay sketch, like the original pencil plan, should only suggest the general forms. It should never be the whole story ready for exact transference.

NEW MATERIALS

There has been added to the list of materials available to the modern sculptor many excellent substances which were not known to ancient sculptors.

The sculptor's imagination is no longer limited to the severe restrictions of a relatively small range of workable material. This should in itself be a source of inspiration. Just as the proximity of Carrara quarries was a stimulant to countless Italian sculptors to work heroically in rich marble and the easy accessibility of ebony and ivory gave inspirational impetus to Congo natives, so these ready-to-hand products of the chemical laboratories should be a force conducive to experimental creative work on the part of today's sculptors.

Many metals of a light and durable nature are at the command of the sculptor—aluminum, chromium, and steel.

Plastics, chemically treated clays, and stone for casting in liquid form are available.

Plastics are less expensive for use as a casting material than are metals and less fragile in many ways. The hazards and uneconomical methods involved in casting metal are eliminated and, in many cases, the beauty and lightness of plastics are preferable.

The "constructivists" are sculptors who have, in the eagerness to disassociate themselves from tradition and thereby escape its cloying restrictions, abandoned the use of the time-honored materials of the sculptor and have utilized virtually every variety of substance individually and in combination to achieve their concepts. Wire, plastics, wood, metals, and manufactured objects of anomalous natures, combined into "constructions" of a highly original nature, have made their work exciting and provocative.

PERMANENCE

The word "permanent" is a relative one. Nothing in nature is immutable, and even the hardest granite is perishable under the blows of time, weather and man's violence.

When sculptors speak of permanence, they refer to an end material, i.e., one that needs no transposing into another for its final state, as well as to a long-lasting substance. Clay, for example, though an excellent working material, is only permanent when it has been subjected to high firing in a kiln. Ordinarily, a clay model serves as a "negative" for casting a more permanent "positive." Were the clay to be allowed to dry and harden, it would inevitably crack and break. Fired, however, it can resist centuries.

Plasteline is a variety of clay treated chemically deliberately for the purpose of making it permanently impermanent. It is intended for reuse, again and again. It is always soft.

Soap used for sculpture is perhaps less arbitrarily impermanent, but it is obviously subject too readily to the effects of heat and dampness.

Wax sculpture, although many pieces have lasted for years and years, is also fragile, perishable, subject to melting and easy breakage.

Plaster is notoriously subject to shattering, but is a good time-resister.

Soapstone, or the commercially sold Sculpstone, is relatively permanent. So soft that it may be whittled with a penknife, it is able to withstand, under moderate conditions of care, time testing of hundreds of years. Ancient Chinese sculpture is rife with soapstone in excellent state of preservation.

Many woods are permanent in the broadest sense of the word, but there are few which will not "check" or crack under severe climate changes. Although we have many fine wood sculptures of remote centuries, few are without serious defects caused by time and weather.

There are so many varieties of wood, from the butter-soft balsa to ironlike mahogany, that it is not possible to make a blanket statement about the relative permanence of wood as compared to say, stone. Even were the relative hardness of each wood to be discussed, the "state" of the wood is more indicative of permanence than is the hardness. I refer to how resinous or how overdry, how grained or how porous. Each piece of each species must be judged individually.

The same must be said for stone. Flaws in granite may make an individual piece much more subject to breakage in working and splitting in weathering than, for example, the comparatively soft sandstone block.

Many stones are great sufferers in sharp weather changes. Metals—iron, steel, copper, etc.—are permanent in a restricted sense because they are subject to rust and corrosion. Very few metals can withstand permanent outdoor life unless periodically treated for protection. Bronze figures seem to withstand time and weather better than do harder metals like steel. However, when given normal shelter and care, all metal sculpture may be called permanent.

PATINA

Patina is the word used to refer to the subtle surface color and feel of the material of sculpture when finished. A patina may be natural or contrived by the artist. If contrived by the artist it must not imply deception, for it calls upon real creative ability and good taste to arrive at a satisfying patina suitable to the character of the piece.

Nothing can be uglier than a badly simulated marble patina given to a plaster surface. Grains simulated to give the appearance of wood to clay can be annoying and only serve to cheapen a material which can have a dignity of its own if properly treated.

Plaster has a dead white dullness which cries for some surfacing which will make it more appealing. It, therefore, calls for treatment which will relieve this dullness and enhance the character of the forms.

Since it is extremely difficult to simulate another material perfectly it is perhaps better to invent one's own patinas and thereby continue the creative process.

Before attempting to apply any patina the plaster must be absolutely dry—a solid patina could seal in the dampness and later cause cracks.

Brush the plaster clear of chalky particles and dust.

Then apply a base dye.

Some prefer analine dyes of one of these three colors diluted in water—brown, green, or black. About three coats should be applied, waiting, in each case, for the dye to dry a few minutes.

There are several brands of bronzing powder on the market prepared in varying hues. Choose the one you prefer for mixing with a solution of clear lacquer and alcohol in about equal parts.

MODELING

IN MODELING with clay the beginner sculptor has the least obstacle offered by the material to the accomplishment of his concept.

The simile "like clay" intended to convey the greatest compliancy in the hands of a user is extremely apt, for it is by far the "easiest" of the sculpture media.

There are many kinds of clay varying in color, consistency, drying and hardening characteristics, and durability. In one way or another some form of modeling clay is available to the sculptor in almost any part of the world. It has been used for pottery and building material in virtually every civilization historically recorded and its properties seem to have been known to the earliest man. The fact that a substance could be scooped from the earth, shaped into bowls, bricks, or figures, and set to dry in the sun or baked in an oven until hard has appealed to the artistic as well as the utilitarian impulses of man.

Long before the brush or pencil was a commonplace, the modeling of three dimensional forms in clay was a highly developed practice.

Drawing or painting an object seen calls for translating into terms of two dimensions that which has body and weight, everything in nature being three dimensional. This translation really calls for a subtle concept not required of the primitive when he modeled the animal he saw or the god he imagined.

With the material readily at hand in the earth at his feet, he inevitably used it as a form of expression, which merely called for a visualization of the object in reduced size, but retaining most of its basic characteristics, those of actually standing or of actually sitting, etc. In drawing, he would have had to symbolize those actions.

ARMATURE

As in every other branch of a highly professionalized field, the armature has taken on a special format that is almost a ritual.

An armature for sculpture is any contrivance that will serve as a firm support for the weight, stresses, and strains of the figure to be modeled. It must be so designed as to be able to bear the increasing weight as the modeling material is added and yet not so rigid as to prevent you from making changes in the movement as the figure progresses and before the material hardens.

You must, of course, first be fairly clear in your mind what shape you intend your armature to support before you build it.

In a sense making an armature calls for the same mental process as making a piece of sculpture. It actually is sculpture. I have seen armatures which should be the finished work rather than the dead object fashioned upon it. It can and often does embody the essence of the movement and form to be expressed and sometimes by implication says more than the clay covering says by detailed information.

For modeling a head the armature must be a central support, built on a baseboard with curved wire spread to form an egg-shaped frame for the clay.

A length of lead pipe or a "one by one" piece of wood, cut to approximately the length of the neck of the head you plan to model, should be fastened to the baseboard securely.

The wire frame is then firmly attached to the upright pipe or wood neck. It may be fastened by thin steel wire to the pipe or by staples to the wood.

Here is a drawing of the way your armature should look.

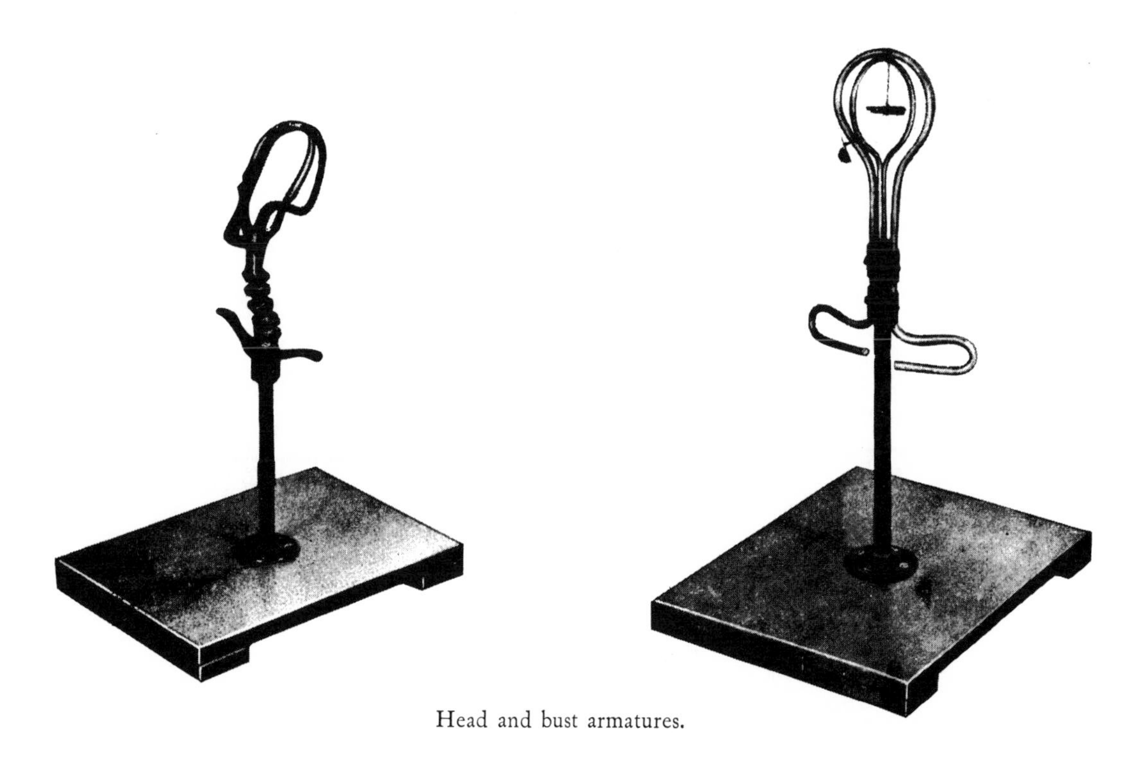

Head and bust armatures.

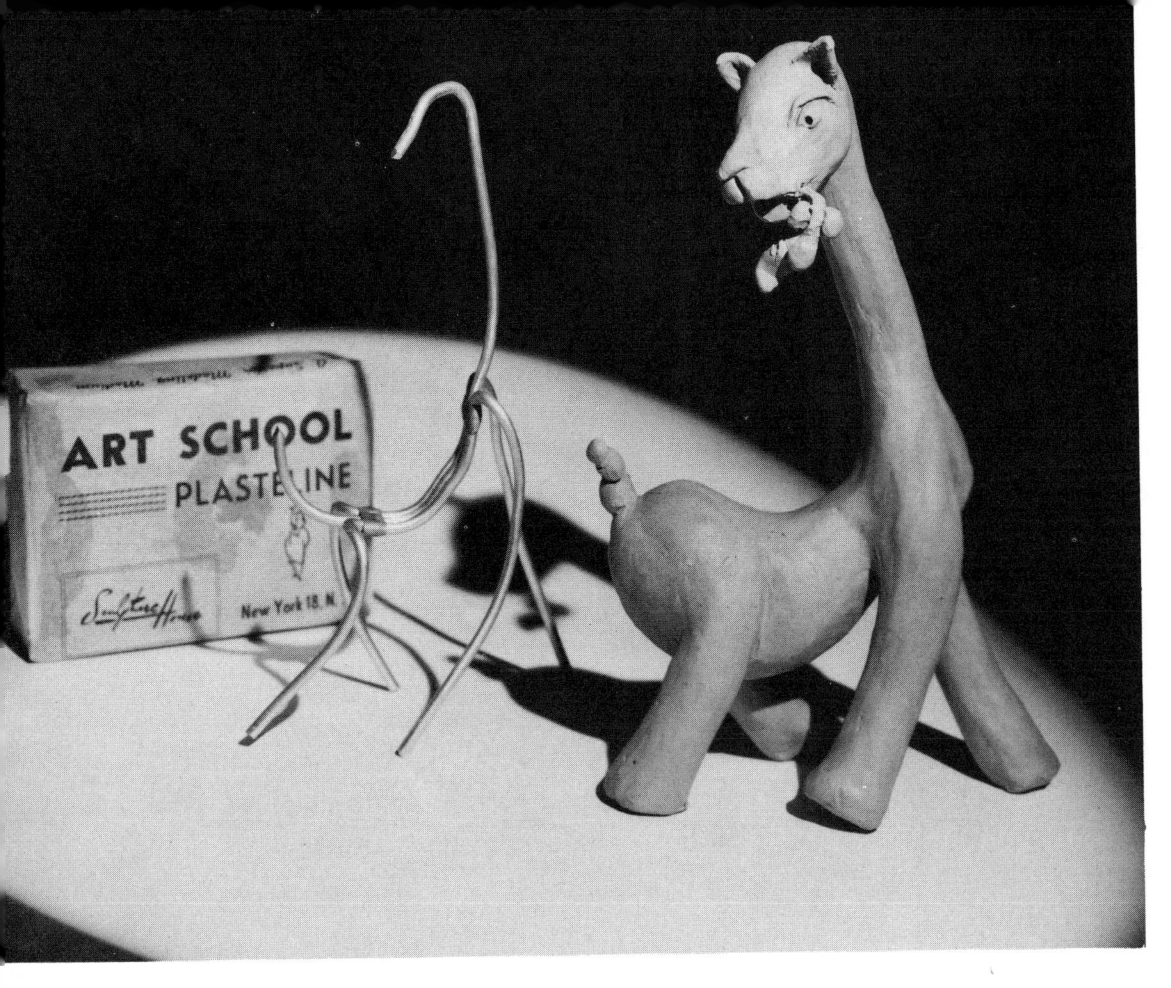

Aluminum, non-corroding wire, available for armature, is preferred by many sculptors to the lead wire.

For children it is certainly more desirable, since it does not stain the hands with lead and eliminates the possibility of lead poisoning.

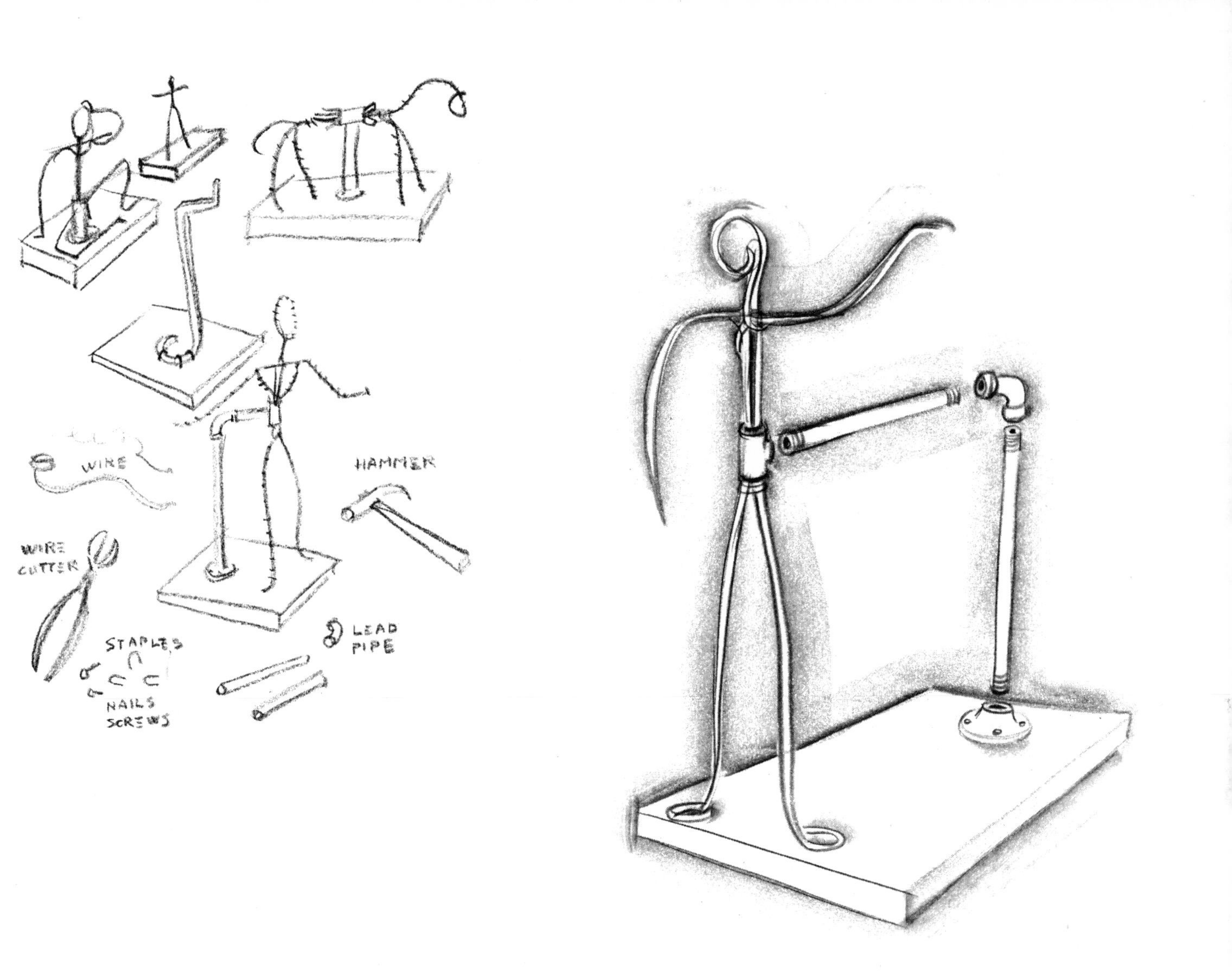
WIRE
HAMMER
WIRE CUTTER
STAPLES
LEAD PIPE
NAILS
SCREWS

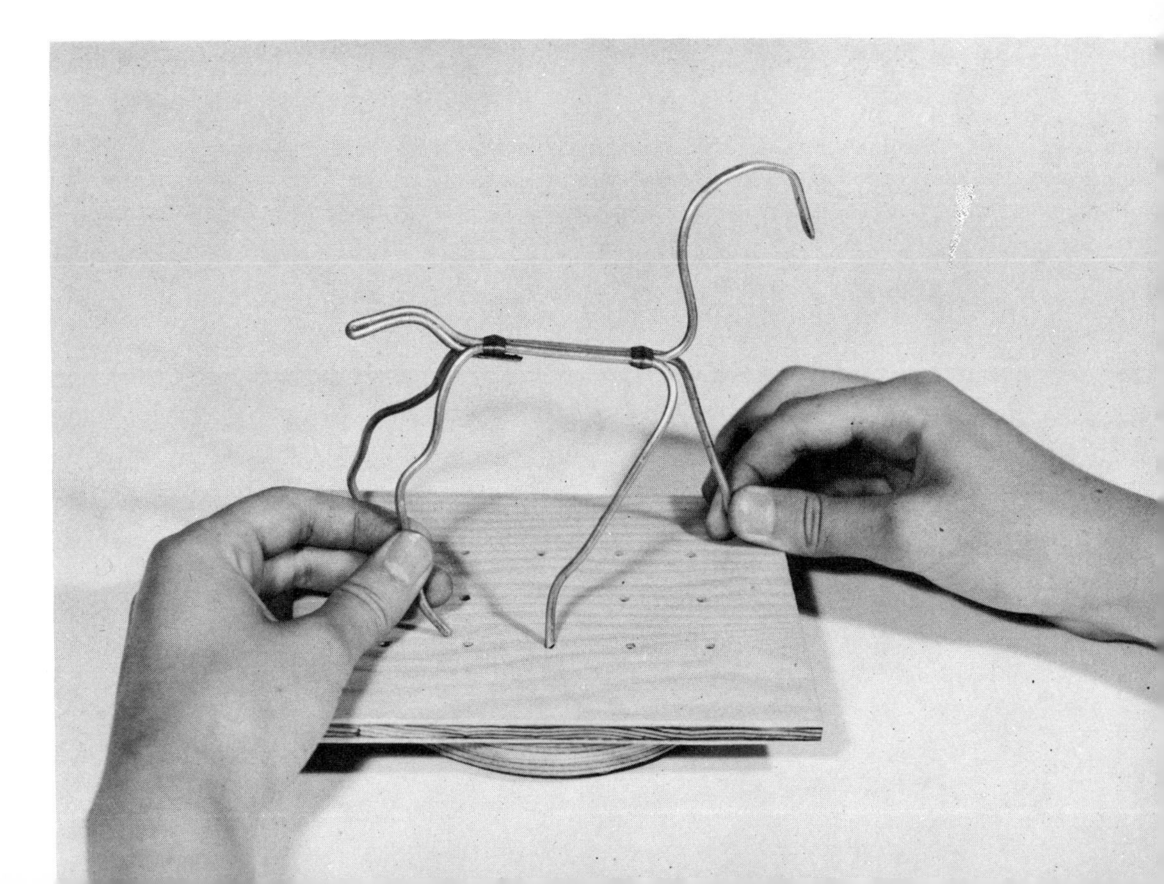

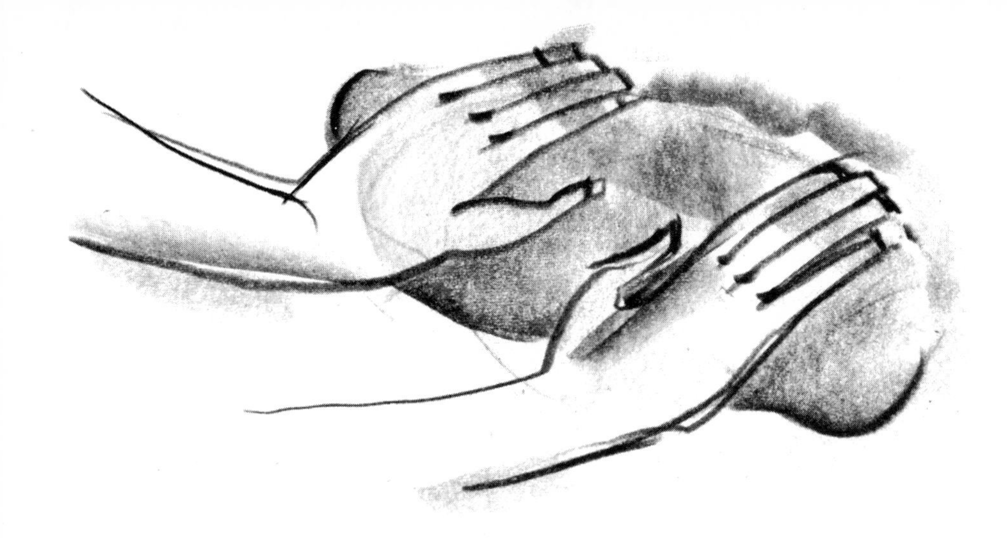

APPLICATION OF CLAY

Each sculptor develops his own special system for rolling and preparing the small gobs of clay just prior to applying them to his armature and as the work progresses.

Some simply break pieces of clay from the mass in the tub and, after kneading them to the desired size between the fingers, press them onto the wire and thus continue to build. These pieces are irregular though not completely haphazard for they are broken off from the mass with the special need in mind.

Other sculptors like to work with pellets of approximately the same size which are almost uniformly pressed onto the structure with a quick motion of the thumb.

If the clay is of a proper consistency, neither too wet to be pleasantly firm nor too sticky, not too dry to adhere easily or crumble unpleasantly into flakes, the actual method of applying the clay should be decided upon by the trial

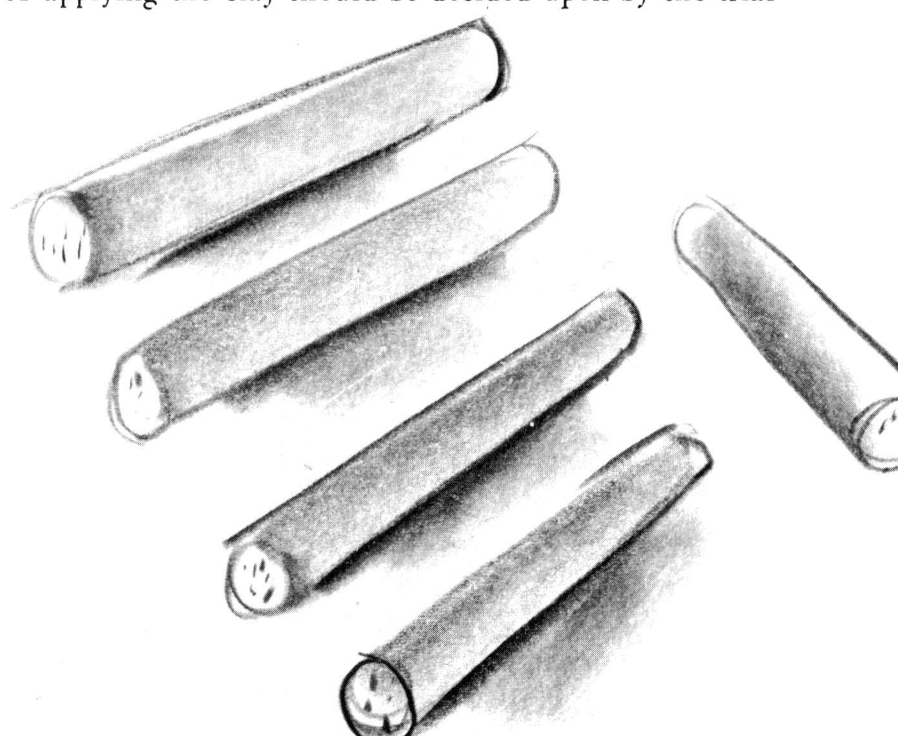

and error approach. When you fall into an easy, comfortable building approach you have found your method.

Clay for the sculptor differs in degree of plasticity and in moisture-holding capacity from the clays used for pottery. Usually they are not suitable for high firing.

Unless the clay used is of the "self-setting" variety, the ordinary sculptor's clay will, if allowed to dry, crack and shrink as the moisture evaporates. It must be moistened periodically every day and kept wrapped in moist cloth over which it is well to put a waterproof cover of plastic cloth.

Clay lasts indefinitely and its quality improves with use. If you can get a good wooden bin, with a cover, lined with tin, in which to keep your moist clay in good working condition, it will help materially in sparing you the annoyance of not having a supply available when you want it. Lacking a bin, you can use an ashcan admirably. It is necessary to have two containers, one for clay suitable for use at once and the other for clay pieces dried and broken from past work, discarded starts, etc. This clay is collected for eventual breaking up and dampening so as to bring it back to good working condition again.

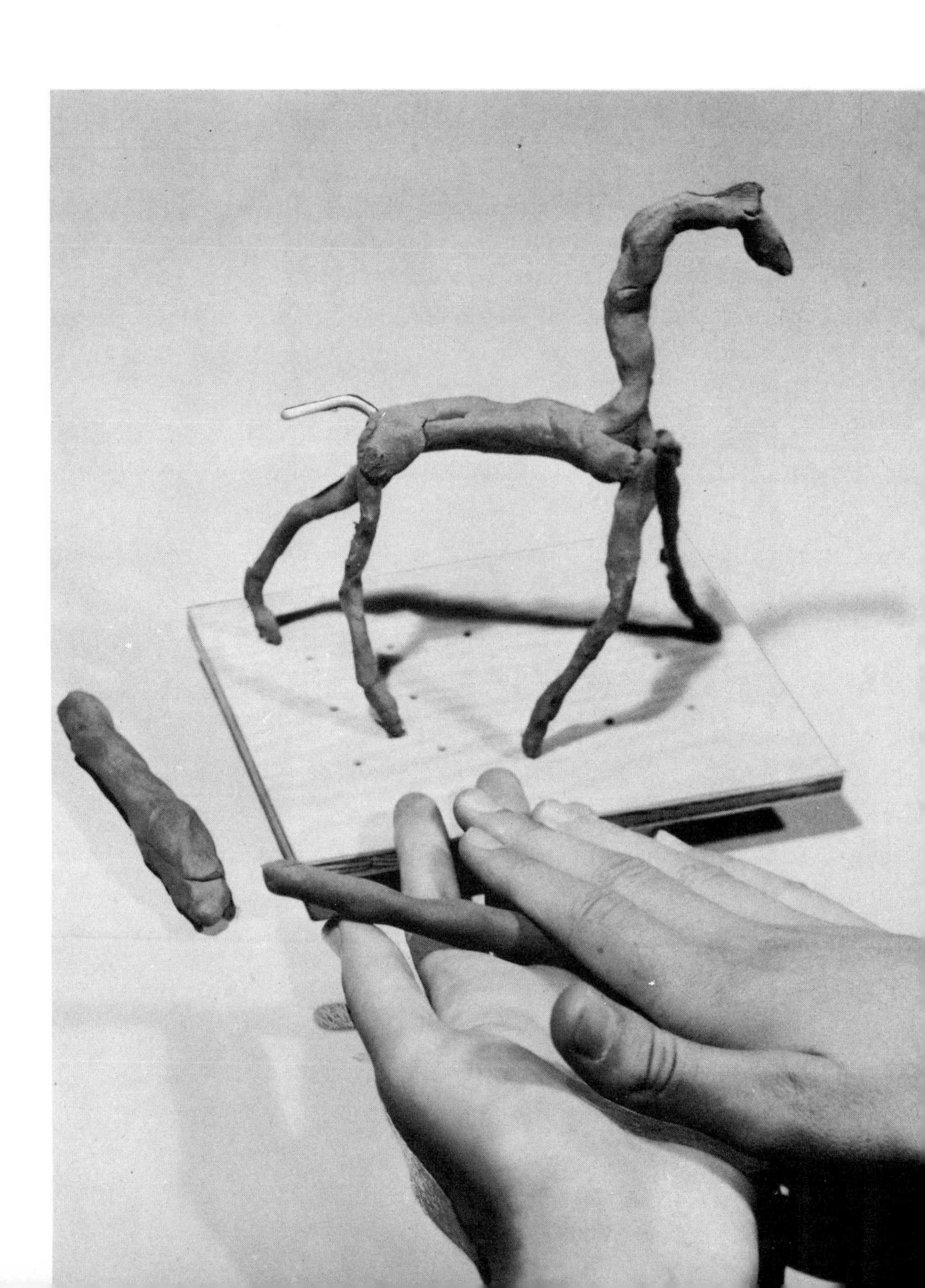

MODELING A CLAY FIGURE

The following series of drawings and photographs deal with the modeling of a standing figure in clay.

The preparation for modeling in clay must be careful for this somewhat messy material can become a nuisance if not kept under strict control. Although a sculptor must not be in a neat, antiseptic studio where he must worry about clay dust and floor stains, neither must he be so engulfed by the sticky substances with which he works that he is hampered and annoyed.

Materials required are:

A tub of clay, kept moist and covered.

A good turntable, and a table for tools, etc.

A few damp rags and some strong wire, all arranged in as handy a position as possible.

A pair of wire-cutting pliers.

A tack hammer—tacks and staples.

A flat piece of wood for the base of the armature, large enough so as to be firm in its stance.

I prefer the self-hardening clay and thereby eliminate the need of casting for preservation.

SKETCH FOR FIGURE This sketch was made from the model. Again, I must emphasize that a professional model, though desirable, is not indispensable. Life is all about you for the studying, and photographs or other sculptured figures are available for study and choice of pose.

This drawing is carried far nearer a state of completion than is required for merely planning a pose and general proportions, but where a more careful study of forms and of the effect of light and shade upon masses helps as a guide for your modeling, by all means make such studies.

In posing your model, as well as in choosing one, think in terms of the sculptural. Strong, simple masses, fluid in line, unbroken by knotty muscles or sharp corners, are the virtues of a sculptor's model.

The pose to be taken should be translatable to clay or stone in the language most suitable to those media. Do not, certainly in the beginning, attempt extravagant gestures and precarious balances. Just as it is difficult for a model to hold a far-flung gesture so it is tiring to behold too flagrant action in some

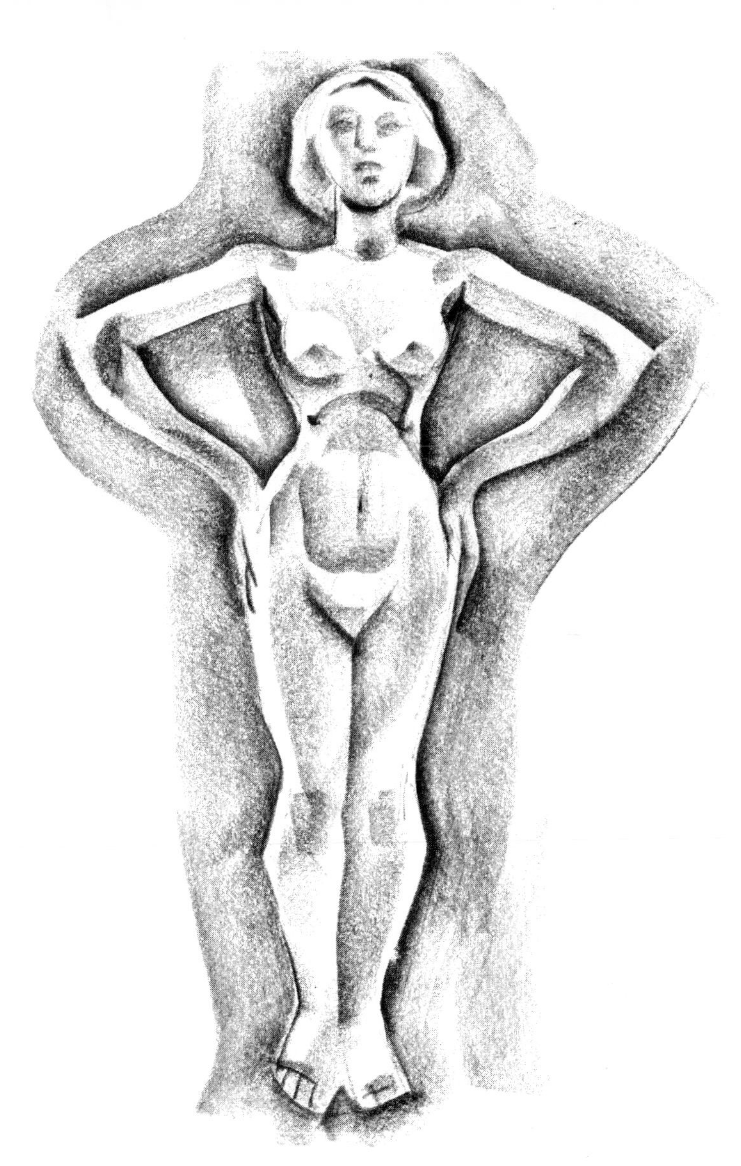

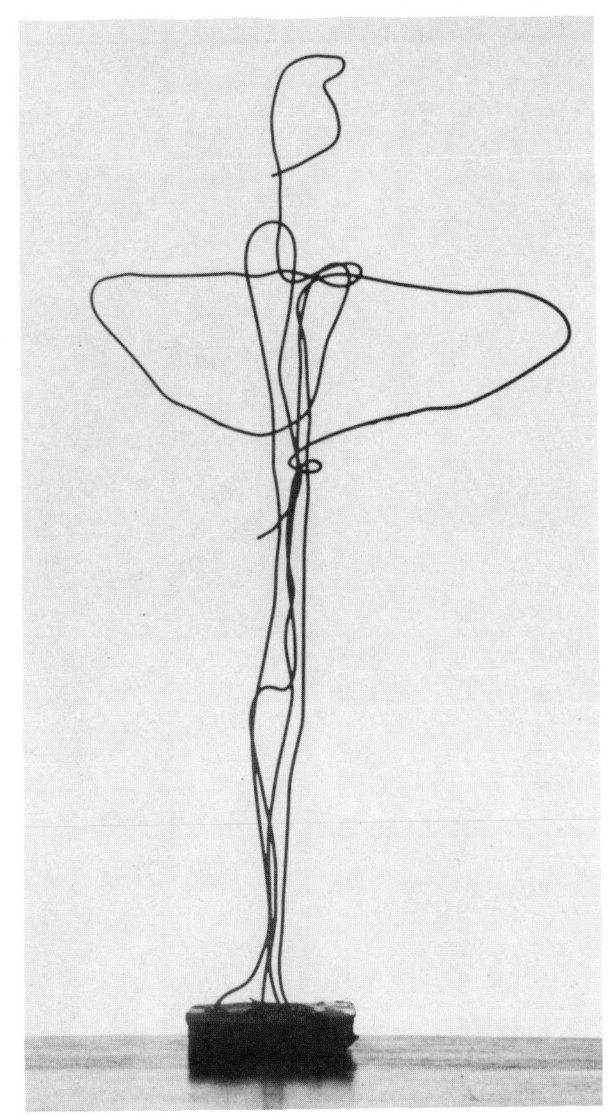

sculpture. Occasionally a sculpture piece of wild action succeeds in sustaining the illusion of that action, but too often it merely becomes static, frozen motion.

Simple and solid should be the key words to your models' poses.

ARMATURE FOR CLAY FIGURE Here is a scroll armature approximating the action of the pose of the previous sketch.

Being for a small figure it does not need a heavy pipe for support.

The entwining lead wire becomes surprisingly strong and the clay acts as a further binder. While the wire is strong it may still be bent, during work progress, as the needs and whims of the sculptor require. The wire is stapled to a firm wooden block which will eventually be covered by the clay.

It is clear that this armature does not attempt to simulate a true bone skeleton. Its only purpose is to support clay.

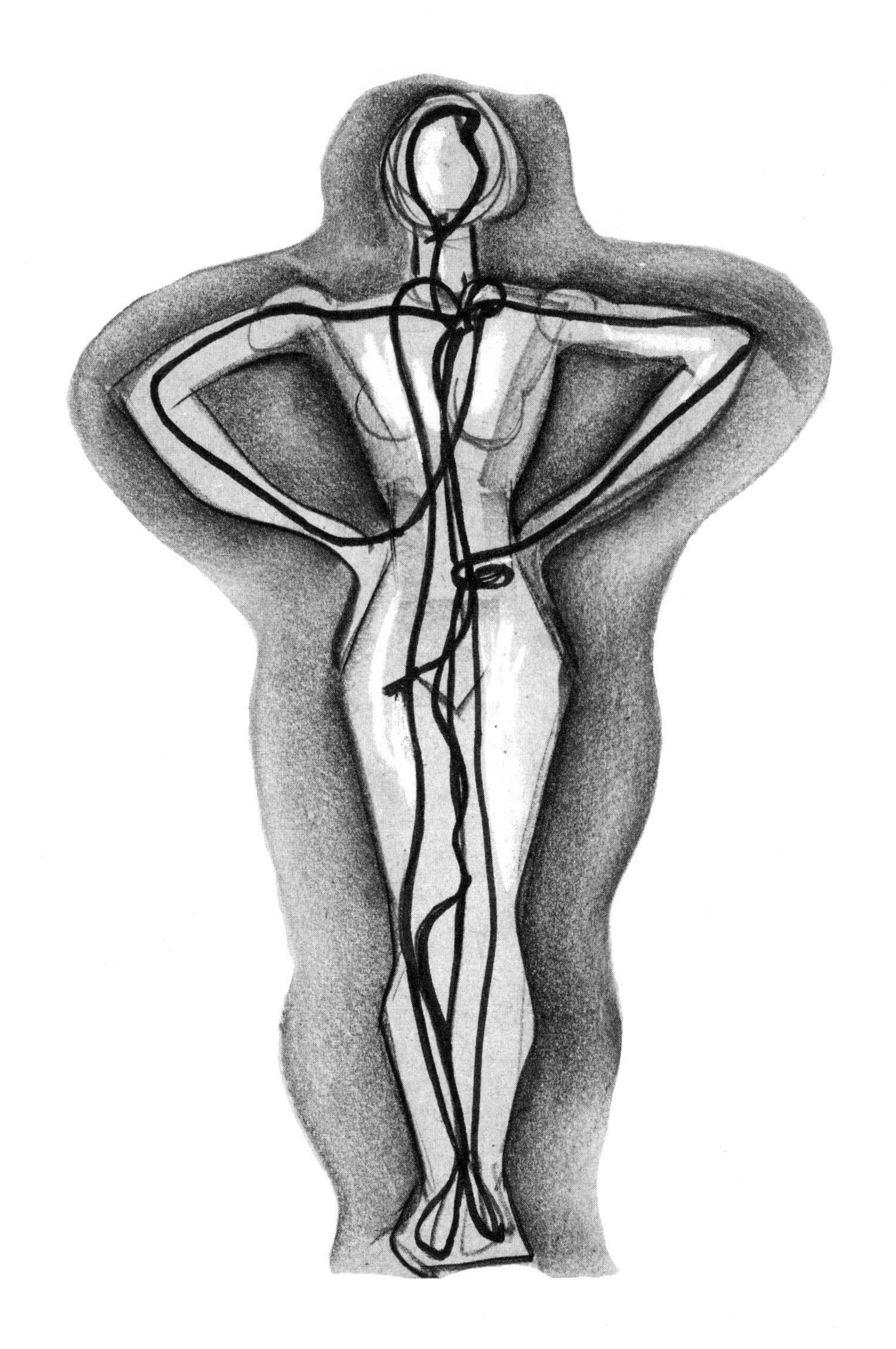

X-RAY OF ARMATURE IN FIGURE This drawing traces the relation of the wire armature to the clay figure. Its convolutions are sufficiently involved to cause the basic clay forms to adhere, but to do so without getting in the way of free creative play with the clay.

Some sculptors insist on a more anatomically true armature, and in some instances it may be desirable, but for figures which do not exceed a foot in height, where great masses of clay do not have to be supported by a thorough skeleton, this free form structure should be quite adequate.

FIRST CLAY STAGE The armature has been completely covered and the stance of the pose has been roughed out.

The first general proportions of the forms have been modeled and the figure stands ready for refinements of shape of forms and features.

This stage is achieved by binding up with small pellets of clay and, in other places, by cutting away with your wooden tools or scrapers.

BACK This back view of the "first stage" shows the early crudeness but the beginnings of a proportioned figure.

The figure should be turned constantly during modeling to keep it in the same state of advancement throughout. When this stage of progress is reached, and the figure is to be left overnight for work the next morning, it must be draped with moist rags or it will dry and become relatively unworkable thereafter and may crack.

In this photograph the figure has been refined to the extent that all the forms have taken their final shape and the arms and legs become modeled in some anatomical detail.

The amount of "finish" desired is strictly up to the individual. A figure may be carried to the ultimate detail and yet lack the realism which may be achieved by simple forms. They need not be crude, but judicious elimination must invariably be preferred to irrelevant detail.

An introduction to the second stage in the modeling—the stage for detail refinements—is as far as the teacher may lead. The next steps are your own to decide upon.

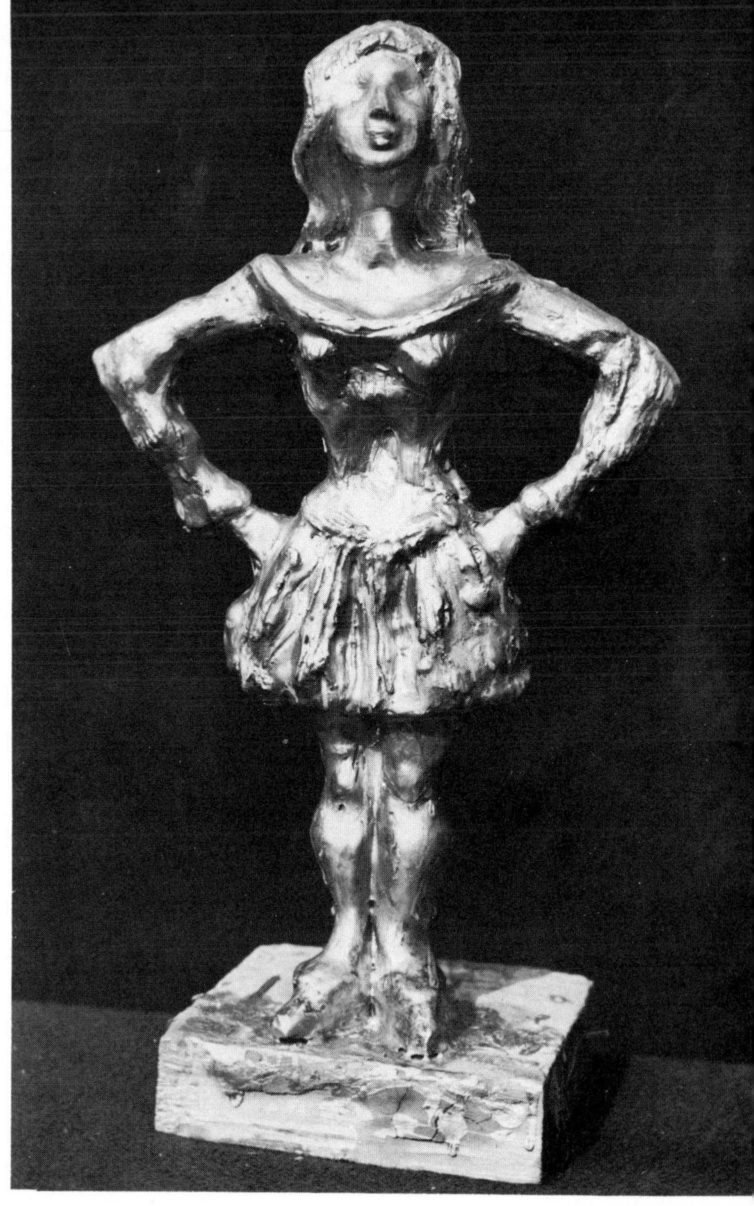

This is the previous figure carried to an advanced state. Though it is not always necessary to model a nude figure and then clothe it, that process often makes for a more solid construction.

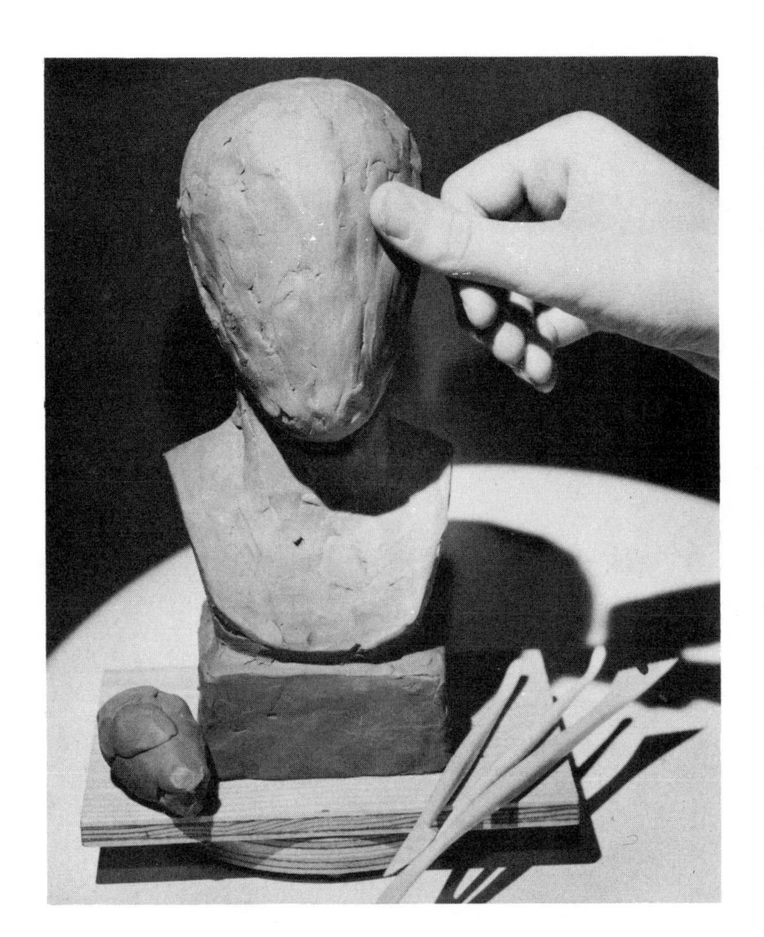

FIVE STAGES IN MODELING A HEAD

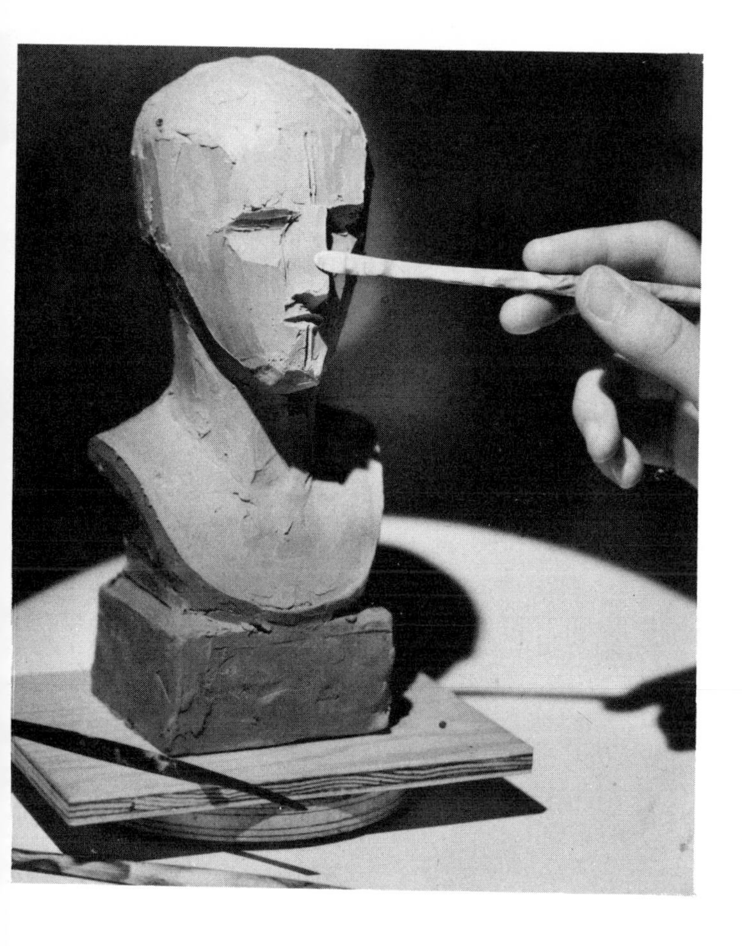

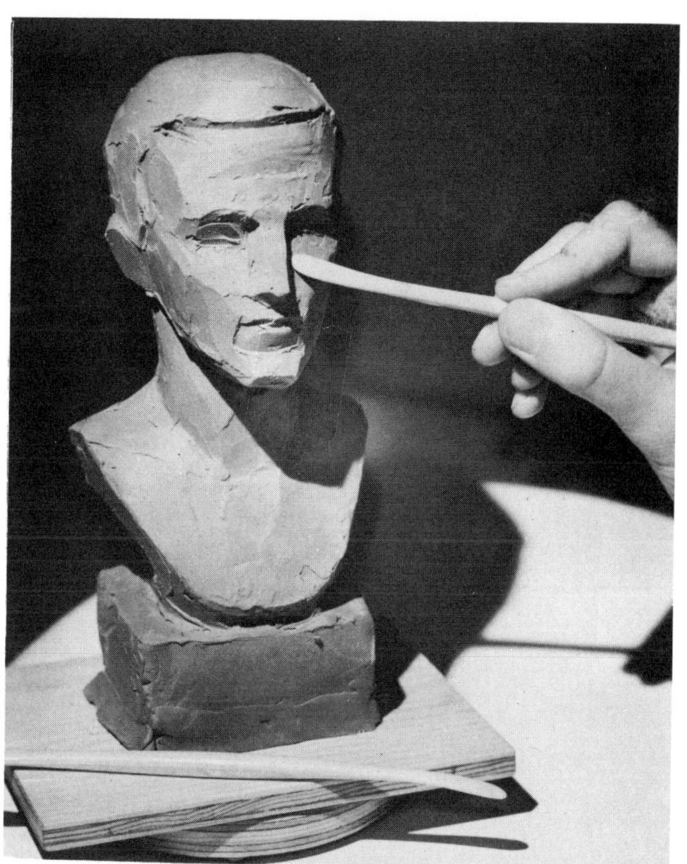

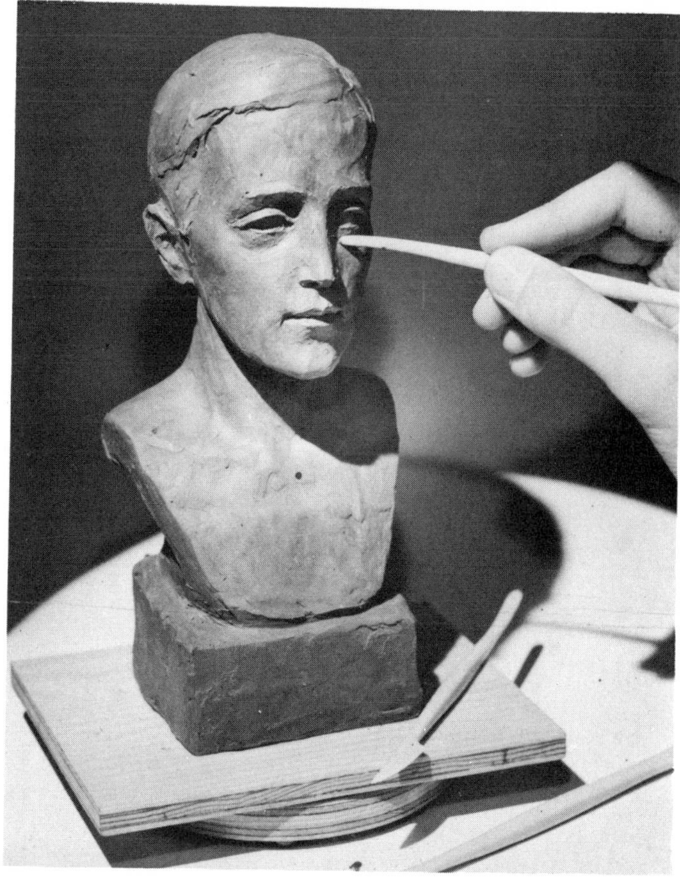

PLASTELINE

Plasteline is a very good starting material for your first figure. Roll out, on any board which is smooth and clean, a series of sausages of plasteline about five inches long and about one inch thick. These will be the firm forms for your figure. Kneading has taken the air pockets out of them and made them relatively solid.

When, during your modeling, they have been joined to each other by spreading firm connecting strips and through their own adhering qualities, the soft material takes on a surprisingly durable firmness.

Plasteline is a commercial preparation available in most art supply shops. It is a mixture of clay and oil which has the property of remaining soft and may be reworked many times. It is a fine material for practice. It comes in wax wrappings in the form of oblong bars and is sold by the pound. It may be had in several colors, usually variations of earth greens, yellows, terra cotta and reds.

It does not always require armature construction to keep it rigid, except where there are required extravagant gestures of thin forms like arms or legs.

FIGURE IN PLASTELINE We shall follow, in the next few pages, the generalized steps in the modeling of a figure in plasteline. First, we approach the drawing of the figure with the ultimate goal always in view—that of the three dimensional figure to be modeled.

The two sketches reproduced above are drawn in as solid and simple a manner as is required for a pre-sculpture drawing. Notice how the planes and large forms are stressed instead of the lesser anatomical details.

Though only the front and back views are shown here, it is well to make side and three-quarter view studies in addition.

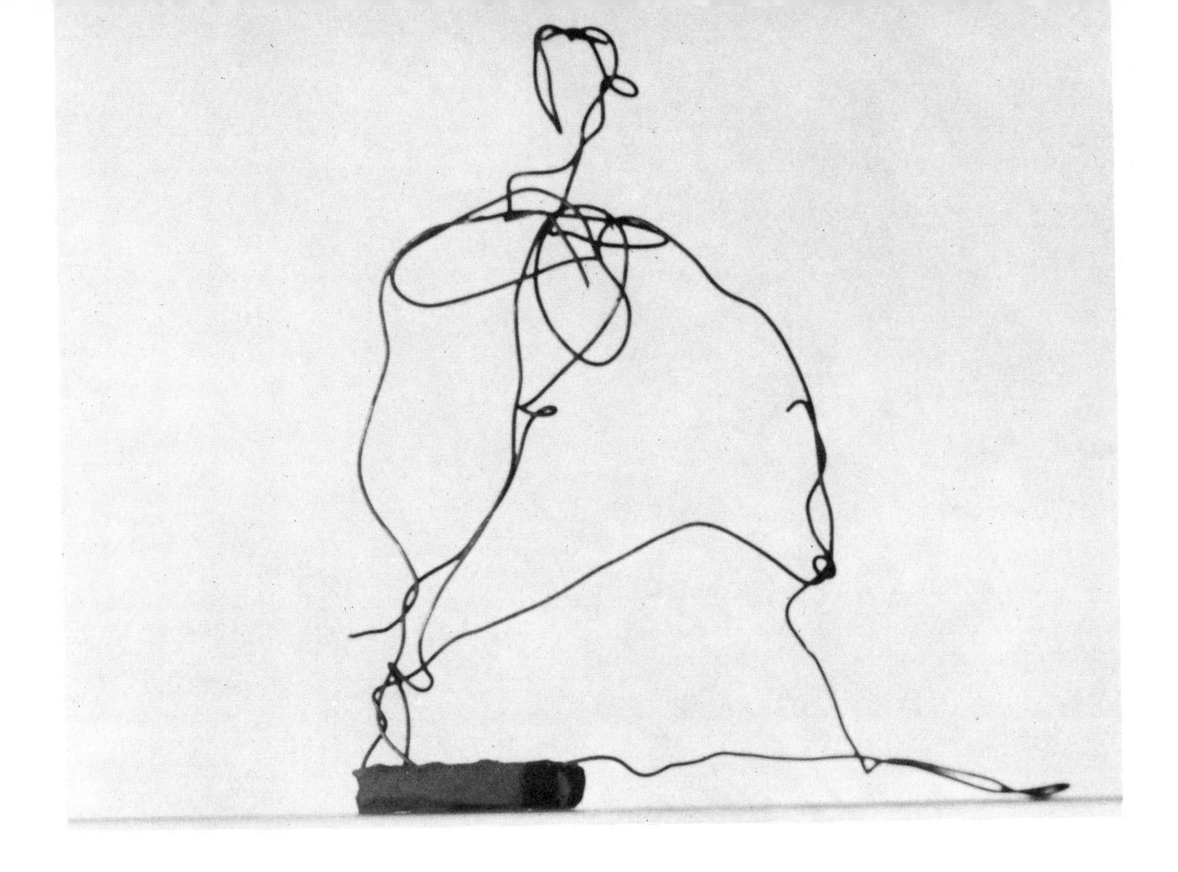

ARMATURE The first step in preparing to model, after your drawings have been made, is the assembling of your plasteline and tools for modeling, in the most accessible, orderly manner, so that you do not add to your difficulties by an uncomfortable setup. You need:

Several pounds of plasteline, a couple of wood modeling tools, homemade or the store-bought type.

A few yards of soft pliable lead wire about one eighth of an inch in thickness.

A small slab of wood to act as a plinth or base for your wire armature.

A few staples and a hammer to tack the armature to the base.

Here you see a very rough generalization of the pencil sketch translated into wire line. No attempt has been made to make an authentic reproduction of the skeleton bone structure.

This informal twist of wire is calculated to support the weight of the plasteline and at the same time to approximate the movement of the figure. It is not so rigid that it may not be changed during the modeling process should one wish to do so.

Its construction, accomplished quickly, nevertheless involved a study of the action involved and an appreciation of the stresses and strains to be put upon it.

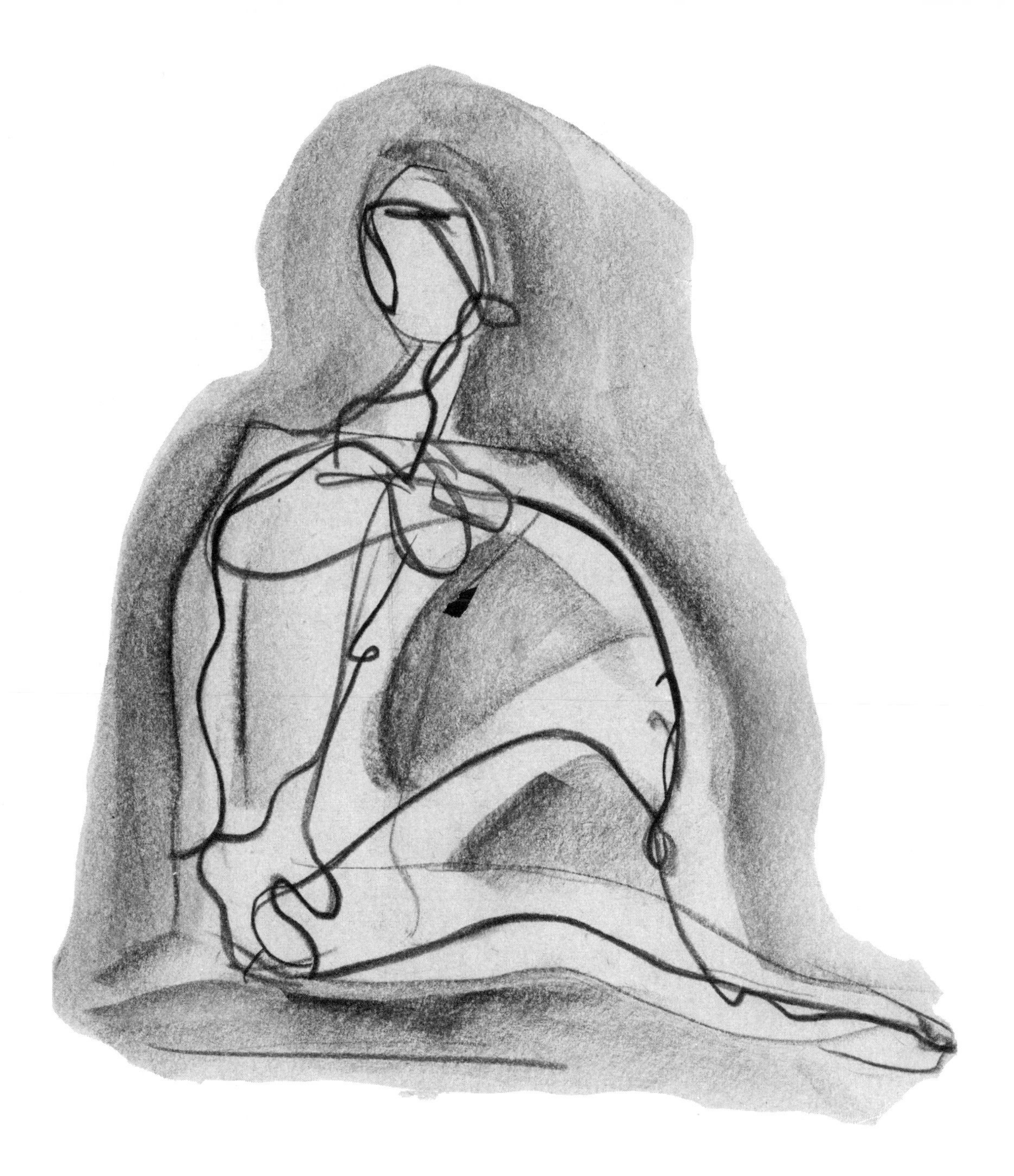

X-RAY Here is an X-ray of the purposes behind the apparently free-twisting "wire sketch."

This is to indicate how the twists of wire aid in supporting masses of plasteline in places where the forms of the body are relatively heavy, as in the chest and buttocks. The arms and legs are single strands of the wire; the head is a rough oval.

Note that this is certainly not a classic armature. It is as individual as a signature and you certainly need not copy it, but it is the type of free scrawl of wire that I have found adequate for small figures, and, I think, you will find it so also.

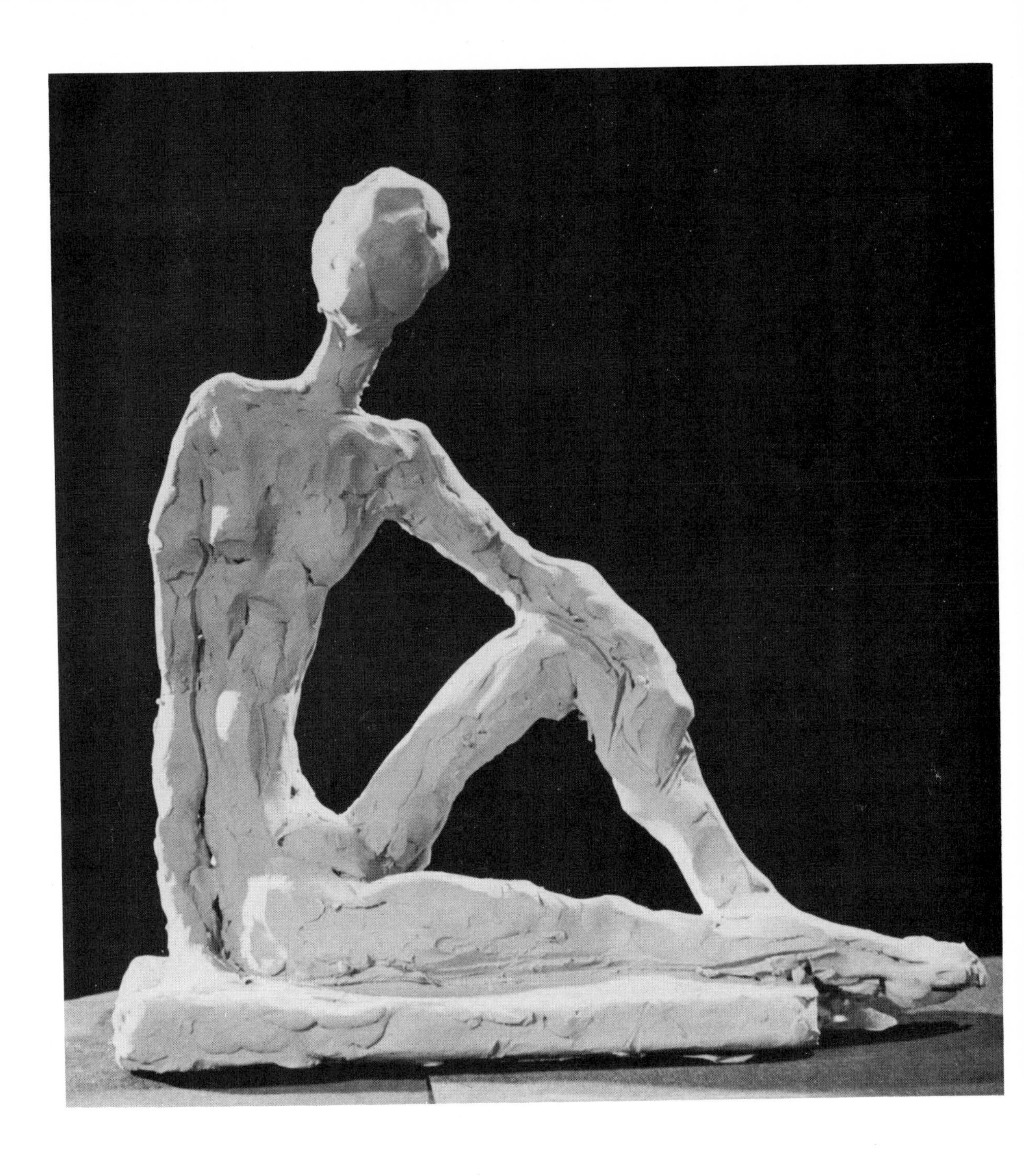

FIRST PLASTELINE STAGE This stage of the figure is the first covered version of the armature. The relative bulk of the masses of the forms has been indicated by slight variations of the weight of plasteline, but the greatest concentration has been on the pose.

Notice the solid plinth which has covered the first wooden block to which the wire had been stapled.

At this stage of the figure's progress the pose may still be varied by gently pressing the plasteline-covered wire strands to a different angle. If the wire breaks through the plasteline, it may still be easily covered.

SECOND PLASTELINE STAGE Here the figure has been carried further.

Notice that the pose has been changed somewhat. The torso inclines farther to the right, the shoulders slant down more than in the first stage, and the angle of the neck and head has been shifted.

At this point, we must concentrate on forms and features which are secondary to the basic ones. The shapes of the limbs are beginning to form and the figure may be carried to any state of detail desired.

BACK OF SECOND STAGE This is a back view of the second stage.

The figure is now proportioned and it is definitely fixed in its pose. Do not work for smoothness of texture or small details until you are sure of the above two steps in your modeling.

Keep turning your figure on the turntable and try to keep all sides at the same state of development throughout the work.

There is no point in showing the following stages since the individuality of the sculptor and his personal techniques assert themselves, and inevitably each work will be different.

WALL PLAQUES An excellent exercise for making reliefs of more serious nature is to make many small "pretzels" of related figures in hardening clay or terra cotta for baking.

These are usually most effective when kept to a small size of, perhaps, 8 inches in diameter.

They need not be made on a base. They are quite effective if the spaces between forms are open and the wall shows through when they are hung. They are usually light enough to be suspended flat against the wall by light supporting finishing nails which do not show their heads.

Here is an example of such interlaced figures used as a plaque.

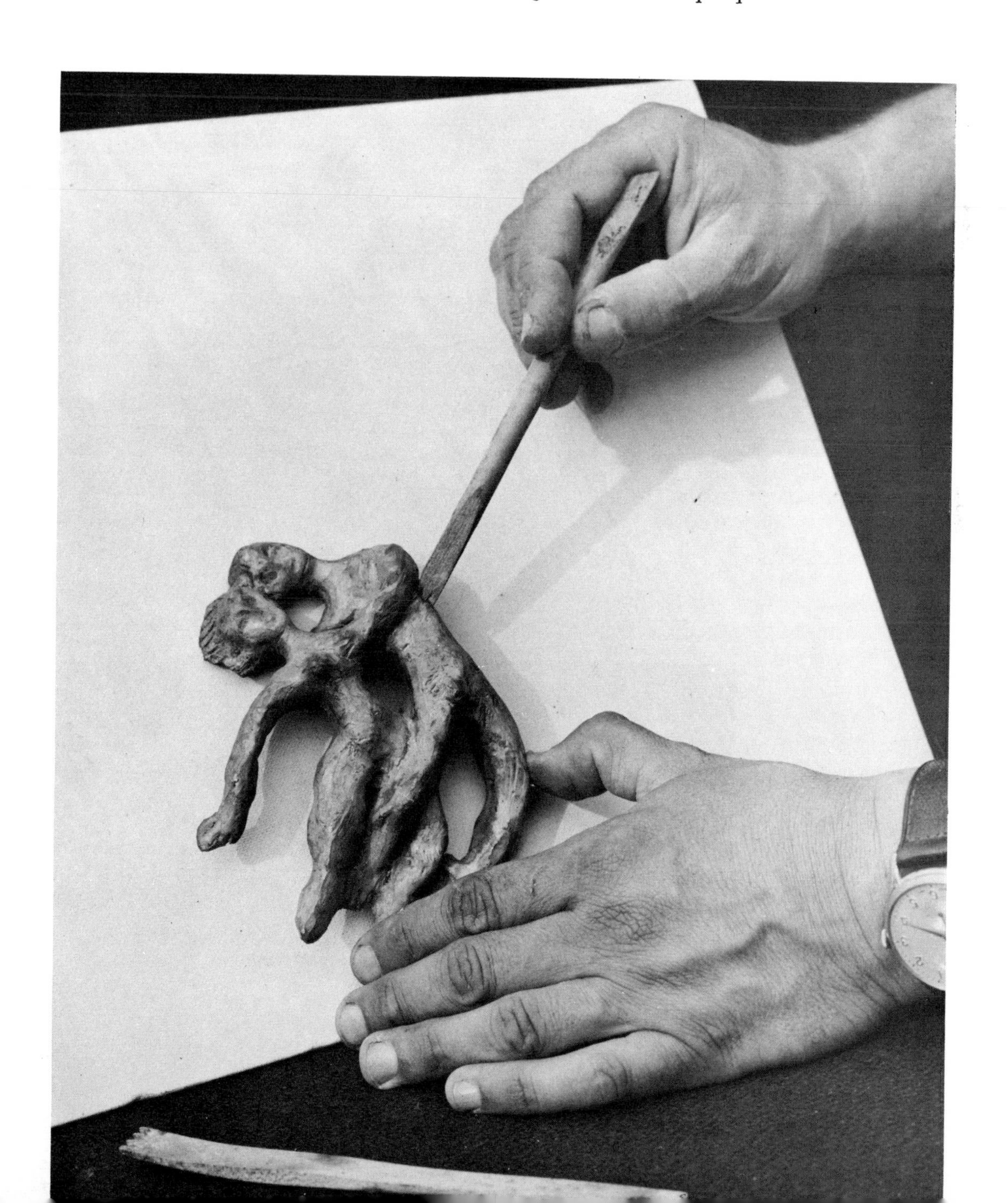

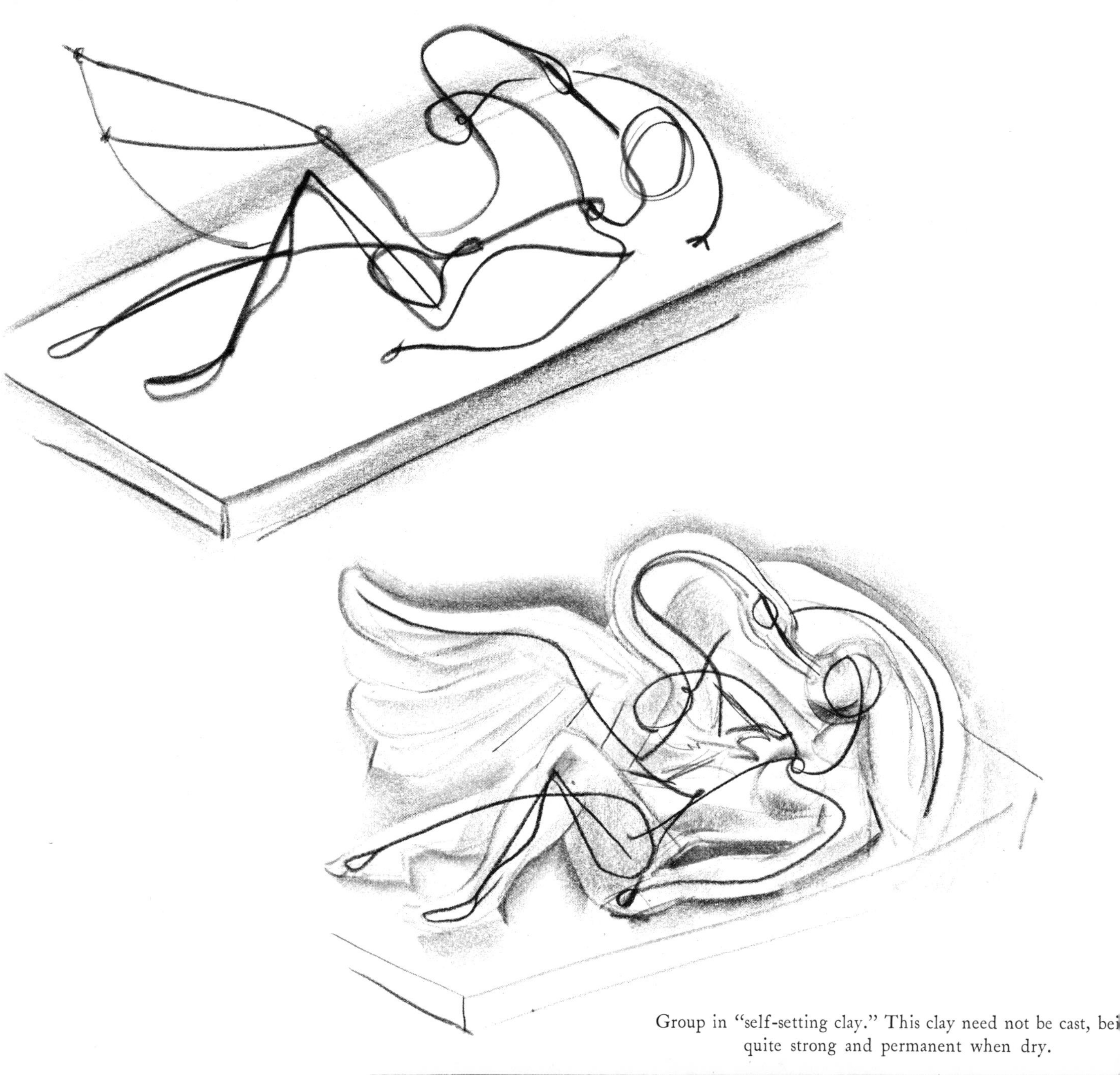

Group in "self-setting clay." This clay need not be cast, bei
quite strong and permanent when dry.

DRAPERY

In simulating draped folds in modeling or carving, avoid attempting realism to the extent of exact reproduction.

Every bit of drape has a definite source of suspension and when this is traced and used as a guide the main vertical folds which hang from it, pulled by force of gravity, become quickly apparent. Indicate these and the secondary few radiating folds, and you will have suggested soft drapery.

The nature of the draped material is better suggested by its natural action than by simulation of actual texture.

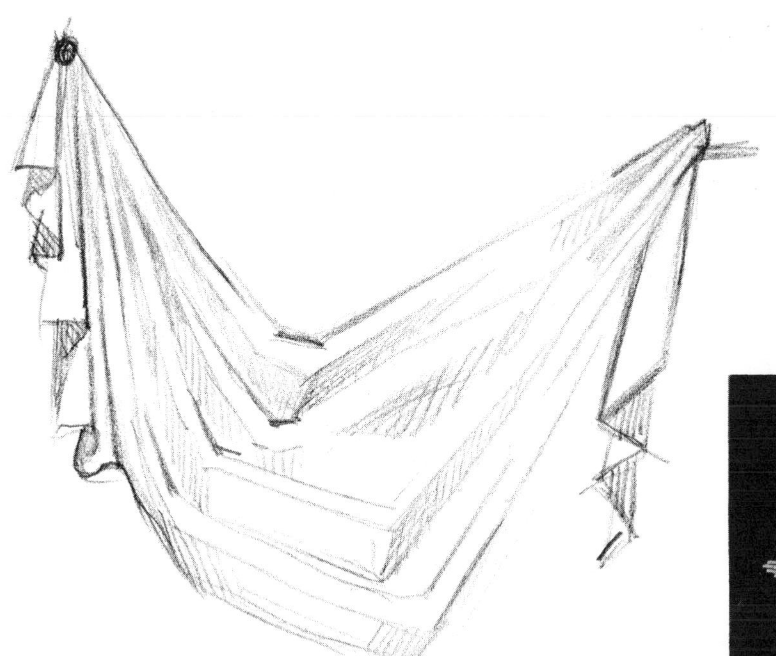

"The Christ of the Andes," Rio de Janeiro.

Classic draped figures.

DIRECT METAL SCULPTURE

Figures executed in their permanent, final form by the sculptor, without the use of casts or any transference agency are called direct sculpture figures. New methods of sculpture in metal have evolved a direct approach to various metals.

Many modern sculptors are sculpturing directly in metal by the following methods:

Cutting—for mobiles, etc.; tin, copper, lead.

Hammering—beaten lead or copper hammered into the desired shape from flat sheets.

Melting—iron or lead or steel melted into shape by acetylene torch, blow torch, or soldering iron.

Modeling—metal materials have been reduced by solvents to a plastic putty form suitable for modeling.

Pouring—liquefied metals, commercially prepared, poured over clay, plaster, or plasteline modeled figures to give a heavy coat of metal, permanent and durable.

MODELING IN METAL

There has been made available to sculptors a really revolutionary material which enables the user actually to model in metal. Of a plastic consistency, this metal allows the sculptor to build up his figure at leisure, while it remains soft and damp by the use of a solvent. When the work is complete, the metal is allowed to dry several hours, and it hardens into a strong, durable, pewterlike character. It is not a synthetic but a real metal though the formula is a manufacturer's secret.

Until the modern miracles of chemistry produced this metal in putty form sculptors were restricted to two forms of producing work in metal. They either had to make a mold and cast molten metal into the shape they required, or they wrought metal into shapes by hammering heated bars or sheets of raw metal, fashioning their objective laboriously from the rough. Both methods are expensive and difficult. With the advent of plastic metal sculptors may model in the same manner as they have with clay through the ages.

The material is put up in cans of varying sizes and of moderate cost. An 8-inch figure may be made with about a pound of plastic metal at the cost of about three dollars for material.

There is also a plastic metal solvent with which one may soften the plastic metal to the most desirable working consistency. Its other uses will be explained as we proceed. The plastic metal I have found most suitable to my needs is called Metal-Modelene, and the solvent liquid, Metal-Modelene Solvent. It may be bought at many art supply shops or at the address listed on p. 177.

ARMATURE As in preparing for modeling in clay or plasteline, an armature is made for metal modeling.

This armature may be of quite light construction since the metal will be put on it in relatively thin coats, each coat being allowed to harden so that the wire of the armature is never required to support much soft, dragging weight.

Notice in the accompanying photo that a small turntable is clamped to the edge of a work bench. Such tables are sold in most art supply stores and are useful for small figure modeling work. The table turns as you model around the figure and saves considerable energy.

This armature is made of light-gauge wire, but it is quite rigid. It is fixed into a wooden base by thrusting the wire ends into two nail holes.

The small pliers shown are used for cutting the wire as well as for twisting it into the desired shape.

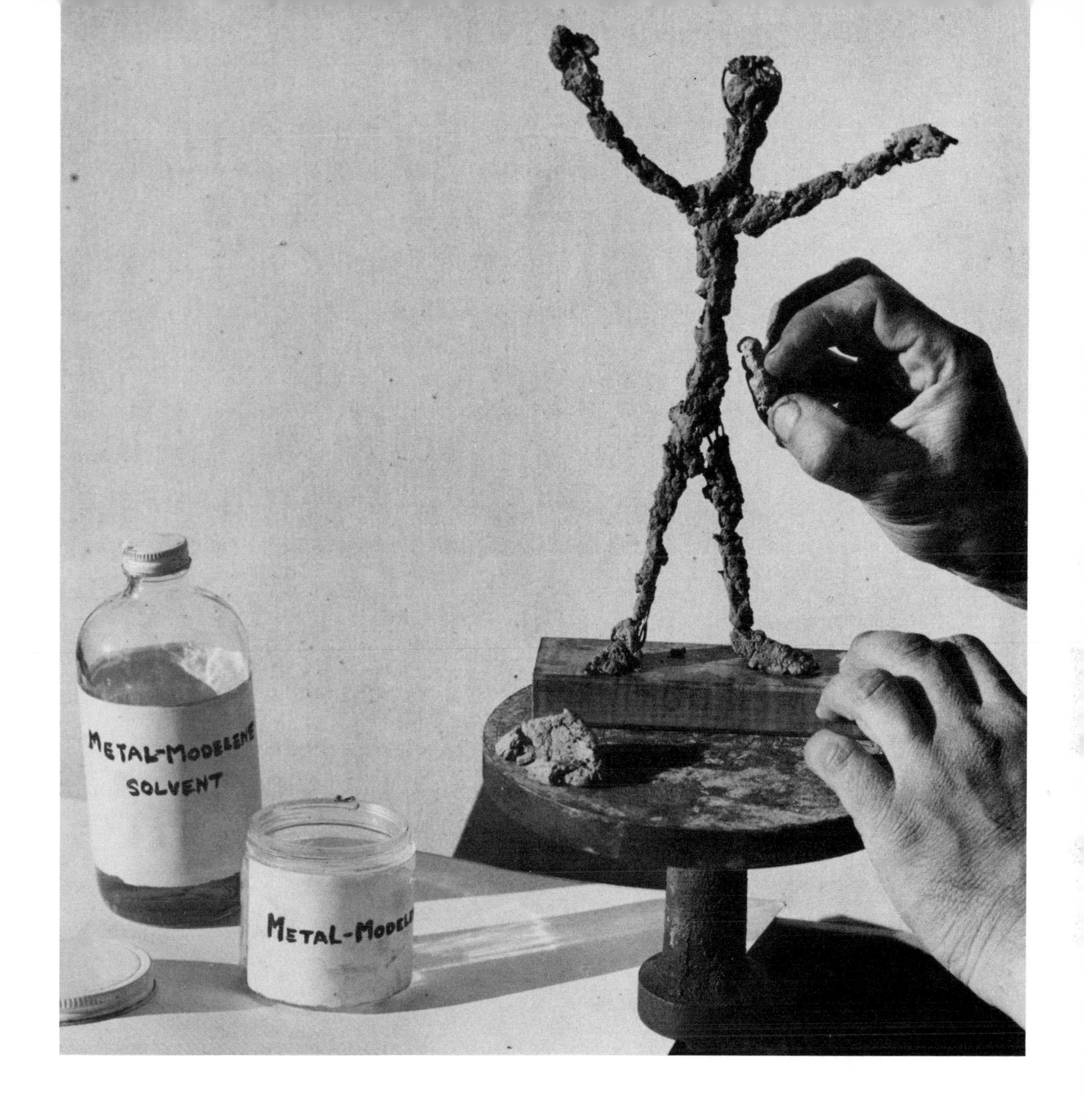

APPLYING FIRST METAL COAT Here the armature is covered with an all-over coating of plastic metal. It has been applied in little gobs, merged to their neighbors by a squeeze with the thumb. Allow this first covering of plastic metal to set for perhaps a half hour before you proceed to build up your figure with more metal.

In this way you form a semihard core which adds to the strength of the armature and facilitates the whole hardening process.

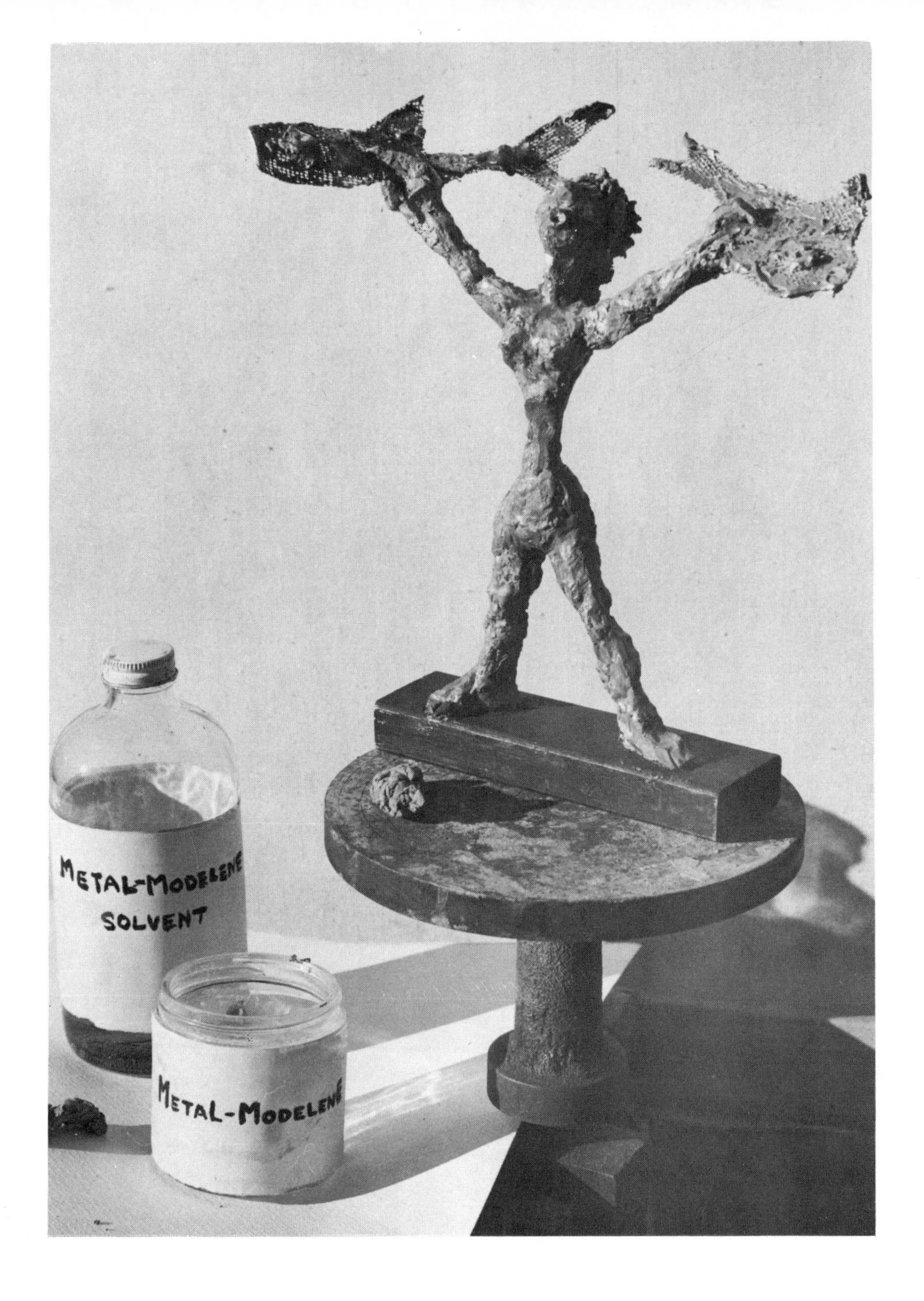

BUILDING THE FIGURE When the first metal coat has dried somewhat, you may proceed with building the figure in detail.

Here is the figure roughly completed. The fish forms are made of metal screening upon which some plastic metal is used to suggest features, but the translucent screen is deliberately exposed, utilizing its texture for the scaly fish effect.

The plastic metal figure is now ready for treatment necessary to bring it to the smoothness or detail modeling desired. When hardened by several hours of drying, it may be filed or sanded to a burnished smoothness.

POWER TOOL SANDING Here, an electric hand tool similar to those used by home hobbyists and amateur carpenters is fitted with sanding emery stone. The metal takes a high burnish. Rough edges may be removed and even form-modeled into the metal with this tool.

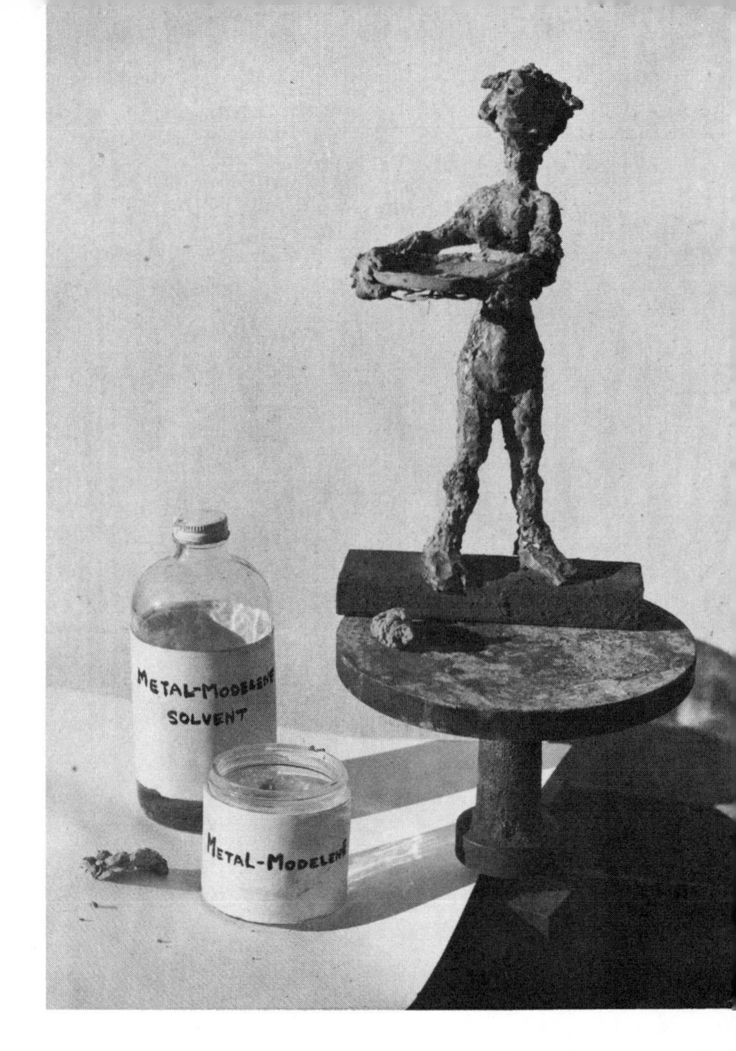
METAL-MODELENE
SOLVENT
METAL-MODELENE

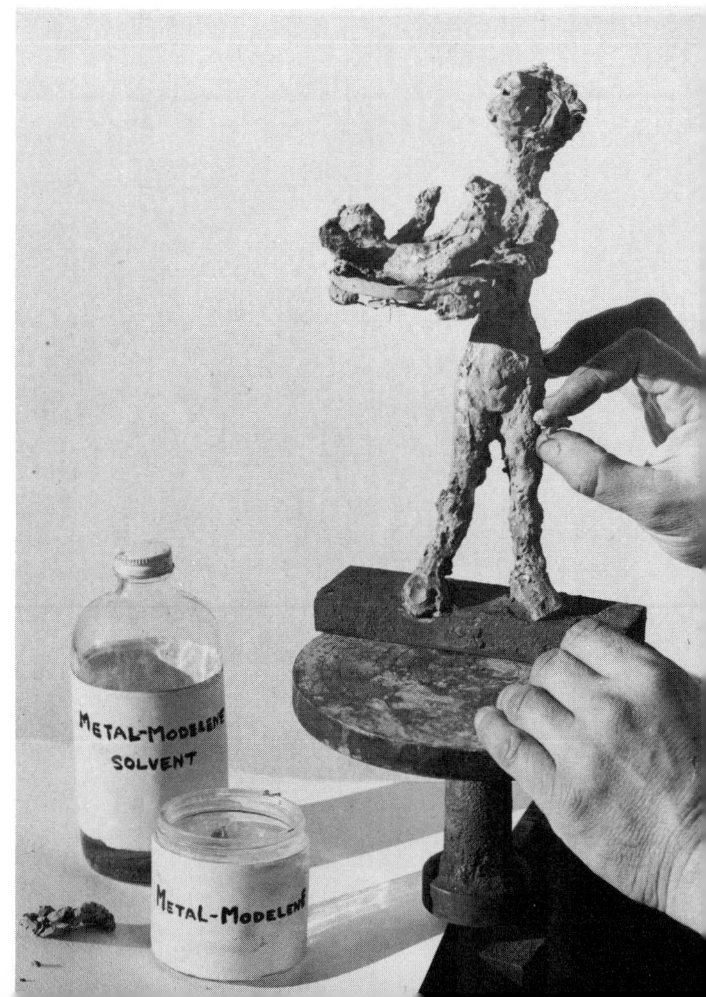
METAL-MODELENE
SOLVENT
METAL-MODELENE

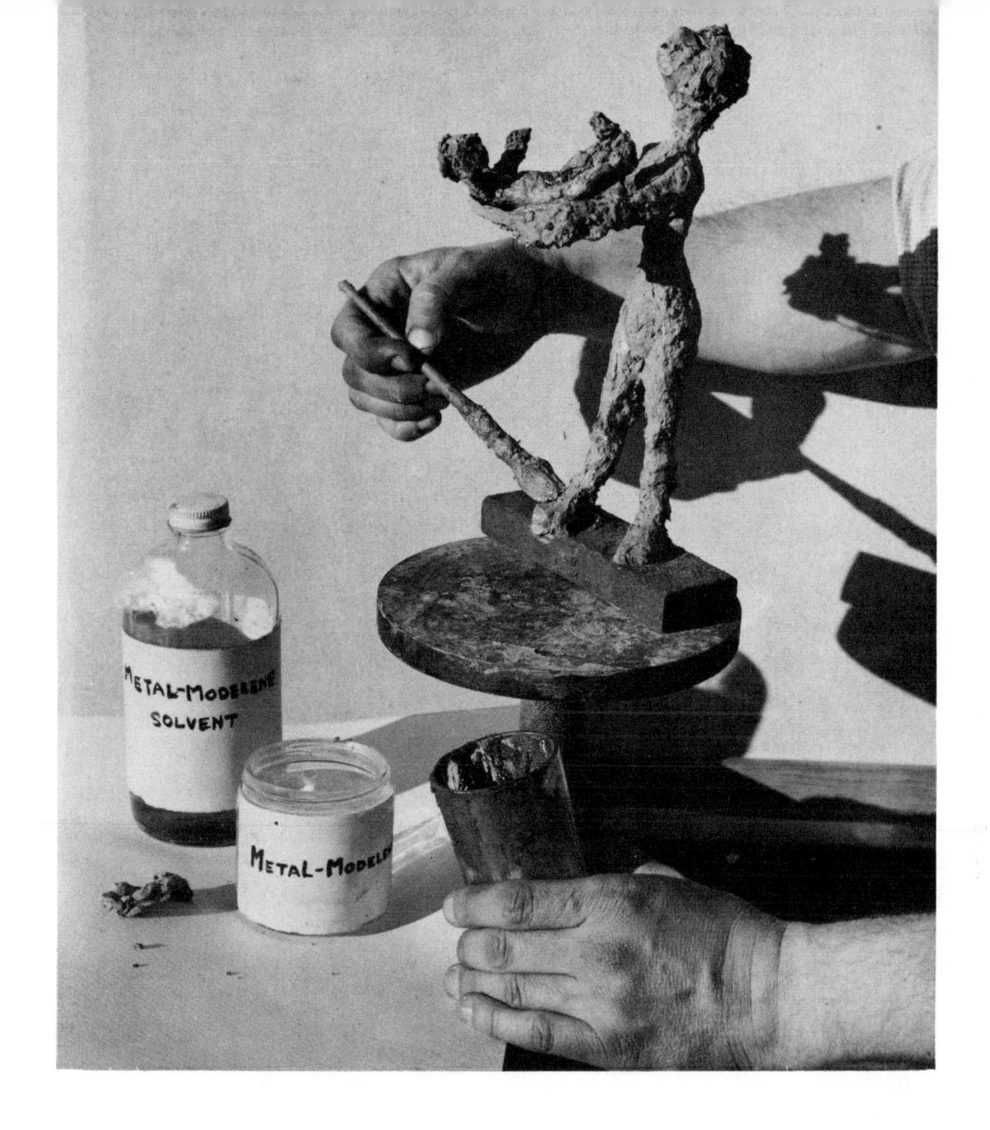

USE OF SLIP

Slip is the term used by sculptors and ceramists to describe a solution of their working material reduced to almost liquid fluidity which is applied as a smooth surface coating or as a repairing substance to fill cracks and pits. It may be applied with a brush.

For modeling in plastic metal, a slip is prepared by diluting a few gobs of the stuff in the metal solvent. When it is in a thick liquid form it may be painted on your figure to give a smooth coat, or it may be used to fill craters and cracks. Another important use for your metal slip is to give a patina to your figure.

The Metal-Modelene substance is of a dark gray color which when dry resembles pewter or battleship gray. Bronze or silver powder may be mixed with the slip, and when it is brushed on the semidry figure, the slip will merge solidly with the under metal, and the bronze patina (or whatever coloring you have added) will become part of the fused whole.

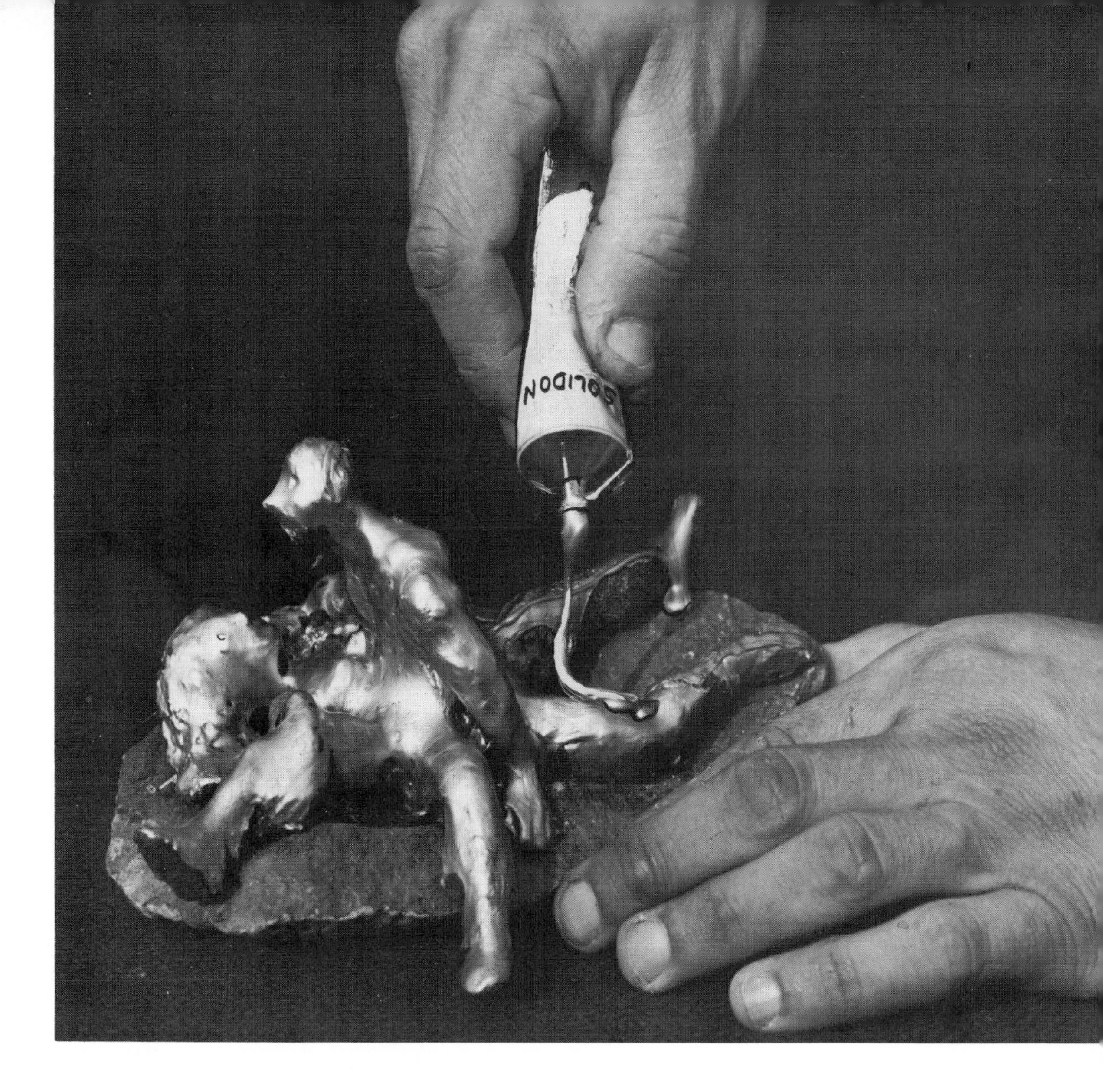

METAL COVERING

Liquid, "cold" metal is available at any art supply store in small tubes or jars. This may be used in conjunction with your melted solder for mending and for reaching relatively inaccessible parts. It may also be used as an independent medium—a quick and inexpensive way of covering a small figure, made of virtually any substance, with a coat of durable metal.

The liquid solder may be controlled with more ease than the hot melted solder and one can arrive at smoother surfaces than are possible with the soldering iron technique.

The liquid metal flows freely and may be applied directly from the tube. The gobs of flowing metal solder should be applied from the top of your armature working downward so that the pull of gravity will spread the thick

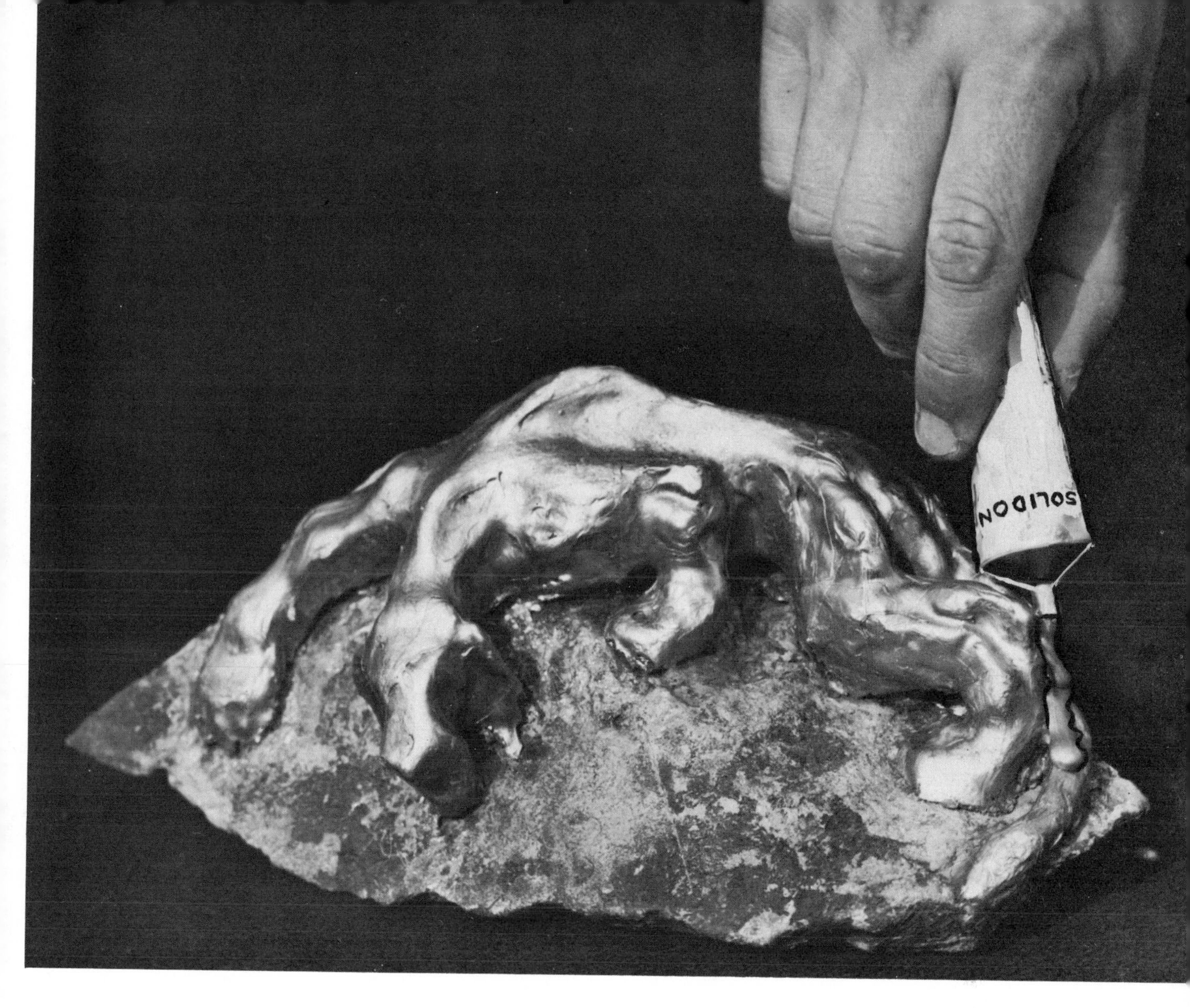

stream evenly as it courses down over the armature or base you have constructed. Any blunt tool may be used as a spreader where the liquid collects in too thick gobs.

The liquid solder drys within a few hours and coat after coat may be applied depending on the solidity you require. When dry it assumes a somewhat shiny silver color. This may be tinted with bronzing powder or "tarnished" into almost any desired patina by washes of color or rubbing and wiping stove blacking on the surface. Experimenting with various tinting techniques will result in discoveries to please your individual taste.

This method of "metal sculpture" is completely new and as open to development as the boldness of your imagination permits.

The art supply stores carry a liquid metal for sculptors called Solidon.

Here are some photographs of stages of the process and some finished pieces.

The liquid solder metal holds this animal piece to the rock base without the use of bolts.

Clay stage.

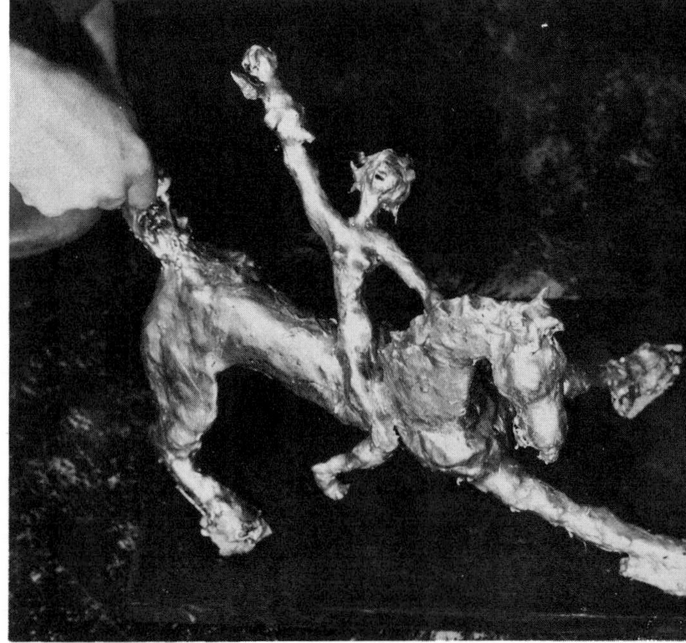

THE SOLDERING METHOD

The new fields of adventure open to the experimentally minded sculptor are ever increasing. With the advent of new materials and the escape from slavish copying of nature the sculptor now may play with substances and shapes with great freedom.

No set techniques have been devised in these new sculpture methods and each sculptor uses them as he pleases and adds to the general fund of methods by the results he obtains in his experiments.

One of the new direct metal sculpture methods, still very much open to experiment, is the soldering method. Here is a general outline of the approach with the addition of a few details which I have found interesting for my own uses and which you may use and develop as you explore the medium on your own.

The materials used are:

A plug-in electric soldering iron—This should be of sufficient wattage to melt heavy solder wire quickly. I have used an 85-watt iron which acts with sufficient speed and heat for most soldering wire. This may be plugged into the usual 110-volt electric plug. Should there be no electricity available in your studio the type of iron which is heated on live coals would, of course, serve as well.

The most popular soldering material is one which has the higher tin content—preferred is the 60 per cent tin 40 per cent lead mixture. I have found the 50-50 is good and even the 40 per cent tin 60 per cent lead is adequate. Solder is obtainable in most hardware stores in wire form on spools of one pound. Where the spools are not available the bar form, though less easy to handle, is serviceable.

Flux paste is a substance with which metals to be covered with solder are lightly painted in order that the solder may adhere more easily. There are also liquid soldering preparations which accomplish the same purpose and are available in most hardware shops. I find that the flux paste is better but in either case they should be used sparingly because when the work is finished and a patina is to be applied the flux causes irregularity in the patina, sometimes rejecting the acids entirely.

Lead foil—Sheets of lead foil, very thin, are useful for covering armature not receptive to solder. These are obtainable at some hardware stores. Where not available tin foil may be used instead though the solder drips do not adhere as well.

Wire for armature—An armature strong enough on which one may build up the metal figure is required. While the metal solder has its own strength the weight is not always equally distributed and a shaky armature may interfere with your work. Heavy steel wire is good but this must be covered by lead foil or tin foil because the solder will not adhere to steel. The same is true for aluminum. Copper wire may be soldered easily and, of course, lead wire, but these are not as firm for a large, heavy armature planned for many pounds of solder.

Where a piece of sculpture is planned to have bulk and wide body forms, a covering of tubes of copper or a galvanized screening may be used. These should be wrapped around the wire armature and held in place by thin wires. Another method of obtaining bulk for your armature is to cover areas with sheet tin cut from cans or bought in hardware stores. Very light gauge tin is needed so that it may be squeezed into the forms desired easily.

A patina for soldering sculpture may be obtained by acid burns which transform the silver metal into a semblance of copper or pewter or bronze, as desired. Experiments with various strengths of acid with the addition of various coloring powders produce a wide range of possible patinas. Use copper nitrate, copper carbonate, or potassium sulfide. Dilute with water to vary strength. Apply with a brush or feather.

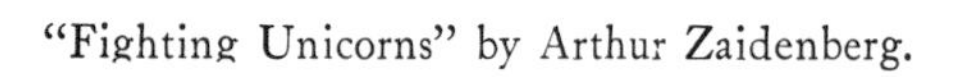

"Fighting Unicorns" by Arthur Zaidenberg.

WELDING METALS

IN recent years welding metal has become one of the most popular media for the sculptor.

The contemporary artist has often turned toward working directly in metal because of the laborious process of carving stone or wood and the obvious limitations of these materials in an age of dynamic soaring of both architectural and mechanical structures. Working in metal frequently allows him to use more imagination and liberty in his work.

Iron, steel, brass, and copper offer unlimited possibilities for the inventive artist. Their malleability under intense heat and the ease with which pieces of metal may be fused and joined to other pieces of the same or different metal make them ideally suited for the direct, forceful expression of creative ideas, whether on a grand or a small scale.

Properly cared for, these metal sculptures are as permanent as stone and far more so than wood. Their natural qualities of color and texture are as variable as stone and wood, ivory or bone.

Metals may also be treated with acids or fused with patinas of other metals to add brilliant hues to their natural qualities.

The tool required for working directly in metal sculpturing is the welding torch.

A description of the nature of this splendid tool, the preparations and care to be taken in handling it, and the methods of its use in bending and joining metal will follow in this chapter, but as a preliminary procedure I would suggest that the student who is interested in this medium familiarize himself with the contemporary welded-sculpture scene.

Look at the innumerable fine examples of metal sculpture in the art magazines and art books available in your public library. Go to exhibitions of welded sculpture and enjoy the wide range of techniques employed.

If after having done so you are inspired to use the welding medium, only then go to the expense and trouble of setting up a suitable welding area in your studio.

The matter of expense is not too serious. For less than two hundred dollars a complete outfit for welding may be acquired. Thereafter the expenses are perhaps less than those involved in carving. Scrap metal is far cheaper than marble or rare woods. Junk piles are all too ubiquitous in many parts of every town and they offer free material for even elaborate welded sculpture if the artist uses his imagination. Some of our modern sculptors have made monumental pieces from the scrap materials freely available in our wasteful society.

If the expense is not too serious, the matter of providing suitable work space is more so. Though welding equipment is not very dangerous to use, the welder must work in areas not too vulnerable to fire. The tanks of oxygen and acetylene which are the source of fuel for the torch are somewhat cumbersome and require a few square feet of space. Room to maneuver with the torch is required. These are the main considerations to be dealt with in undertaking welding.

Should you be able to overcome these few and far from insuperable difficulties, the welding-sculpture process will amply repay you with its great qualities in terms of freedom of expression, permanence, and beauty.

The hunt for stone or wood desirable for sculpture, especially for city-dwelling artists, has become more difficult in recent years. Such materials have become both rare and expensive and their bulk and weight unfeasible for the crowded living conditions of today. In addition, these materials and their natural limitations are less suitable to the experimental and libertarian ideas of modern artists.

Precious patinas and subtle textures have lost much of their appeal in our mechanical age and have given way to the symbolic manmade strength of iron and steel.

The easy accessibility of scrap metal and its readily malleable nature, subject to quick bending and twisting and shaping into strong and permanent structures, appeal strongly to the artist striving impatiently to express his message without the impediments of painful muscular effort and time-consuming whittling and chipping into the depths of materials which have the added disadvantage of possessing restricting boundaries.

An additional advantage—and in my opinion the one which has truly liberated the sculptor from the age-long principles of the solid-mass concepts of sculpture—is the possibility of "drawing" with metal directly, as one could do previously only with the linear tools of the artist—pencil and charcoal or brush and paint.

Working directly with twisted wire, hammered and forged metal, or heat-bent and welded rods, the sculptor has added a rich quality virtually nonexistent in the carving and modeling eras of sculpture.

That thousands of sculptors have eagerly taken to the use of direct metal work is not surprising considering all the virtues of these new materials and methods.

You will require:

A work bench, table high, which is made of metal or at least covered with a sheet of steel.

A small vise and several clamps for holding the piece you are working on since you require both hands to be free for your welding.

A pair of leather gloves, gauntlets preferred, is necessary to avoid hand burns. You are bound to get a few from picking up hot metal by mistake and other accidental heat contacts. These are acceptable occupational hazards and unless they are serious enough to require medical attention home unguents for burns will suffice as treatment.

Buy or make a leather apron to further protect yourself and your clothes from sparks.

Pliers and a hammer (for straightening rods too thick for hand bending when you do not wish to use the torch for such purposes) should complete your basic tool requirements.

The metals you will need for your welding sculpture will be dealt with on another page.

For light sculpture welding the minimum kit is quite adequate.

It usually contains the following pieces:

1. Three torches of varying size.
2. Torch holder and two hoses to be attached to the oxygen and acetylene cylinders (which are not part of the kit).
3. Two sets of regulators which are to be affixed to the cylinders and which indicate the amount of gas in each cylinder, plus the pressure gauge to indicate the amount of each gas flowing through the hoses to the torch.
4. A pair of goggles, indispensible for protection of the eyes, both from the intense glare of the flame and from flying sparks.
5. A sparker for igniting the torch.
6. A cutting torch for cutting heavy metal.
7. Some kits contain a special wrench for affixing regulators, tightening connections, etc. Monkey wrenches and regular pliers should not be used.

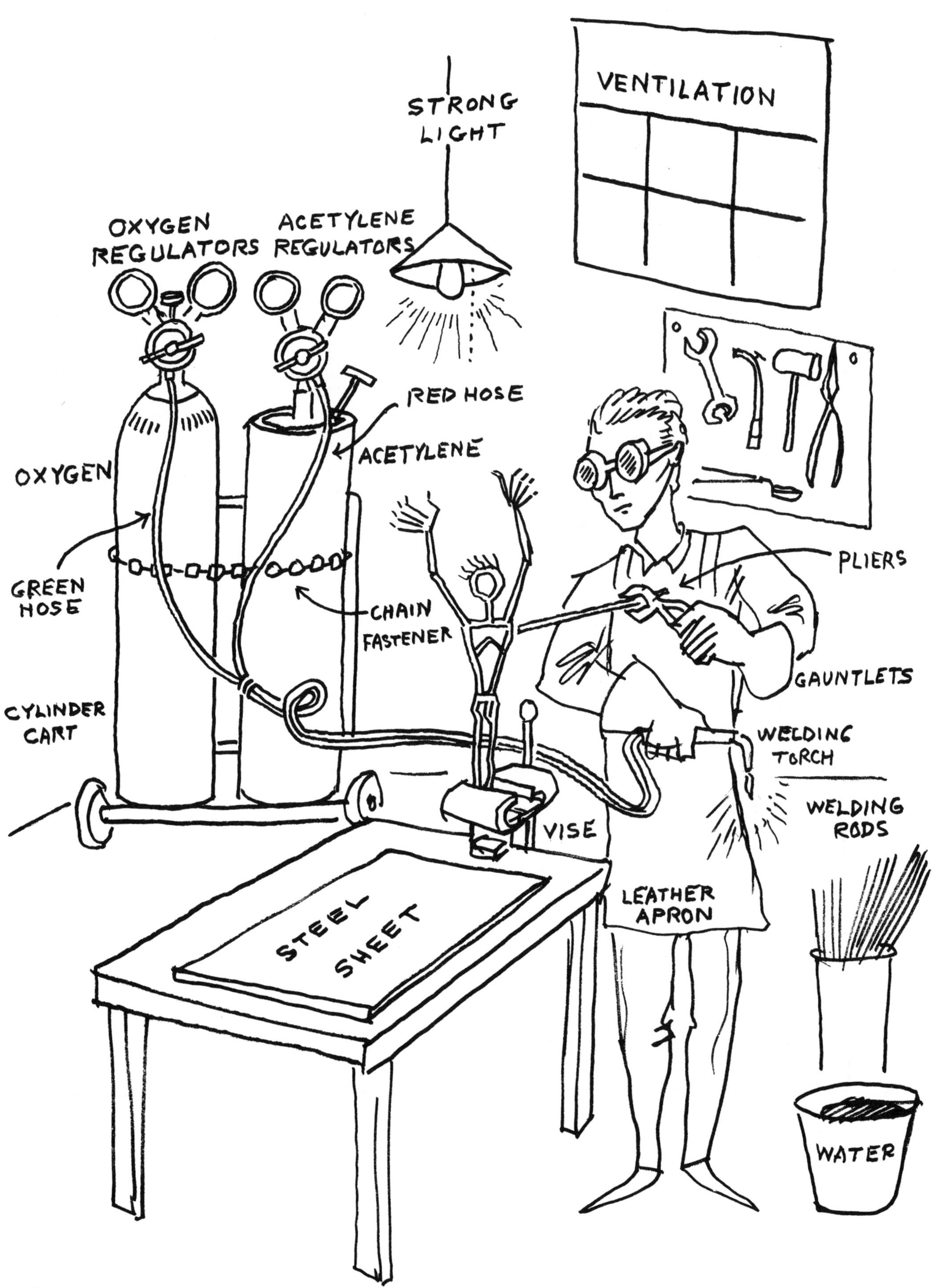
VENTILATION
STRONG LIGHT
OXYGEN REGULATORS
ACETYLENE REGULATORS
RED HOSE
ACETYLENE
OXYGEN
GREEN HOSE
CHAIN FASTENER
PLIERS
GAUNTLETS
CYLINDER CART
WELDING TORCH
WELDING RODS
VISE
LEATHER APRON
STEEL SHEET
WATER

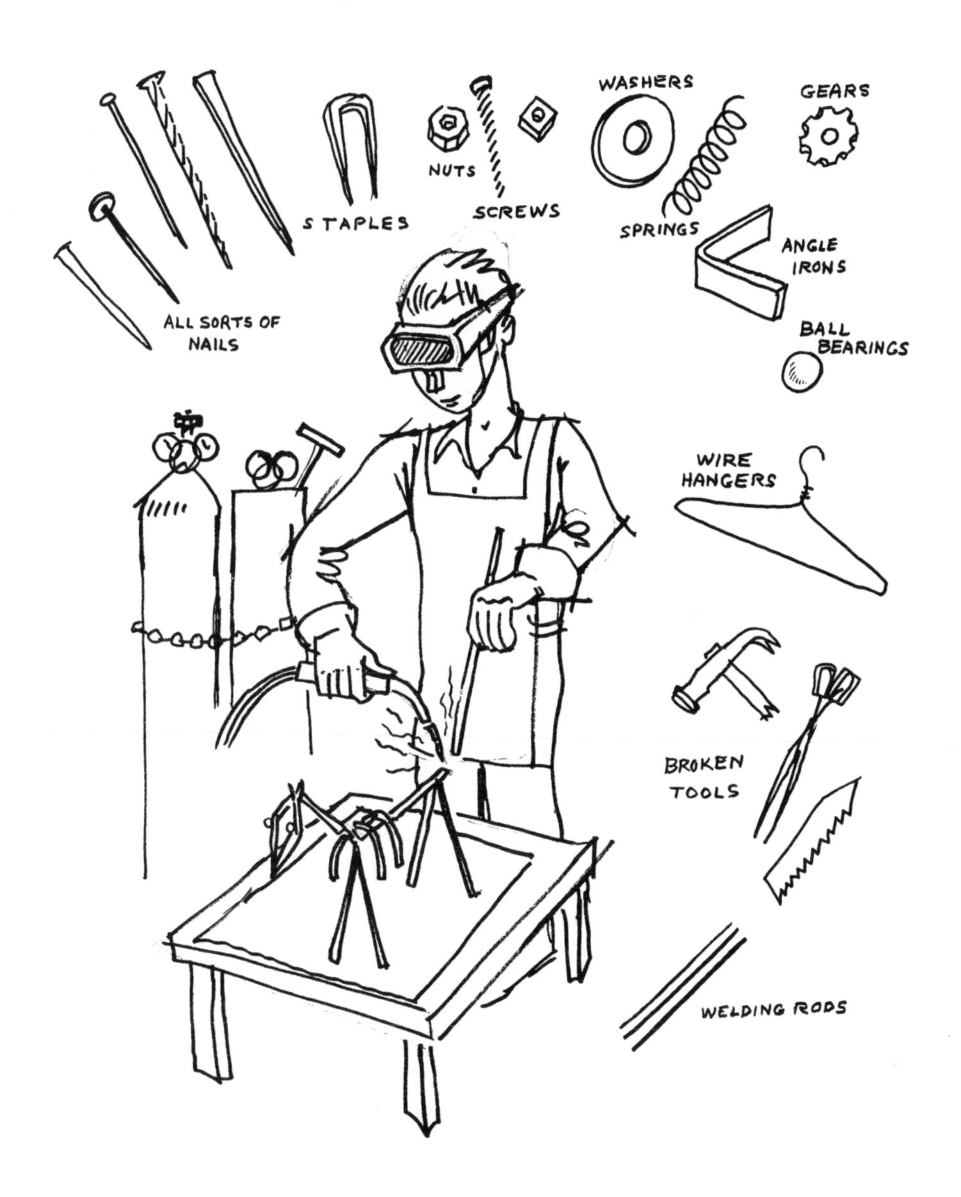

MATERIALS

For the imaginative welder-sculptor all metal junk is a rich source of working material. Broken old garden tools, rakes, trowels, shovels, and the entrails of old cars suggest themes and anatomical parts for the implementation of those themes.

From iron and steel supply yards rods and heavy steel wire may be bought cheaply by the foot or yard and in many varying thicknesses. Light-gauge steel sheets for the more solid areas of your work are also readily available at these yards.

For the less adventurous student sculptor the welding cylinder supplier usually carries an assortment of soft metal welding rods. These rods, actually intended as metal additives for the professional commercial welder, are excellent structural rods for the sculptor. They are easily fused together with the torch, and the sculptor may bend them and "draw" his figures in steel line. Solid areas may be added, using steel sheeting, if desired.

The novice at welding should begin the study of the process by practicing the basic step in constructing in welded iron or steel: joining two flat pieces of steel (or iron) by "beading" drops of molten metal from a slim welding rod at the juncture edges of the two pieces of metal.

This process, as studied in commercial welding schools, is one upon which the instructors demand long practice until the seam is made with great precision. For the student sculptor, however, the seam need not be made with commercial precision and satisfactory joinings may be learned with an hour or two of practice.

The method is as follows:

Holding the torch flame close to the two steel edges until they turn a cherry red, move the torch along, closely followed by the slim welding rod tip which drops the beads of metal to fuse the edges together.

Nails of all sizes and weight, shape and form are fine materials for welding. Screws and bolts, staples and wire hangers also offer possibilities for unusual structures. In short, as you go on with your welding sculpture, you will find yourself eyeing avidly everything made of metal, because all such things are grist to the welder's mill.

TAKE CARE

In dealing with any flame one should be careful, and it follows that in handling your torch, which exudes a flame of 5,000 degrees of heat, precautions must be observed with special care.

Do not be frightened of your welding torch. It is made of sturdy metal and the dangers are rarely other than those of your own lack of caution. The cylinders of oxygen and acetylene are constructed of heavy steel and the valves are strongly set in their place.

The sources of danger are:

1. Inflammable objects close to your work area, vulnerable to the sparks thrown out during welding or cutting.

2. Burns to your hands and arms by careless handling of hot metal.
3. Leaks from your torch valves and hoses or at the valves and connections of your regulators or hoses.
4. Improper turning on or turning off of your equipment as you begin or conclude your work.

Let us briefly deal with these four hazards (and I call them hazards only until care in dealing with them becomes an easy habit, whereupon they cease to be hazards).

YOUR WORK AREA It need not be very big for most welding purposes. It should contain a work table covered with a sheet of steel or, better still, be made entirely of metal.

The table should be large enough to affix a small vise at one side for gripping your sculpture piece during work.

A handy hook rack for pliers and the parts of your welding equipment not in immediate use.

Space for your two cylinders of gas, the oxygen and the acetylene, and the two hoses which run from them to your torch.

This whole work area should be free of inflammable objects such as paper, books, rags, and, above all, oil, grease, or chemicals which burn.

A simple precaution for security would be to acquire some sheets of light-gauge steel and lean them against the walls of your working area.

BURNS Inevitably you will pick up hot metal rods or heated pliers or be lightly burned by an occasional drop of molten metal. These are trivial for the most part and an occupational hazard. To preclude most of these burns wear leather or asbestos gauntlets and a leather apron over your clothes.

Get into the habit of using pliers to handle metal rods and pieces of steel and keep an open pot of water at hand for cooling hot materials and tools.

LEAKS Test for leaks frequently. Your regulators, hoses, and torches should not leak if properly tightened but during work they may loosen. *Do not test with a match.* Mix a small dish of soap and water. If you hear or smell a leak, apply the soapy water to each valve and joining nut. The soapy water will bubble if any gas is escaping.

Follow carefully the instructions for turning on and off your torches and valves.

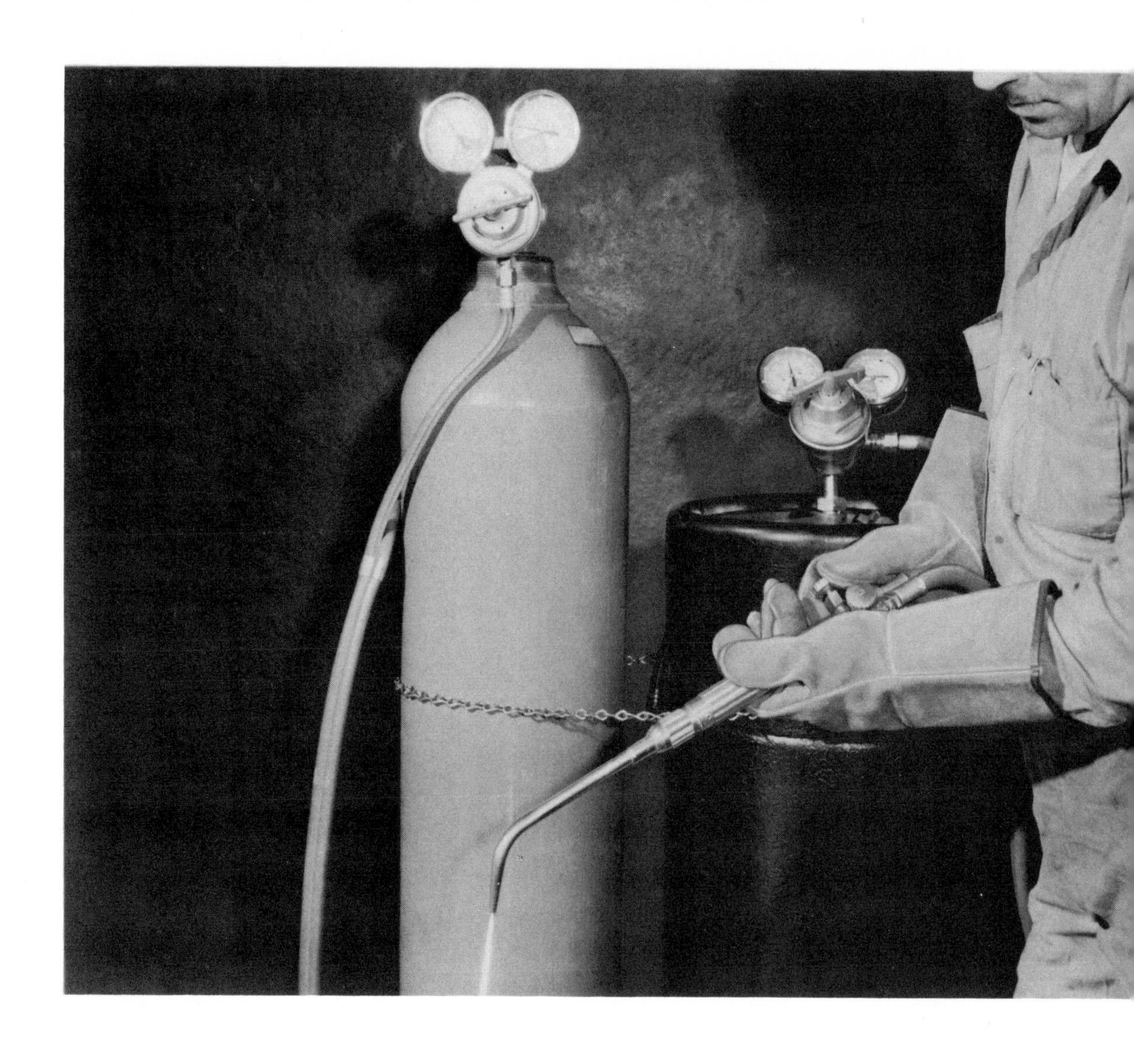

THE CYLINDERS OF OXYGEN AND ACETYLENE

There is an oxyacetylene cylinder supplier in virtually every area of the United States and in all but the most primitive towns in most countries. Your local garage has need for the cylinders for routine metal joining, hence the many suppliers.

Incidentally, it might be a good idea, before you obtain your equipment kit, to ask a friendly garageman to show you the simple methods of using welding torches and of turning the cylinders on and off, regulating pressure, etc. He is in a position to point out the nature and small hazards of the welding process.

The cylinders of oxygen and acetylene may be rented from the supplier in your area. The terms are variable and in most cases the supplier will deliver them to your studio and call for empties for refilling. Cylinders come in various sizes and the decision as to which to rent depends on the size of the project in mind.

The cost of rental should not amount to more than the cost of brushes, paints, and canvas to the painter.

STARTING TO WELD

In every kit of welding equipment there is a book of directions telling how to assemble the various parts of the regulators, hoses, torches, etc. These instructions vary somewhat depending on the special character of each manufacturer's kit. It therefore becomes impossible to attempt to outline the assembly methods for all varieties of welding equipment here.

I would suggest, however, that you follow those instructions with great care both for safety and so that you get the best results from your equipment.

What follows is the starting method after the equipment has been set up and is ready for work.

The accompanying drawing indicates the parts referred to in the following steps.

1. *Slowly* open your acetylene valve with the "T" wrench (A).
2. Look at the left-side indicator of your regulators (B). The needle will show the amount of acetylene in the cylinder.
3. Turn the handle on the pressure release valve (C) to about five pounds on the right-hand gauge (D).
4. *Slowly* turn the wheel valve on the oxygen cylinder (E) by *hand*.
5. The amount of oxygen in the cylinder will be indicated on the left-side regulator (F).
6. Turn the indicator handle (G) to about five pounds on the pressure gauge (H).

Your torch is now ready for ignition preparation.

On the torch, with the flame end pointed away from you and aimed down, open the wheel valve (I) on the left side of the torch about one half turn.

Holding the sparker in your left hand, put the tip of the torch close to the pan and squeeze the sparker handles (J). The torch will ignite with an orange flame of burning acetylene.

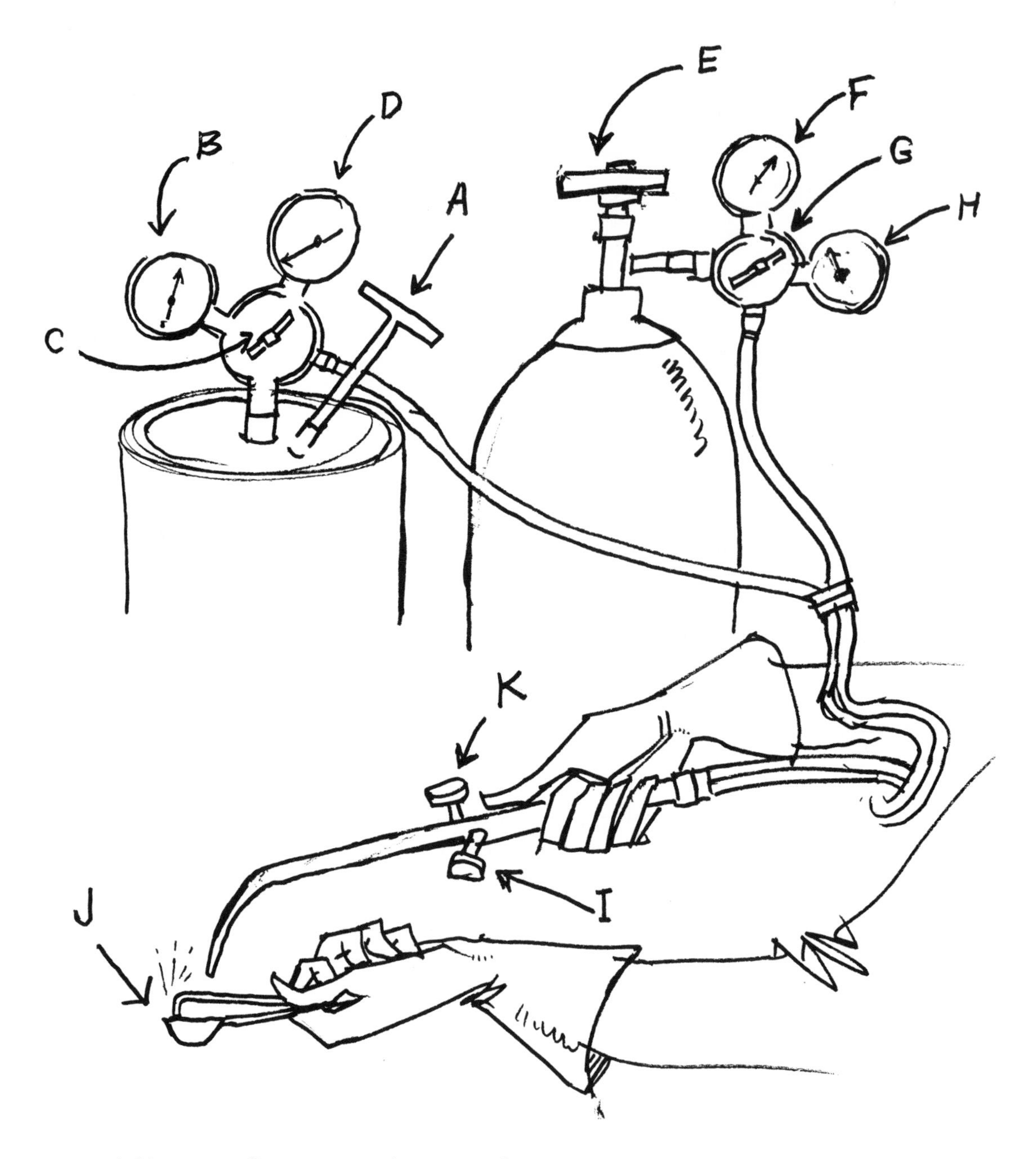

Adjust the flame until there is a faint smoke at the end of the jet of fire.

Now half turn your right-hand torch valve (K).

The two gases, acetylene and oxygen, combine to emit a blue-white flame.

The description of the required flame and the methods of adjusting it will follow.

Shut off your welding apparatus carefully as follows:

1. Close the wheel at the top of the oxygen cylinder.
2. Open the valve for oxygen on the torch and the indicator pressures will go down to zero.

3. Turn the screw handle on the front of the oxygen regulator until it is loose.
4. Close the oxygen valve on the torch. Now the acetylene cylinder.
5. Close the cylinder valve with the "T" handle.
6. Open the acetylene valve on your torch until the acetylene regulators indicate zero.
7. Turn the screw handle on the front of the acetylene regulator until it is loose.
8. Close the acetylene valve on the torch.

Your equipment is now safely shut off.

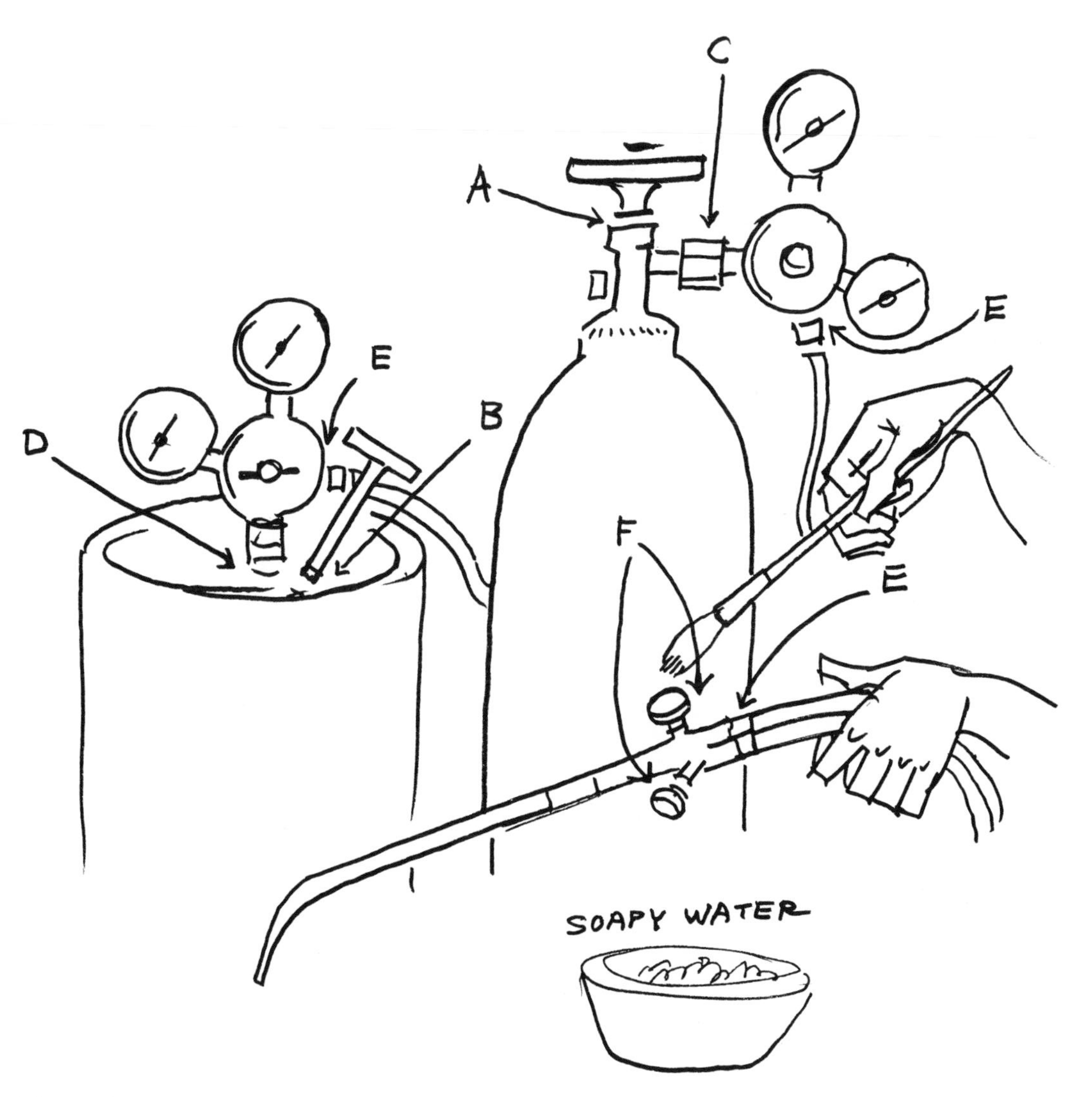

Testing for leaks.

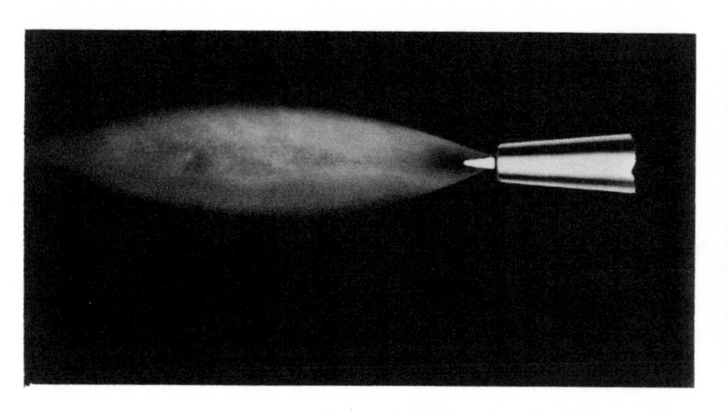
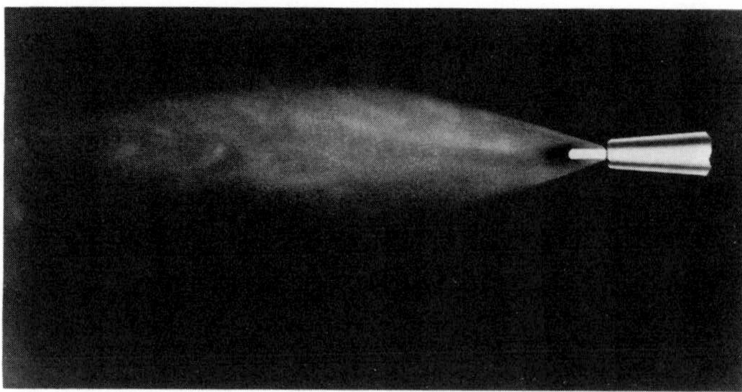

THE FLAME

The part of the flame most used in the welding process is called the neutral flame. It is the area which is made up of equal parts of acetylene and oxygen and is the white cone close to the tip of the torch.

When additional acetylene is added to the mixture by turning the acetylene control valve on the torch, a "feather" of flame is added to the neutral one. This area is used for lesser intensity of heat for various purposes during the welding and bending of metals.

When more oxygen is added to the equal mixture, the neutral cone is shortened and the feather decreased. The smaller cone is very intense in heat and melting and fusion are more quickly accomplished.

The size of the torch (of which the usual kit has three) you use for your welding is determined by the thickness and hardness of the metals to be welded.

As you proceed with your welding practice, the special character of the work you do will help evolve the exact nature of the various flame intensities you require. Your own "handwriting" will appear in your welding and no teacher can set hard and fast rules for you to follow invariably.

Frequently your torch will make a loud and, when first heard, a startling "pop" and go out. This may be caused either by working too close to the metal you are welding, inducing a backup of heat in the torch nozzle, or it may be due to tiny bits of molten metal in the tip of your torch.

If the latter is the cause, flick off the metal drip with a bit of wire. If there is enough drip to actually clog the torch tip, a wire may be inserted (gently) and the torch tip cleaned. Special "keys" for cleaning the torch tips may be bought at your dealer's.

If the pop was caused merely by the backed-up heat of too close working, reignite your torch and hold it somewhat farther from your work.

THE CUTTING TIP

The area to be cut is preheated to a cherry red by the mixture of acetylene and oxygen emitted from the holes in the cutting tip in preparation for the actual cutting.

The center hole emits a jet of oxygen when the lever on the cutting torch is pressed.

The intensified heat of this jet along with the mixed flames of acetylene and oxygen from the preheat holes accomplish the cutting process.

The cutting torch is held in position so that the cutting jet of oxygen can be brought into play by pressing the lever.

The two levers at the base of the cutting handle are first turned on to emit the mixture of oxygen and acetylene necessary for the preheating previous to cutting.

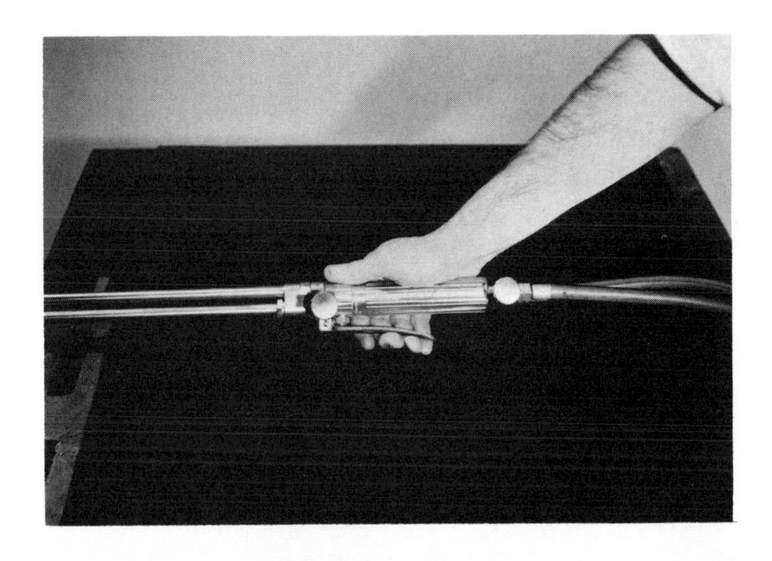

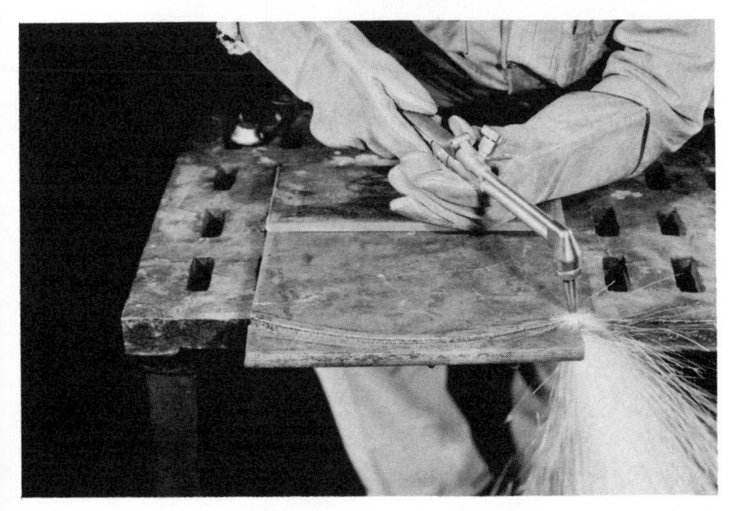

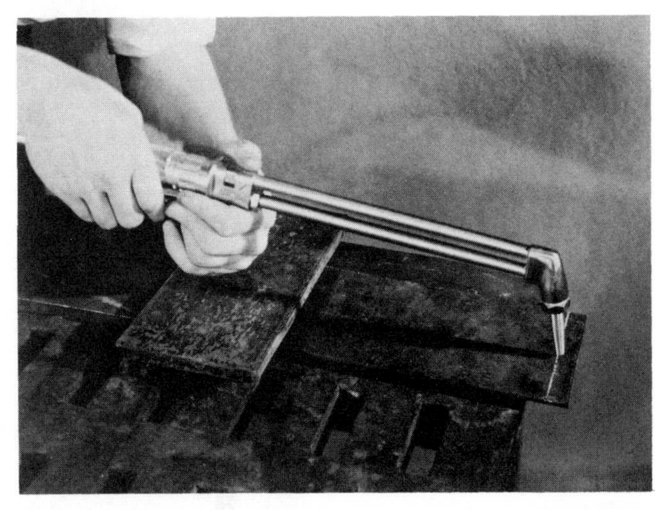

CUTTING A HOLE

WELDING FIGURES

These would serve to act as the scaffolding upon which the ultimate figure would be supported and as a guide to the stance and action of the figure as you add the detail which will take the figure farther, to the final stage you have in mind for your sculpture.

In this piece can be seen how the original concept may change in the welding process as easily as in painting in oils.

Rough sketch.

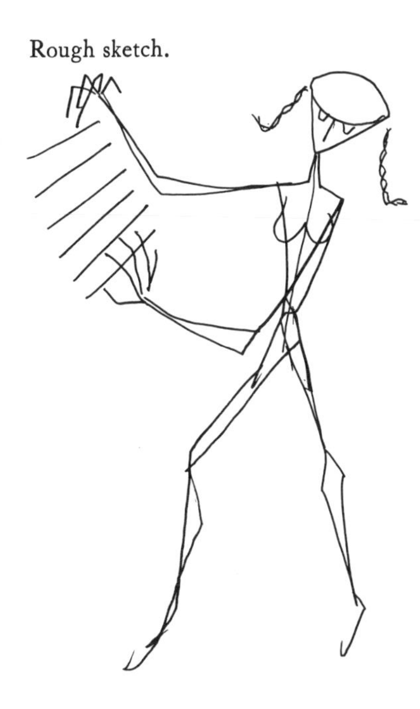

The figures in this series are first shown in the "matchstick" state in various positions.

"Accordionist" by Arthur Zaidenberg.

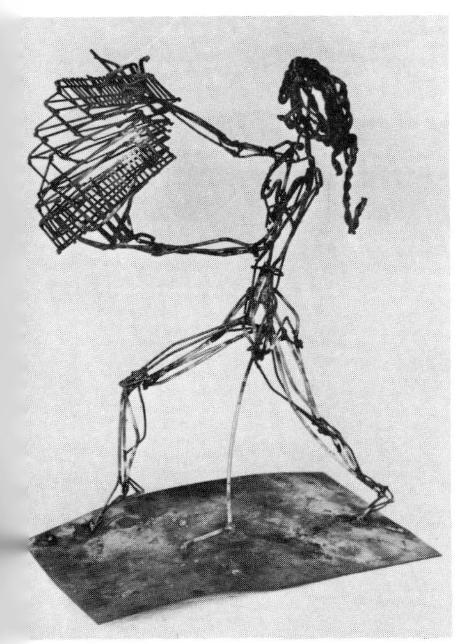

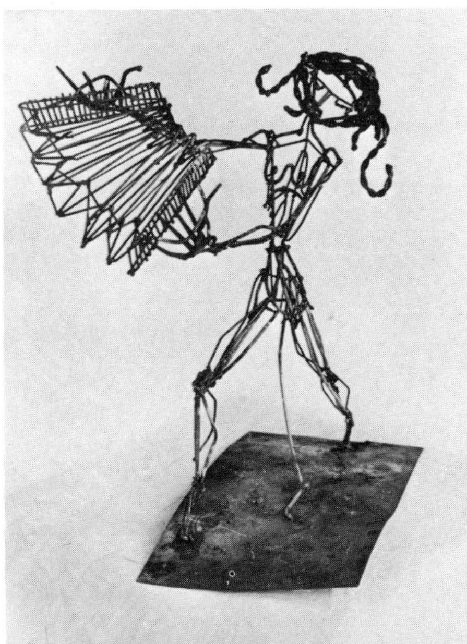

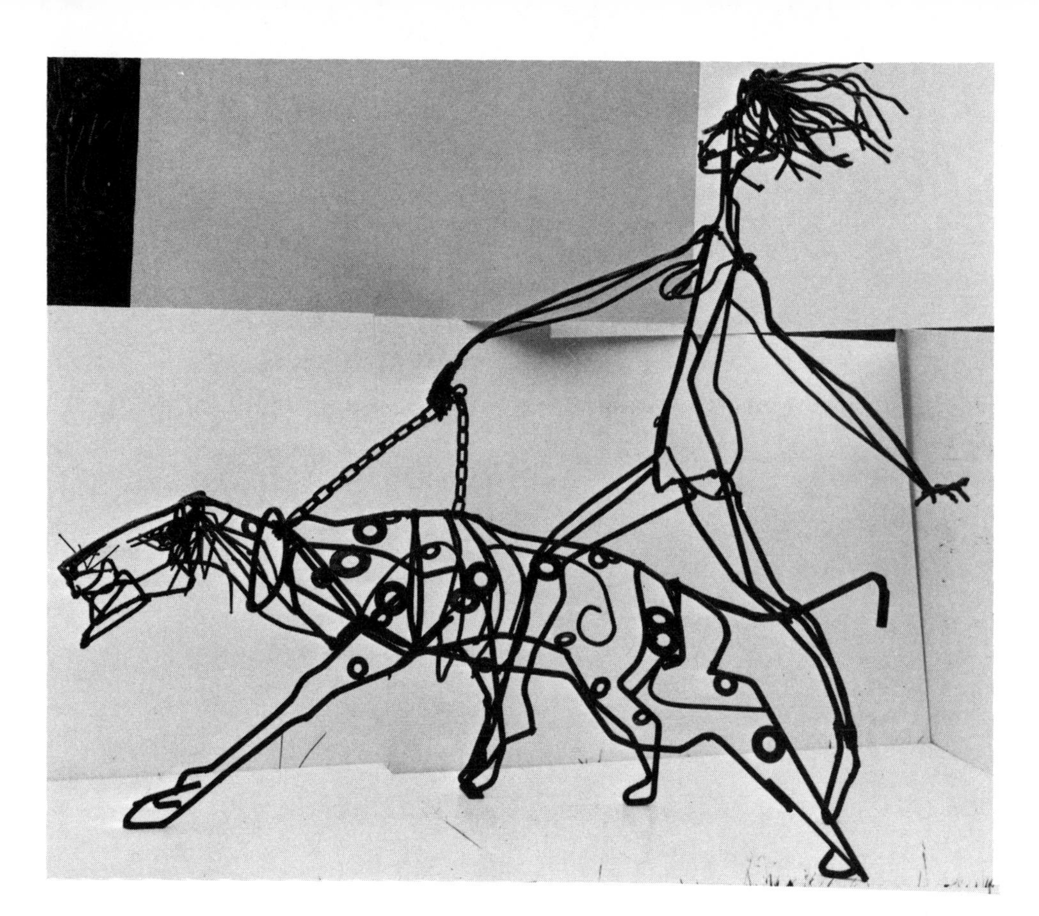

"Diana the Huntress"
by Arthur Zaidenberg.

"The Accordion"
by Arthur Zaidenberg.

"Cellist" by Arthur Zaidenberg.

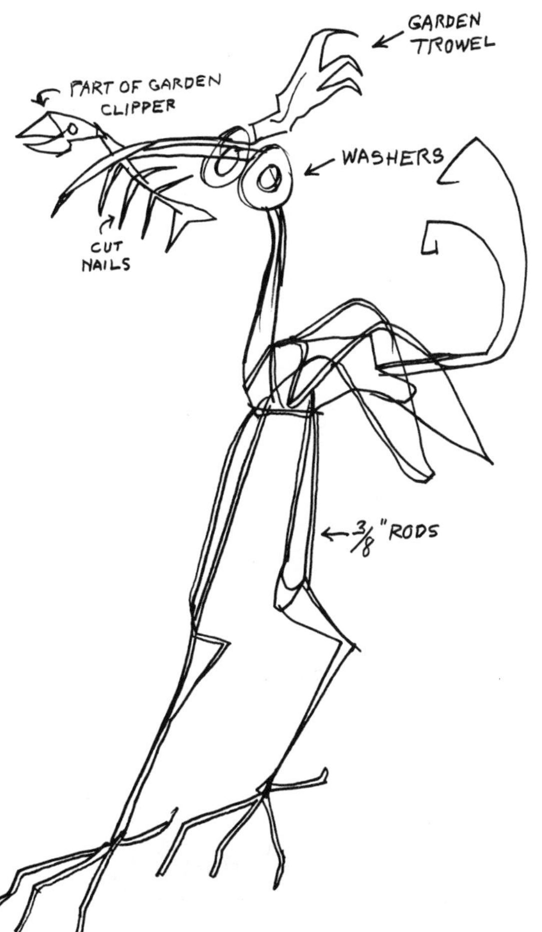

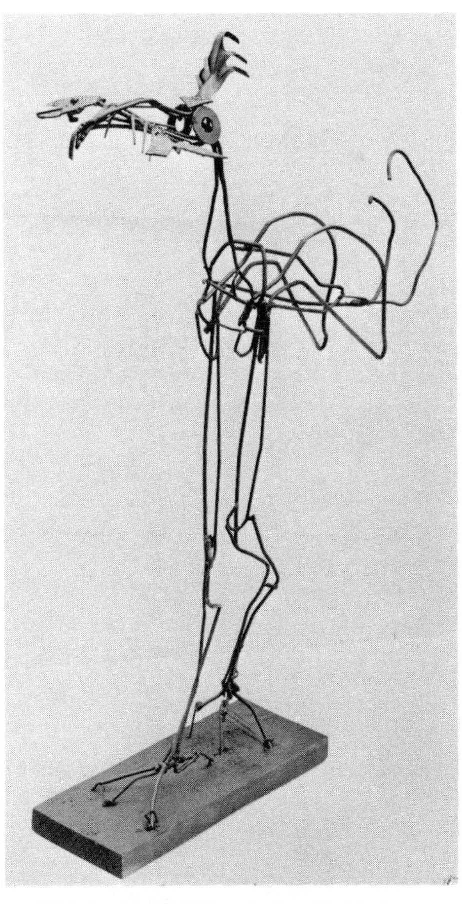

"Bird with Fish" by Arthur Zaidenberg.

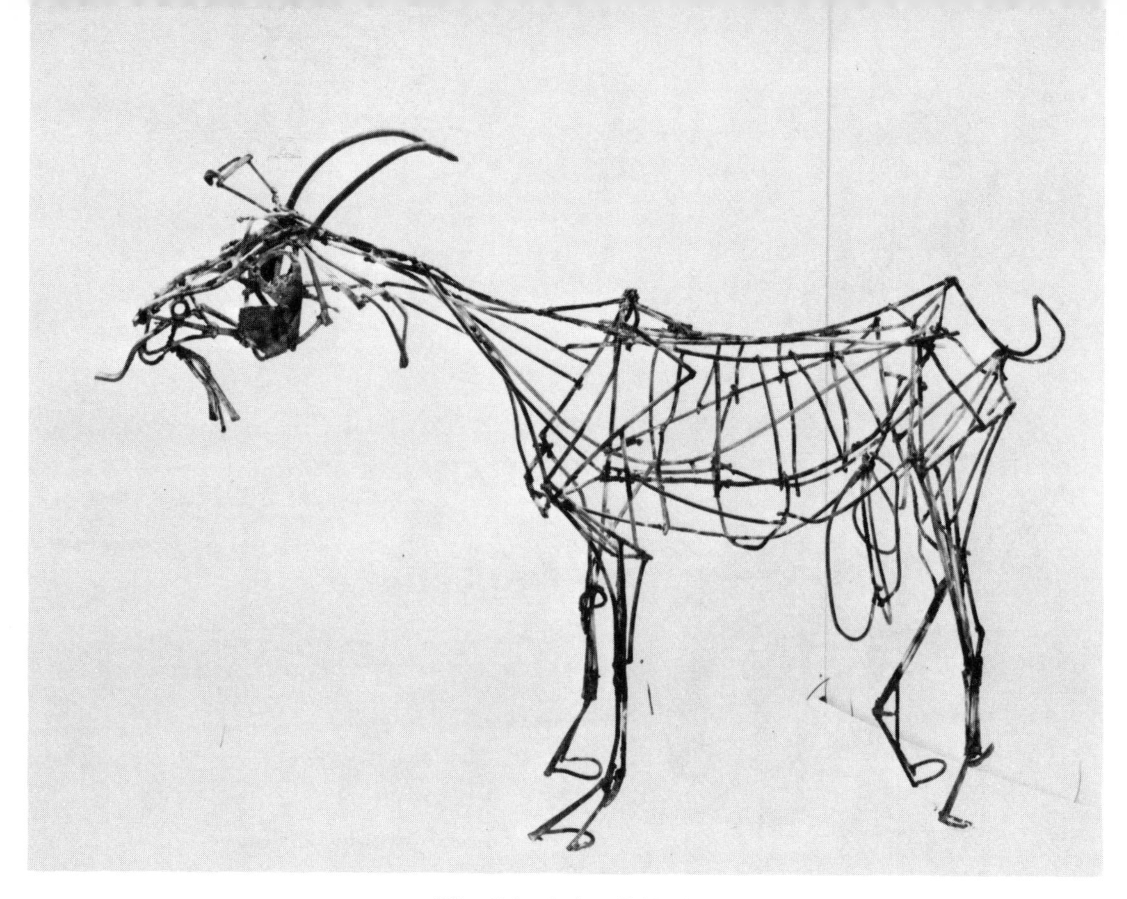

"Goat" by Arthur Zaidenberg.

"Guru" by Arthur Zaidenberg.

A series of figures in line executed in heavy rods of steel and iron.

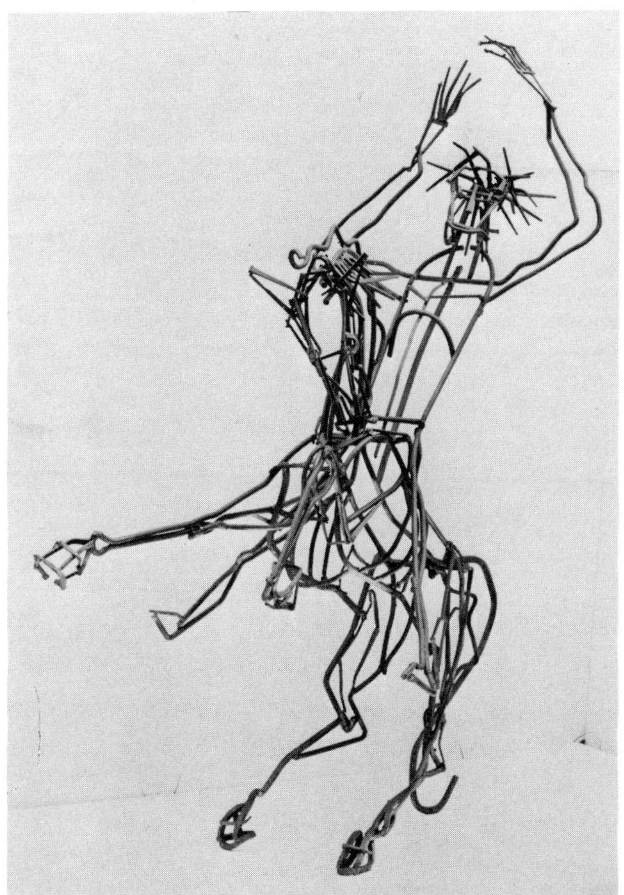

"Horseman" by Arthur Zaidenberg.

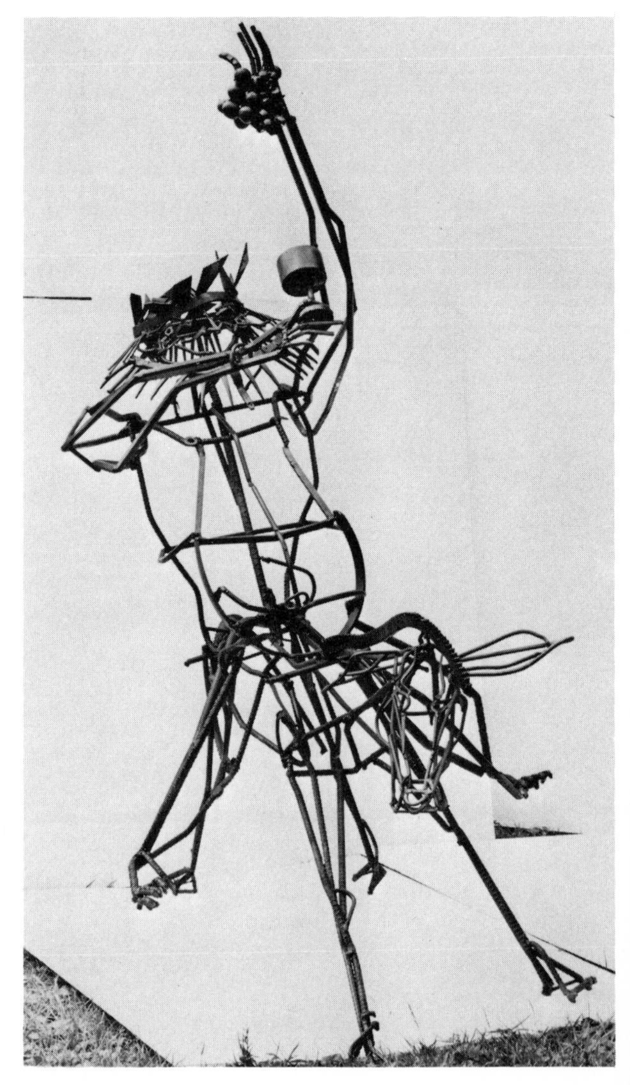

"Silenus" by Arthur Zaidenberg.

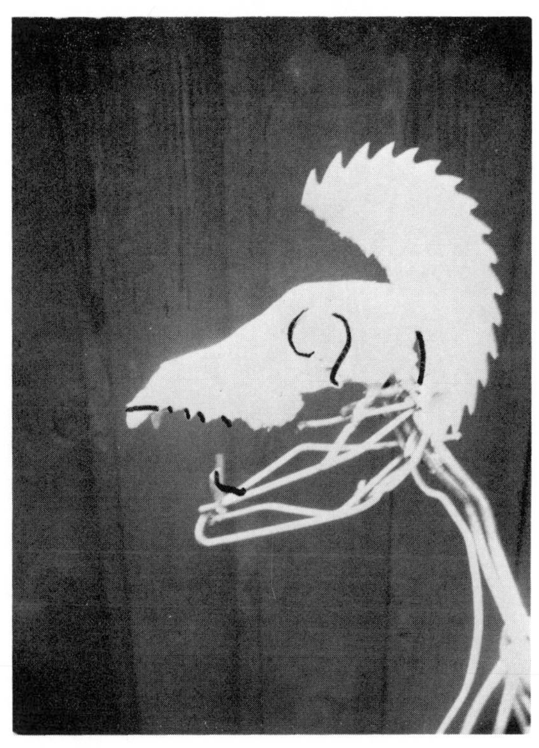

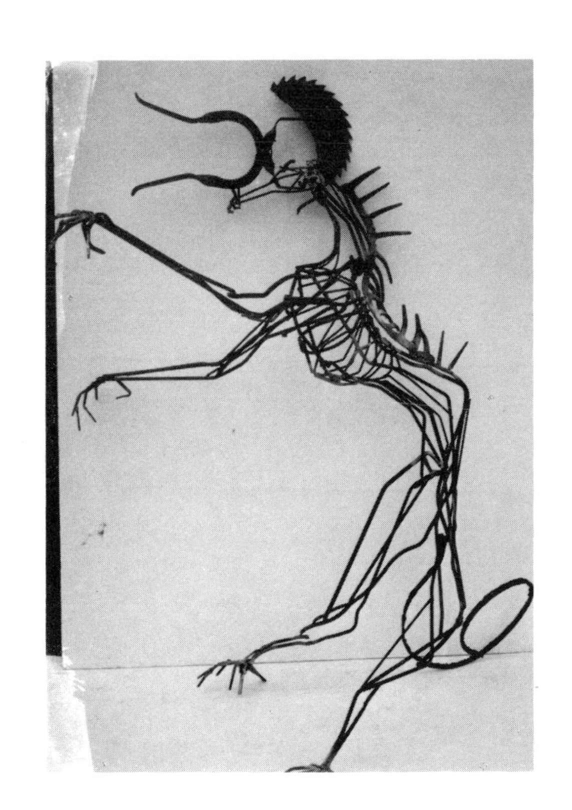

"Beast" by Arthur Zaidenberg.

"Guru II" by Arthur Zaidenberg.

On the cube base of this piece are shown the beads of welding-rod metal where they joined plate to plate to form the four sides of each of the two blocks of which it is constituted.

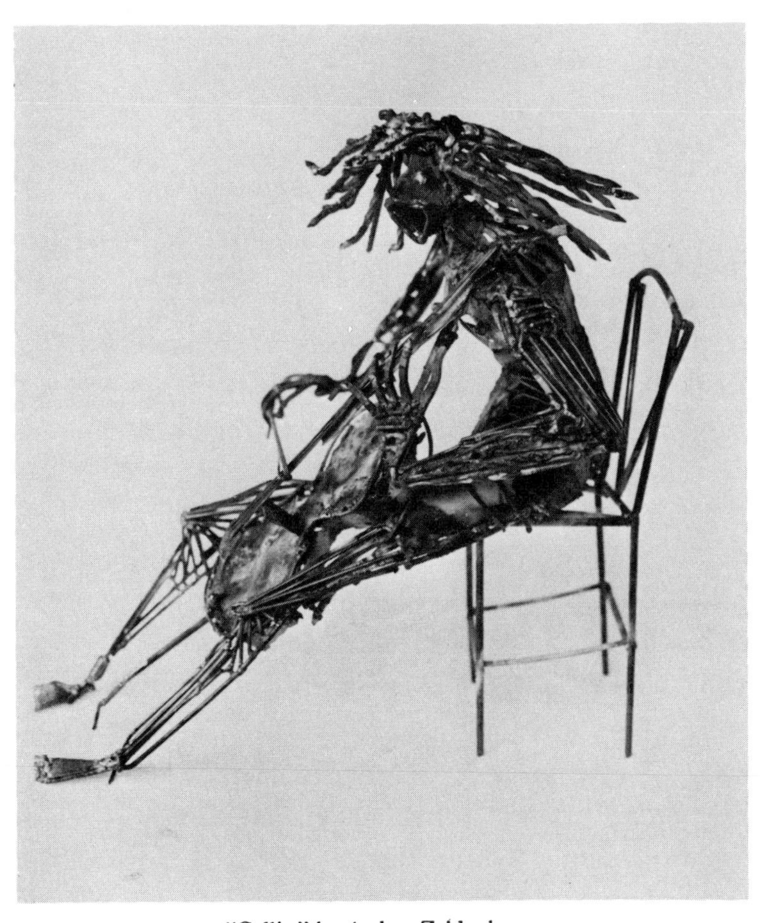

"Cellist" by Arthur Zaidenberg.

"Guru II" by Arthur Zaidenberg.

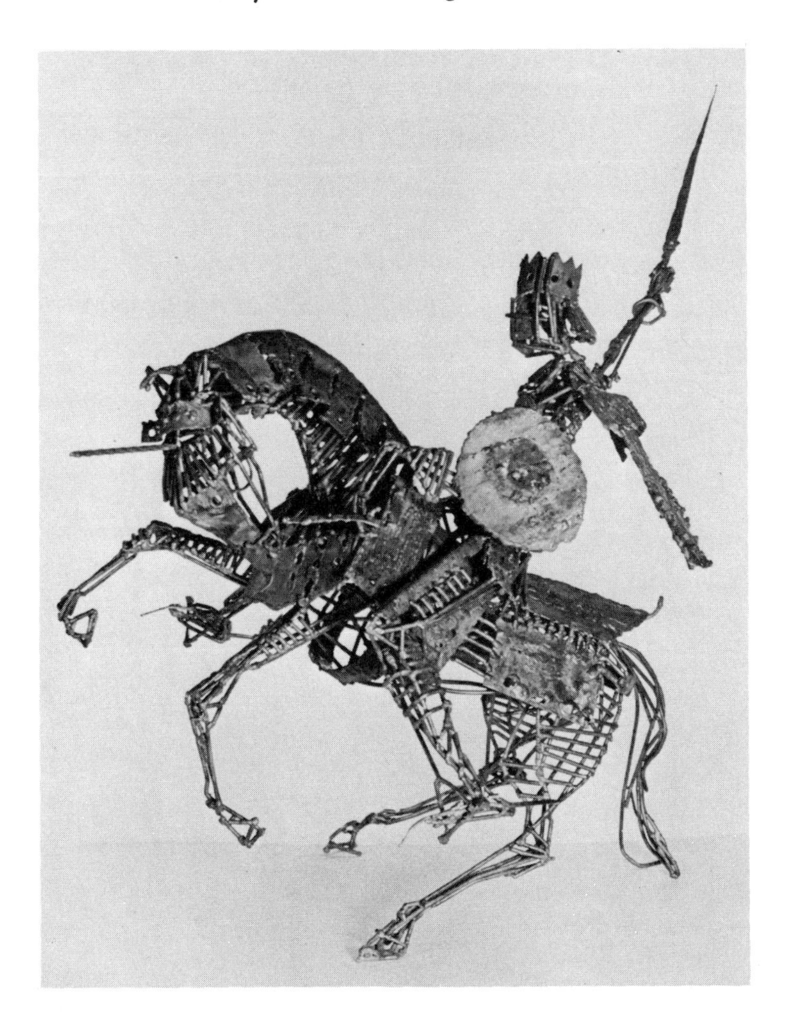

"One of the Four" by Arthur Zaidenberg.

BRAZING

Ferrous metals are those containing or derived from iron.

We have been discussing the process of joining two pieces of ferrous metal, steel in particular, to each other by the fusion method, i.e., by melting the edges of each section with the oxyacetylene torch until they flow together and make one piece. In some cases we added metal from the welding rod to the edges to further strengthen the joints, but this, too, is the fusion method.

Brazing is an additional method of joining metal parts, which does not require the melting together of those parts. Joints that have great strength may be made using the brazing method. These joints are made by using bronze rods, which melt at a considerably lower heat than steel yet will effectively join two metals whose melting point is higher.

The welding torch is used for the brazing process. In order to braze weld using the bronze rod you must use a *flux*. Flux is obtainable in either powder or paste form and is sold in all welding supply houses. Be sure that it is the flux used for brazing. There are other fluxes, suitable for soldering only.

When joining two pieces of metal which have a higher melting point than the bronze rod, the rod must be preheated with the torch and dipped into the can of flux before you apply it to the metals to be joined.

Another use for brazing rods—and this concerns us more from the art point of view—is to coat parts of iron or steel sculptures with areas of beautiful bronze to add color and special texture.

This process calls for use of the torch on the surface to be brazed until the heat produces an orange-red glow. Then the brazing rod is applied, using the torch until the bronze begins to flow over the preheated steel or iron surface, producing a beautiful patina.

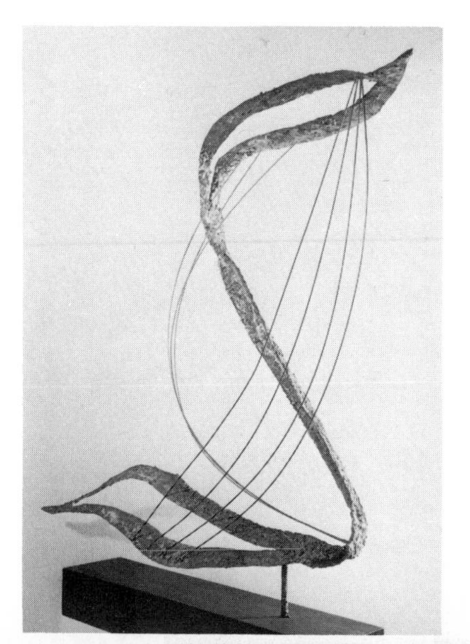

"Flight" by Amy Small. *(left)*
Cut steel shapes of light-gauge metal covered with a texture of dripped solder. The thin wires are bronze welding rod soldered to the steel shapes.

"Path of Flight" by Arthur Zaidenberg. A ribbon of steel has been bent with oxyacetylene heat and a pair of pliers into this graceful spiral path of a bird in flight. Color and texture were added by brazing.

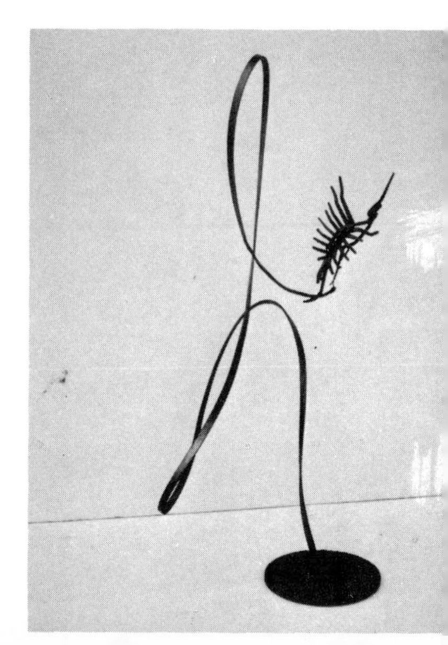

THE HEAD

The head in drawing is essentially an oval shape; in three-dimensional sculpture it would be an egg form.

If you wish to sculpt a more or less "realistic" head you must plan a scaffolding of metal rod bent and joined into an approximation of the skull and upon that build your outer surfaces of planes and contours solidly of either slices of light-gauge metal or a close pattern of rods.

However, the imaginative welder may invent and stylize, and the medium of metal welding lends itself admirably to such an approach.

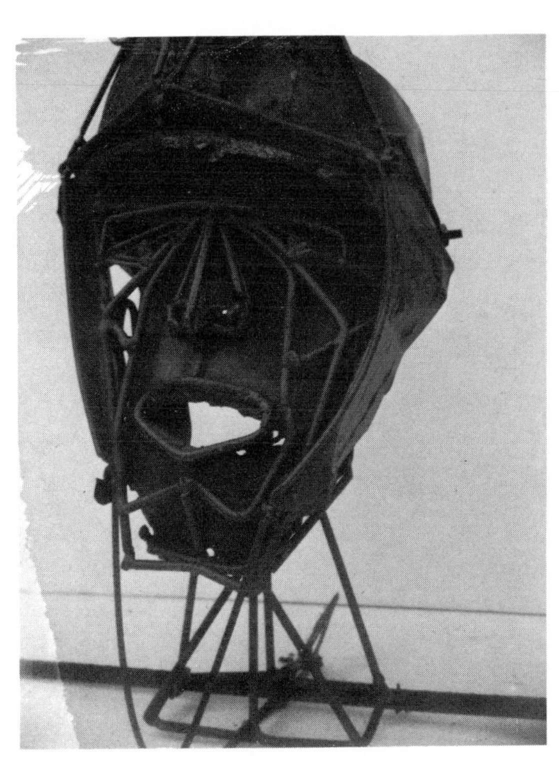

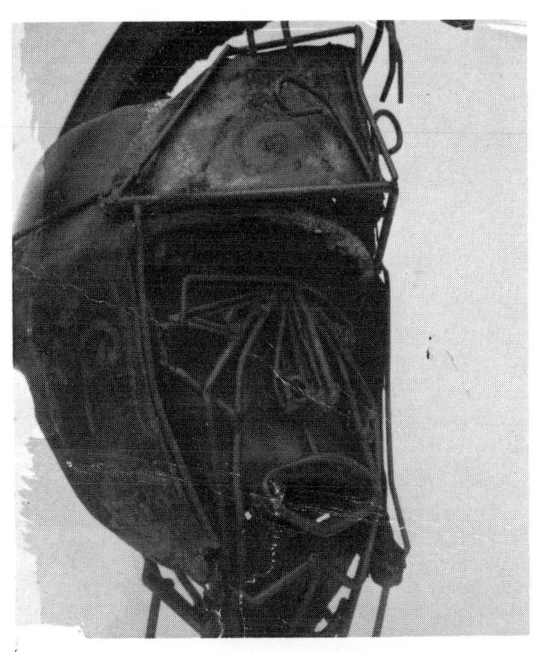

"Warrior" by Arthur Zaidenberg.

"Eli, the Fanatic" by Arthur Zaidenberg.

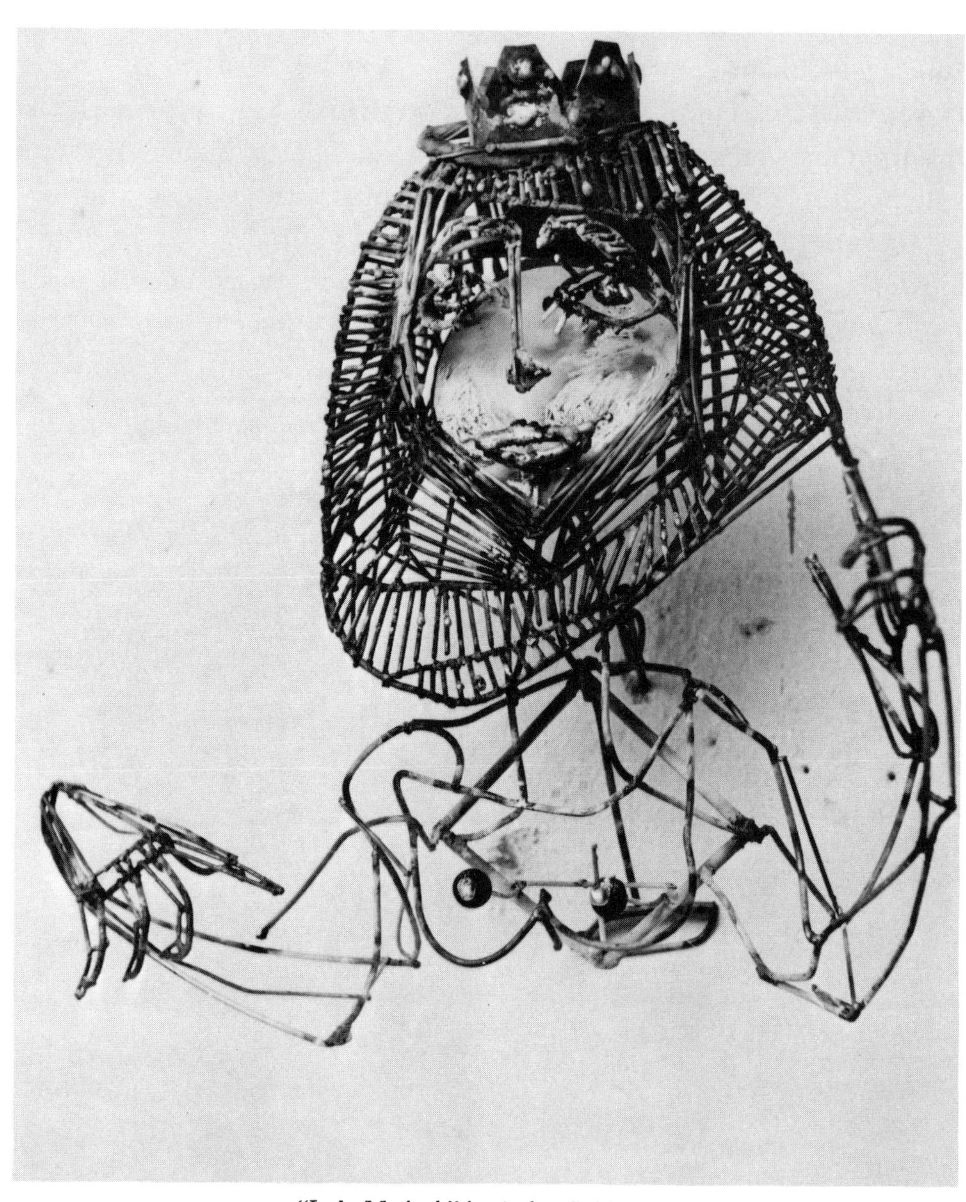

"Lady Macbeth" by Arthur Zaidenberg.

HAPPENINGS IN WELDED METALS

The science of kinetics deals with the motion of masses in relation to the forces acting upon them.

Though sculptors are rarely scientists in the purest sense of the word, many have experimented with the arrangement of forms in motion. To the frequent mobiles and undulating "stabiles" have been added many interesting experiments with motor-driven kinetic sculpture, using gears or changing weight distribution to produce action in a piece of sculpture. This has added an intriguing new dimension to the works of art.

Some delightful examples of water circulation are shown in the following pages. A small electric motor impels a stream of water to flow, which causes changes in balance of parts of a sculpture structure. There is a continuous movement of forms. These sculptures, which the artist calls "water happenings," also have an additional feature—the steady, appealing sound of moving water.

These welded fountains are designed by Hans van de Bovenkamp and are made of brass, copper, and silver alloy.

"Water Fantasy."

"Arabesque."

"Rainbow." Kinetic water sculpture by Hans van de Bovenkamp.

This group of welded metal fountains by craftsmen in Woodstock, New York, are reproduced to show their decorative character in relation to their surroundings.

CASTING

IT is a common illusion of the layman that the sculptor whose work is reproduced from wax or clay by casting into bronze or any other metal merely hands the modeled piece over to the commercial caster and receives back one or more copies of a finished metal sculpture without any additional toil on the artist's part.

The fact is that very often the serious sculptor's main work actually begins where the foundry's ends.

Many of the sculptors who work first in the impermanent waxes and clays for casting attend the casting ceremony and participate actively in the attaching of the sprues, which are the passages through which the molten metal is poured into the mold. They supervise the mixing of the metal to be poured and after time has passed and the metal has cooled, they work with the foundrymen to remove the casting coat of clay.

When the cast figure emerges, a highly personal effort by the sculptor begins: the repair and welding of inevitable small flaws in the cast figure, the grinding and polishing by hand to produce desired texture, and the application of acids and other chemicals to obtain the color and patina which only the artist may evolve to his satisfaction.

LOST-WAX PROCESS

This is an example of the method used for casting since classical antiquity. It is called the cire-perdu or lost-wax method.

The original piece is modeled in wax. It is then covered with a heavy coat of clay, with a small aperture left for the wax to run off when heated.

When the wax is all gone, molten bronze is poured into the clay cast and the aperture is sealed.

After many hours of cooling, the clay cast is chopped away, revealing the bronze replica of the original wax model.

Only one copy of the original may be made in this manner.

"Leap-Frog" by Tommy Beere.

PLASTER CASTING

Plaster casting is a very old craft, and its general use throughout all ages and in virtually every part of the world is due to the fact that it is relatively a simple process of reproduction.

It was inevitable that this obvious method of reproduction of a modeled form would be discovered in almost every earthly locality since it is one of the everyday phenomena of cooking. A *pasta* when baked and dried takes the form of the bowl in which it was made.

Reversing the process, the clay of the bowl, when soft and wet, receives the imprint of the hard substance it encircles, and takes an incised impressing of that substance's protuberances and penetrates that substance's declivities. When the clay dries and hardens, the impressions left in the inner surface are ready to reproduce the shape of the original substance. Most clay is impermanent and subject to cracking when dry. Plaster is preferable as a more permanent record of the original clay study.

To reproduce the clay form exactly, a mold must be prepared. The most commonly used mold is called a waste mold—waste because during the process of evolving the plaster reproduction both the clay original and the mold are destroyed. By this process obviously only one reproduction is possible. Its value lies in the exact, relatively permanent facsimile of your original study obtainable by this method.

There are other methods of casting by which you may, without destroying the mold, obtain many reproductions.

However, the waste mold method is most exact and rarely is there a need for multi-reproduction of one's work. If such a reproductive method is required, it is far better to employ a commercial casting company to make a durable mold for quantity reproduction for commercial purposes.

MATERIALS FOR WASTE MOLD

Plaster of Paris is bought in most paint supply shops in powder form. Break up lumps and sift through your fingers until it is of even consistency.

Brass shims are used as a thin wall to separate the two or more parts of your mold. The brass may be bought in strips from sculptors' supply shops or from hardware stores. Thirty-eight-gauge brass is firm yet thin enough for easy cutting with scissors. Where brass strips are not available, tin may be used.

Iron pipe about ¼ inch thick to be used as armature is used in clay to strengthen and hold together the walls of the plaster mold.

Bluing, the ordinary wash-day bluing, is used to tint the plaster layer closest to the clay model. When, later, in removing mold by chiseling away the plaster, you reach the blued plaster, you have a warning that the cast area is close and you must chop carefully.

Strips of burlap may be inserted in the plaster mass to aid in strengthening where a mold is complicated and weak walled. Strips of iron are also used for the same purpose. Burlap is obtainable everywhere. Your grocer will give you old potato sacks.

Basins. Two for mixing plaster.

Brush.

STEPS IN CASTING

First examine your piece of sculpture in order to decide at which points your mold may be separated into sections. Each piece of sculpture presents a special problem. The protruding forms and the deep cuts must be studied so that the divisions of the cast will not be impeded when each section is dried and lifted from the original.

A simple head or a figure without many variations from a large simple mass may be divided by protruding brass shims.

If your piece of clay sculpture is not quite dry it would not be difficult to insert a band of brass shims into the surface of your piece. The line of shims must follow the line of separation points you have decided upon. Your shims should be about ¾ inch wide and when inserted about ⅛ inch into the clay, you will allow for a plaster covering of ⅝ inch. The plaster will probably cover the shims at various places and you may have to scrape the dried plaster with a knife to uncover them again.

Half fill a large basin with water. Put enough bluing in the water to tinge it a deep blue.

Sift the plaster of Paris between your fingers, breaking the lumps, if any, and spread over the surface of the water. Let the first covering of plaster powder sink to the bottom and then repeat until the plaster fills the water. Let it absorb for about a minute, then stir with a spoon carefully avoiding air bubbles. When you have a thick smooth cream, it is ready for making the first blue coat. Make a scoop of your fingers and throw creamy gobs on your original model, starting at the top and working down, filling all the hollow parts until the piece is completely covered with the blued plaster to the thickness of about ¼ inch. Allow it to set.

Now mix a batch of white plaster—without bluing.

Cover the blue plaster with a thin coat of white plaster.

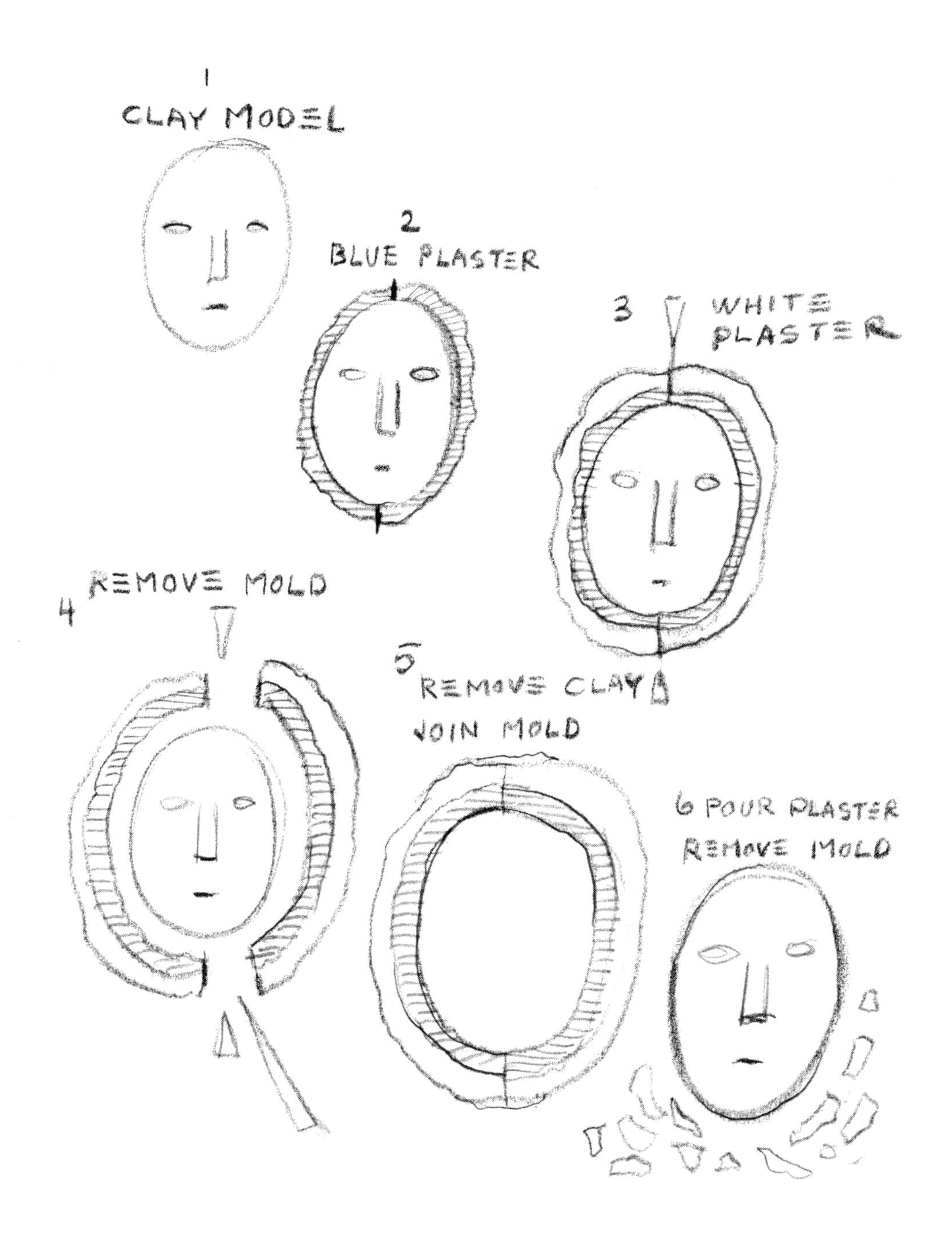

When this has begun to dry somewhat and is still sticky, quickly throw on an evenly thick coat of plaster over the whole figure to the thickness of the shims.

When this final coat has set to its full hardness you are ready to remove the sections of the cast by prying them apart at the shims.

SEPARATING THE SECTIONS

It is at the point when your cast is ready for lifting off the original that you scrape with a knife to uncover completely the line of brass shims.

At the division lines, along the shims at several points, cut a few wedge-shaped incisions. These will serve as markers for reassembling the cast parts later.

Wet the lines of the separation boundaries liberally. Allow the water to soak in.

You are now ready for prying apart the sections and lifting them from the original. This is a delicate operation. Forcing may break the mold. Insert the edge of a chisel between the soaked division lines and pry carefully, a little at a time at various points. The parts of the mold will lift off after the lines separate completely.

Now scoop out of each half of your mold interior all the fragments of clay which may have adhered to the plaster and wash the whole interior thoroughly.

Now give your mold sections several coats of green soap diluted in water until a glossy film of soap fat is apparent. Allow for drying. Then cover this whole interior with a thin salad oil film.

The cast parts are ready for reassembling. Fit the two sections together, making them "register" perfectly. The wedge-shaped notches must join exactly. Seal the joints with burlap strips soaked in freshly mixed plaster. When these strips dry the mold will be held together tightly.

The base, being open, is where the next step in your casting process takes place. Mix an amount of plaster sufficient to fill the interior of the hollow mold, though you will not make a solid casting. Rotate the mold slowly so as to swish the plaster into all parts of the interior. Try to prevent air pockets from forming by pouring the plaster in a slow, steady stream.

Now pour it back into the mixing bowl. A coat of plaster will have covered the mold interior.

Repeat these pourings, again and again, until a thick coat of plaster has built up within the cast. Strips of burlap may be inserted between these layers in order to strengthen the plaster. When a good thick area of plaster has been built within on the sides of the mold, you have made a strong, hollow casting of your original work. Let this dry until it has hardened.

A plaster cast mold being separated to reveal the exact reproduction of an original piece.

The mold now must be chipped away from the cast replica of your work. This is a delicate procedure. It is done with a chisel and mallet. Do not use too sharp a chisel because it may penetrate too far and mar the surface of your cast. Until the blued area of the plastic has been reached, you may chip freely. When the blued plaster is uncovered, you are close to the cast figure.

Special care must be taken from now on. Chip gently until the cast figure is revealed.

PLASTER

Plaster of Paris is the familiar white powder which has so many homely uses in our everyday life.

When mixed with the proper amount of water it takes on the consistency of heavy cream and when it dries it hardens to a uniform solid. This solid is no longer easily soluble in water and for most purposes may be said to be waterproof.

For sculptors it has two special virtues.

The main virtue is that when cast in a mold it takes every protuberance and declivity into its own mass, and when dry reproduces these features exactly in reverse. Having dried, it is, with normal gentle handling, permanent. It is, therefore, used as a medium for reproduction of less permanent or perishable works completed in other media. These works enclosed in a mold made of plaster give their imprint to the walls of the mold. The mold dries, is removed and then filled with fresh wet plaster. When this in turn dries, the outer plaster is removed and the "fill" now is an exact reproduction of the original work. This process is described in more detail in the section of the book on "Casting."

The second virtue of plaster of Paris is that it can be used for carving or modeling directly. The wet plaster when dried assumes any shape into which it has been confined. In this way, through the use of a wood mold, one may make blocks of solid plaster in any shape desired.

These may be carved easily with a penknife and the result is a reasonably permanent carving in a solid form.

Another way in which plaster is used as a modeling medium to begin with and a carving medium in finishing is to "slap" gobs of somewhat thicker plaster (less water content) onto a prepared armature. When covered, this has the general shape of the figure desired. The refinements are then whittled into shape by use of a knife, after the plaster has dried.

Plaster of Paris, when mixed with about the same volume of water as its own volume, will dry and set quickly and become hard in about twenty minutes if the atmosphere is dry.

MAKING SIMPLE MOLDED FORMS OF PLASTER

Small plaques of bas-relief or intaglio design are easily made with plaster of Paris poured into molds of modeling clay or plasteline.

When a medium of sculptural reproduction is as simple and as flexible as this process you may easily invent special uses for it to suit your caprices.

Here are outlined a few simple steps in making bas-relief plaques.

The materials needed are as follows:

One can of modeling clay or plasteline. I should suggest that the plasteline is preferable because of the fact that it does not dry and may easily be used over again without too much trouble.

About two pounds of plaster of Paris powder.

A smooth board surface upon which to work.

A penknife.

Some cheap drawing paper sheets.

Make a pencil square on a sheet of paper. This will serve as your pattern for the base of your mold and the ultimate shape of your plaque.

Fill the rectangle with a ½-inch covering of clay—directly on the paper. Trim the edges evenly along the lines of the rectangle drawing.

Now press out four strips of clay about 1½ inches in width and of the same length as the sides of your rectangle.

Squeeze these strips against the ½-inch depth of the sides of your flat rectangle of clay and you will have formed a box 2 inches in depth, open at the top.

Draw with your knife or pencil point any design or figure you wish reproduced, directly into the flat inner bottom of your clay box. Incise the drawing perhaps ½ inch. You have now made the mold for the poured plaster of Paris.

PREPARATION OF THE PLASTER

Pour a sufficient quantity of plaster of Paris powder into a mixing bowl. Add an equal volume of water little by little, stirring the powder and water gently. When you have a thick creamy consistency free of air bubbles, your plaster is ready for pouring.

Now pour the plaster slowly into your clay mold. Try to pour an even distribution of the liquid plaster until the clay mold is full to the brim.

After about twenty minutes' wait, the plaster will have set.

Now remove the clay walls one by one. Then gently lift the finished plaque of plaster from the clay base of the mold.

There will be a perfect bas-relief of your incised design taken from the clay onto the surface of the plaster.

RUBBER MOLDS

A new method of casting small figures is that of making a rubber mold which when dry peels off; when resealed, the empty coat of rubber is ready for plaster to be poured in. The steps are:

1. On your clay or plasteline original, draw a pencil dividing line to indicate the seam for the rubber mold.
2. Insert a brass or tin dividing strip in your plasteline or clay (about 1/8 inch). If the clay has hardened, tape your brass edge up on the model.
3. A liquid rubber separator is painted over the model before the first coat of liquid rubber is applied. This will prevent sticking.
4. Paint or pour a coat of liquid rubber on the model, covering it evenly.
5. Allow to set somewhat, then repeat the painting or pouring process until you have applied about six to eight coats, depending on the thickness of each coat. When you feel that there is an even, heavy coat on your model, let it set firmly. The mold has covered the brass shim and formed a flange.
6. Slit the rubber at the flange until it reaches the shim. Open the mold at the seam and peel off like a coat.
7. Reseal the mold at the seam firmly with tape and a thin coat of liquid rubber.
8. The base of the mold is open to receive the pouring of plaster or whatever casting material you decide upon.
9. Pour and allow to dry and set.
10. Open the rubber mold at the seam and peel off. You now have a cast of your original model.

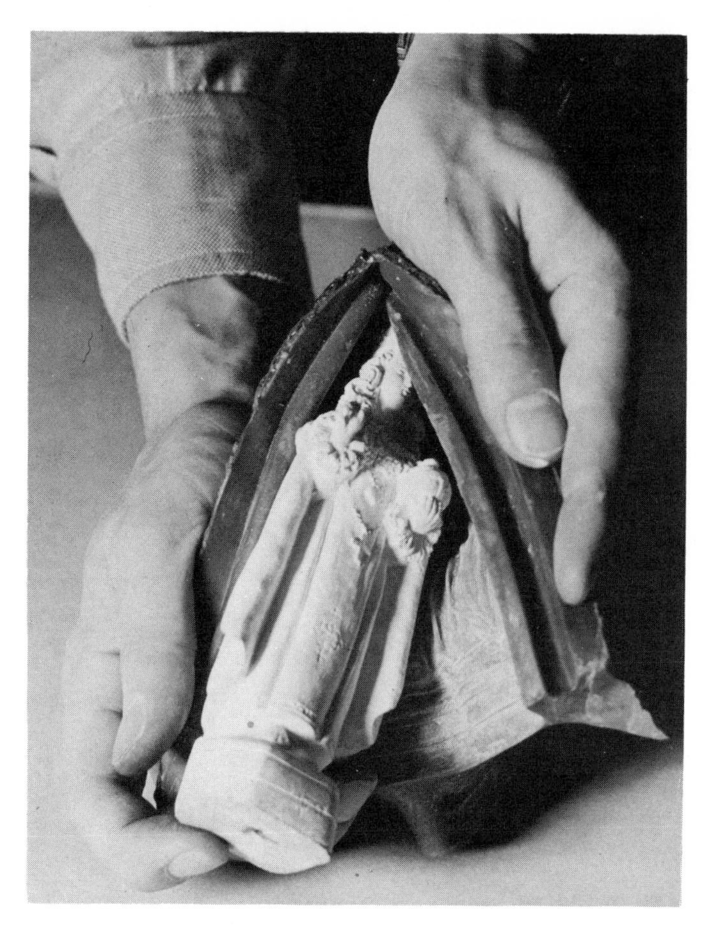

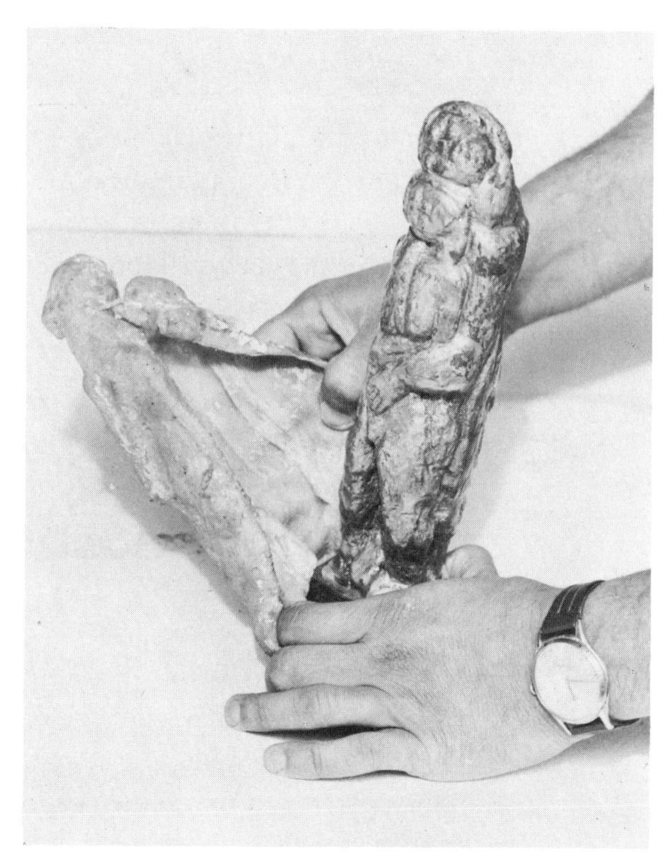

Removing a rubber coat mold and revealing the cast plaster reproduction.

CASTING IN STONE

A variety of cement with which there has been mixed stone particles ground to powder and to which has been added coloring matter to give the semblance of various stones is now available to sculptors for casting. It is said to be extremely durable and may be exposed to outdoor weather as readily as stone.

When the cast stone has dried, it may be chiseled and filed. The casting stone is sold in powder form and is mixed with water until the desired pouring consistency is reached. It dries slowly and becomes extremely hard.

Marble statuette of a woman. Cycladic, about 2500 B.C.

CARVING

UNLIKE modeling, the building up process, carving is a process of setting free forms imprisoned within a large form, that of the wood or stone piece with which you start. Resisting matter opposes your intrusion. It opposes, with its natural armor of unyielding hardness and with the more subtle opposition of grains and texture variations, your entrance into its depths to change and twist its original shape.

Basically, it is by the strength of the blow and the sharp edge of the chisel that the changes are accomplished, but knowledge of the special type of opposition offered by each hard material must be added to mere strength in order to realize the best possibilities latent within your material. You may learn much about the peculiar traits of each variety of wood and stone from reading, but essentially, it is a matter of the "feel" of each piece which gives the cue to the best approach. The weight of the blows struck, the grains to follow, and the size and variety of tools to be used are determined by the soon discovered character of surface to be penetrated.

Woods are, of course, softer than stone, yet certain species of wood are far more resistant to carving than some stone varieties. Some very hard stones chip cleanly and are controlled with greater ease than are considerably softer stones. Within each generally classified species of stone are many variations which preclude definite statements as to their nature, statements which can serve the student as an invariable guide. Experience can be a positive guide if freshly renewed by each problem. Your previous experience with one piece of stone will be subject to adjustments necessary to deal with a change in character and grain of another piece of the same species.

This must not suggest to you that nothing may be learned by experience or that the problems are so many as to make the tyro as competent as the veteran. It merely means that fresh vigor and the experimental approach are more valid than documentation.

The nature of the block to be carved contributes much to the original concept and is the main determinant of the figure's limitations. Unlike paint, which is the complete self-effacing servant, unobtrusive in the forming of decisions as to subject matter and completely obedient in the execution of the concept, stone and wood, or any other material to be carved, impose their character very forcefully on the artist.

The chief restriction which the material imposes is, of course, the aesthetic one. Subjects suitable for modeling in clay or plasteline are sometimes unsuited to stone and wood. Often a concept which would be exquisite in wood would not have half the quality in stone. The same aesthetic considerations apply where different varieties are concerned. Granite is suitable to subjects not desirable in marble. White marble suggests subject matter less attractive in black marble. Each species of material has its own suggestive virtues, and the "materialistic" compulsions are always to be considered.

However much this may be true, one must not let the material be the complete master in forming decisions as to subject and conception of that subject. A vigorous or subtle approach, as the case may require, may often overcome aesthetically and physically the limitations of material. The Egyptians achieved lightness in hard granite, and the Chinese made monolithic massiveness in fragile porcelain.

But it is best to meet the natural demands of material halfway and plan your concepts for the type of material you have or get the material suitable to your preconceived ideas.

SOAP SCULPTURE

Soap is, of course, an impermanent material, not intended for the ages, but with ordinary care it may well outlast plaster and clay pieces, for it does not crack and crumble with changes of weather. It is certainly more permanent than plasteline in that a touch will not alter its shape. I have known soap, subjected to slow dehydration by sunning, to become as hard as soapstone.

Just as clay and plasteline are the study media for modeling, so soap may be considered a fine study material for carving. The same problems of visualization require solving in soap as they do in stone or wood. Except for the grain problems and the brute opposition of the harder substances, all the essential factors to achieve one's concept are the same in soap as in any other carving medium.

Soap is obtainable virtually everywhere in one form or another. If you live near areas where it is manufactured you may be lucky enough to be able to get it in large bars of various colors. It may be cut with an ordinary pocketknife and if, in finishing, an ivory smoothness is desired, a minute under the water tap will produce results comparable to hours of polishing a harder substance.

Its butterlike consistency allows for clean, controlled cuts with a minimum of danger of chipping or of cracking off larger pieces than desired, as often happens in stone. It is strictly a carving process, i.e., cutting down to the figure rather than building up (though soap is cast into the commonly seen bath animals for children).

Once the concept is visualized in the mind's eye and indicated with a few scratched lines on the outer surfaces (all four sides), the carving process is easy and direct. One may reach the general shape in a few swift cuts and any amount of fine detail is possible without breaking if a certain amount of basic engineering is borne in mind. An extended, unsupported form may break off easily; a too thin area may be unable to support a heavy form, etc. Be reasonable in your demands of what is essentially a fragile substance, and it will be surprisingly tractable in your hands.

The drawings made within the traced dimensions of the soap block cannot, of course, be exact in their points of contact with the outer sides of the block. There must be a certain amount of mental visualization of the appearance of the figure within the block while using the drawings as approximations as to position of the high, middle, and low projections of forms.

Here are demonstrated a few pieces of soap sculpture in various stages of realization.

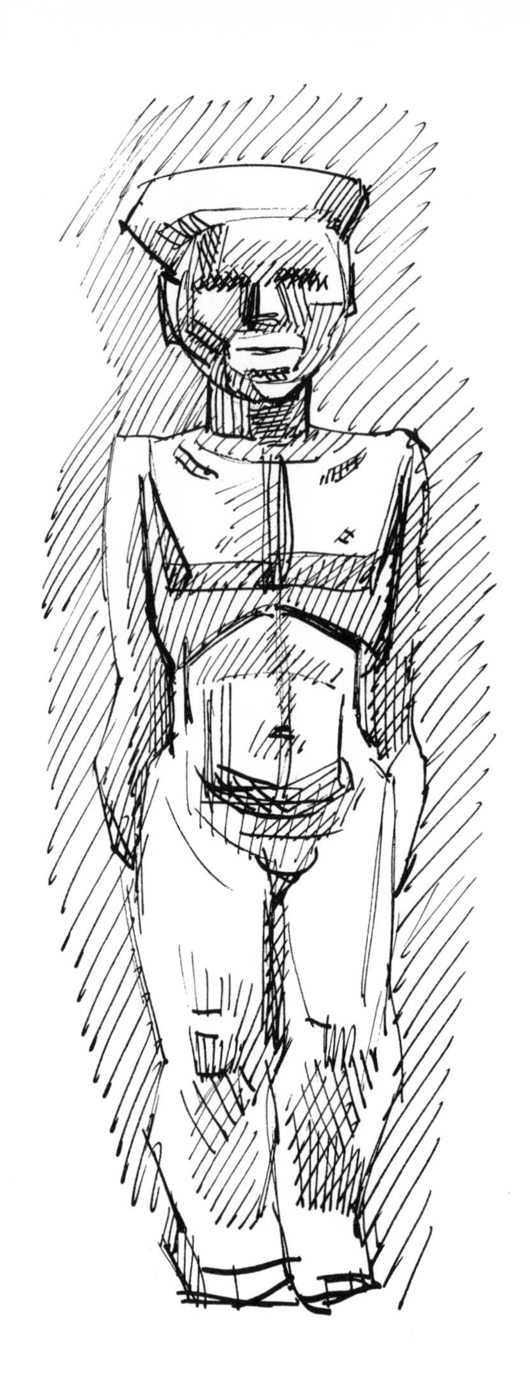

SOAP FIGURE This preliminary drawing is shaded so to act as a guide to the varying height of the planes and protruding points of the figure seen from directly in front of the soap block.

Try to "fill" your block with the figure, that is, use as much of the block as you can and only cut away what is needed to be cut. Many beginners give themselves unnecessary work by making a small figure within a big block.

This soap figure is being carved with a small pocketknife and a razor blade as can be seen in the photographs.

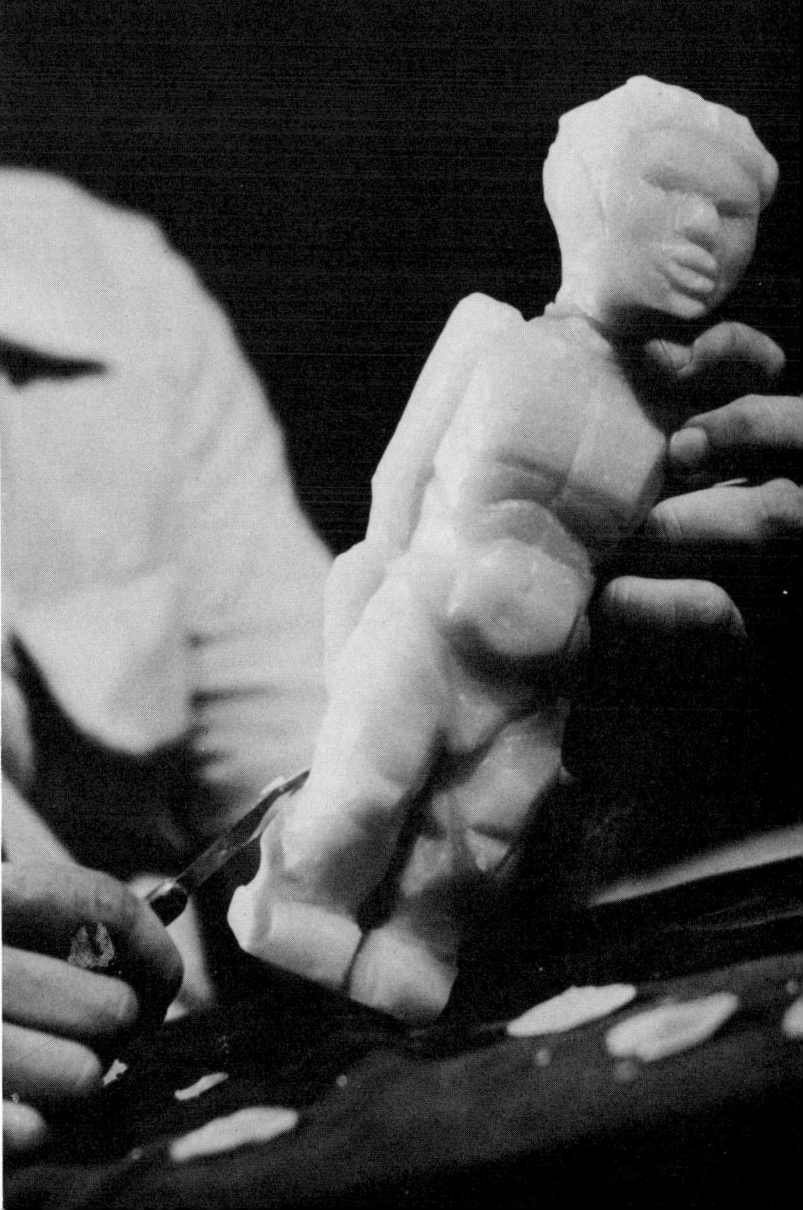

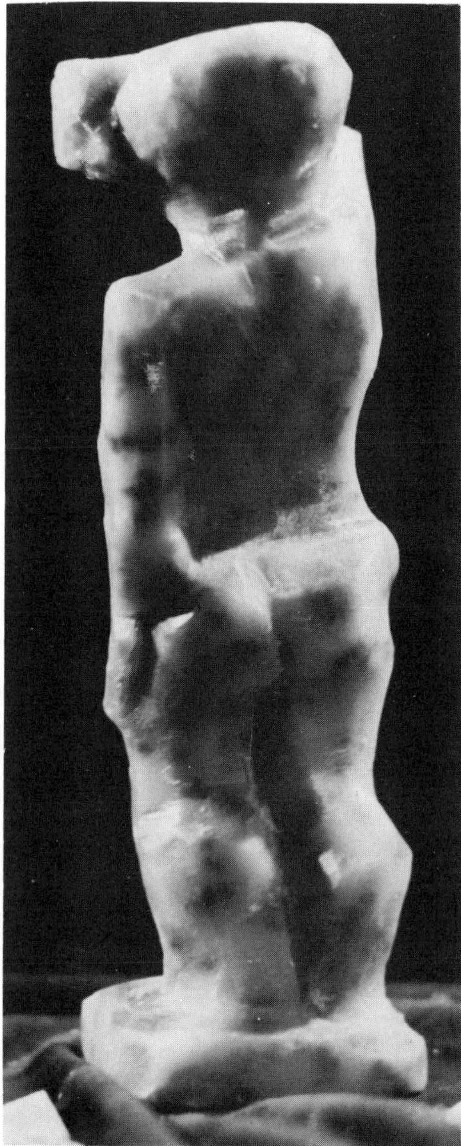

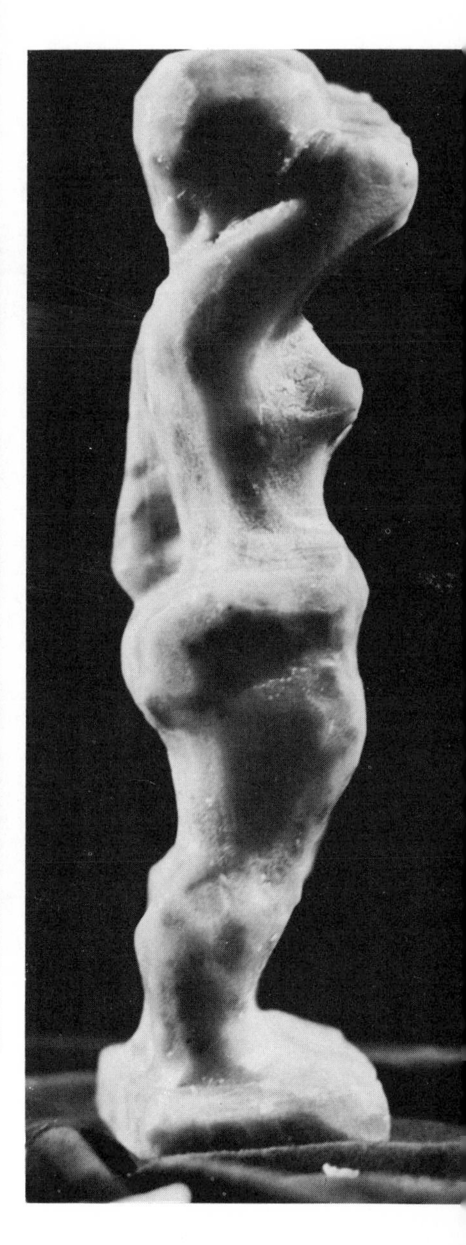

Three views of a solid figure carved in a cake of soap.

The broad planes have been emphasized and have been allowed to remain in their squared, blocked-out state to indicate how the soap may be sliced in large slivers to arrive quickly to a state where finish and details may easily be added.

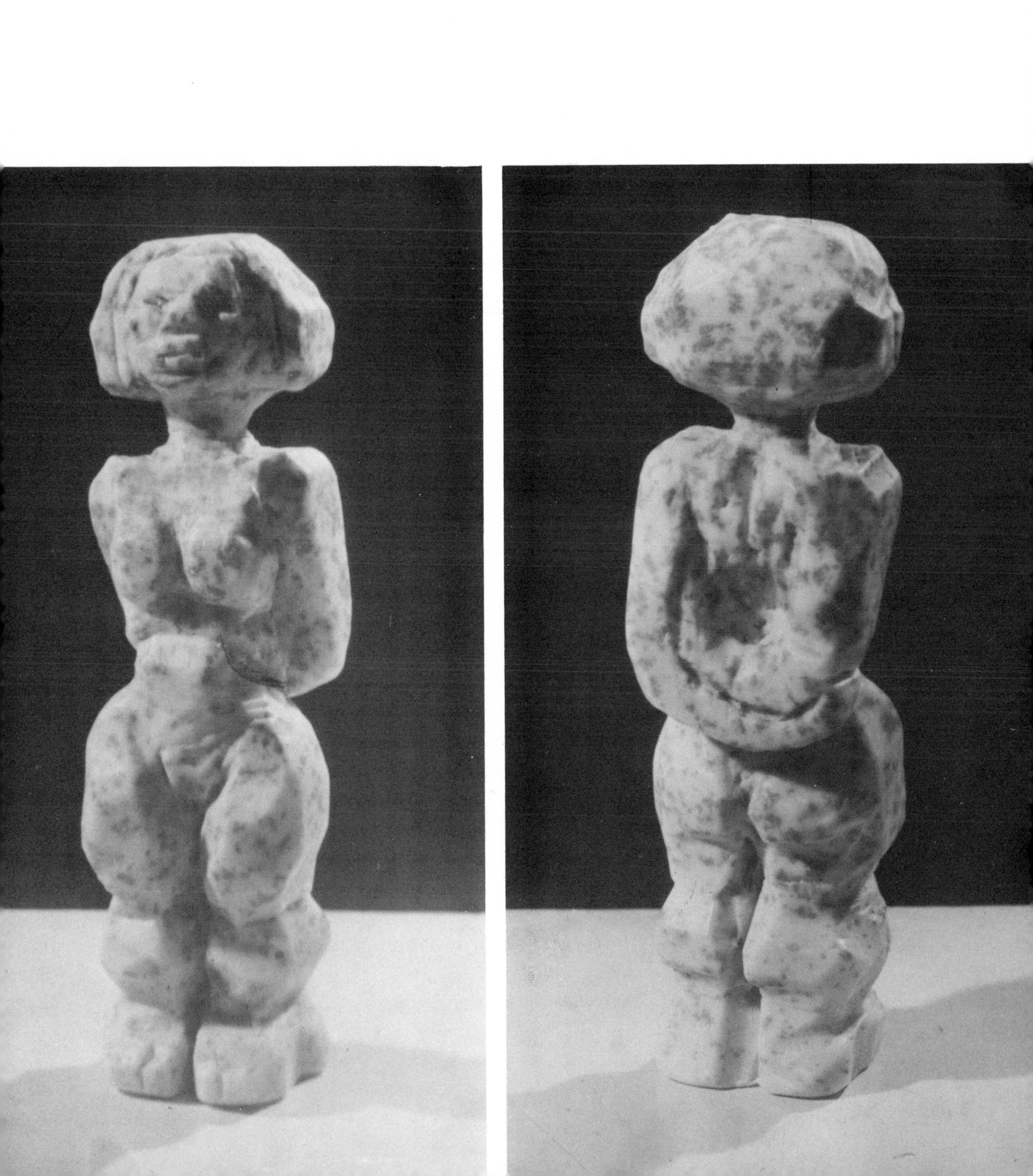

SOAPSTONE

A great boon to the amateur sculptor has been the popularization of varieties of soapstone by commercial companies. They have appeared in art supply shops everywhere, blocks of soft beautiful stone along with simple tools for their cutting. It is to be counted among the few notable contributions to the artist's lot that commercialism has made in our material world, comparable to the enterprises which have made available good prepared colors in tubes and the uniform blocks of plasteline. The distribution of a wide choice of Sculpstone (the trade name for many varieties of soapstone) in not too expensive blocks should make for a popularization of the carving medium. Soapstone is durable and soft, a combination devoutly sought in carving material.

It may be cut with a penknife. Its grains present a relatively small problem for consideration in the cutting process and the hazards of chipping and splitting are small.

The stone is available in many colors and textures, some of which simulate (without artificial effort, but by their natural appearance) much harder stones such as marble, jade, etc.

The same carving problems pertain as in soap.

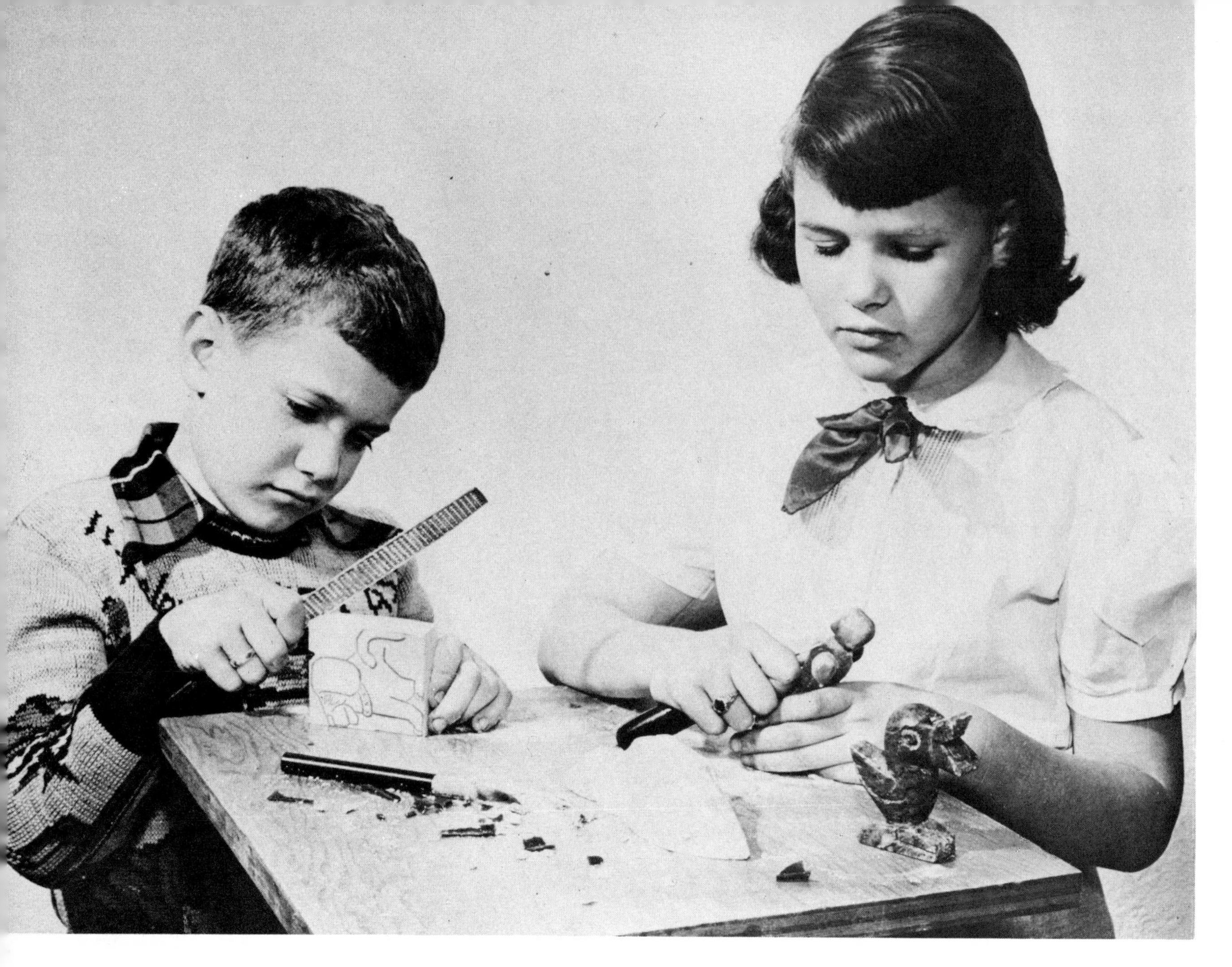

Children work in soapstone.

Jacques Heliczer, sculptor, works on Sculpstone.

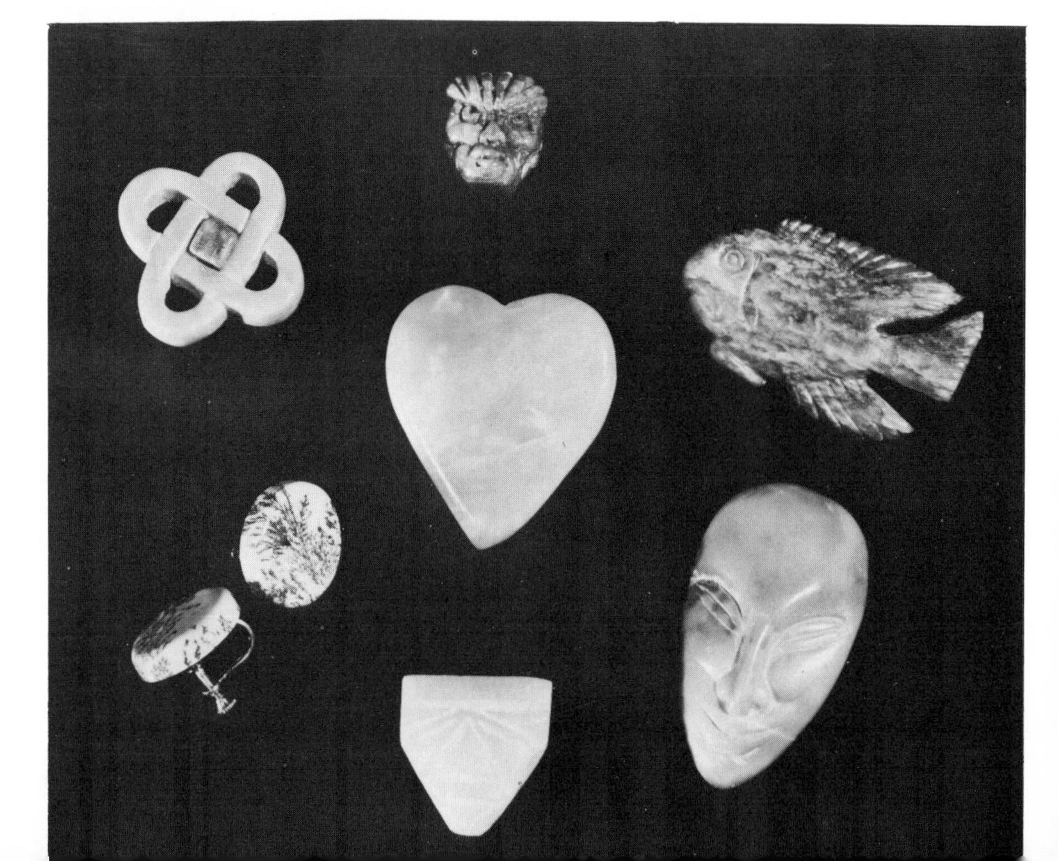

STONE

Lying within your block of stone is a beautiful shape in a rich three dimensional volume, prepared to say for centuries to come, "I was released by the skill and imagination of an artist who tore me out of the surrounding stone where I have been hidden for countless centuries."

It is a great privilege to enter below the surface of a stone which has taken millions of years to form. It should not be taken too lightly. Beautiful stone must be treated with the reverence due its age and dignity.

But do not let it frighten you. It will oppose you at every turn, fighting hard with its rigid resistance and tricky reins to prevent you from finding in its labyrinthine depths the forms you seek. That opposition only adds to the fun and, more important, to the quality.

It is difficult to be trivial in stone. On the way to trivia, should you have the bad taste to desire it, you must pass through stages of the monolithic simplicity which inevitably comes before overworking, excessive detail, and smallness of concept destroy it.

The sculptor is fortunate who can follow this inverse process of reducing rather than building. He is given an opportunity to stop on his penetrating way and examine what he has uncovered and to decide, based on his sense of taste and restraint, when he has done enough chopping to reveal the forms desired in their purest and strongest character.

The Egyptians knew when to stop magnificently. Their stones have the great virtue of implication rather than overdocumentation.

Stone in itself has the virtue of implication. It implies strength, dignity, permanence. Do not try to do in stone what can be better said in a less restrained and restraining material.

STONE SPLITTING In order to work on a stone quite close to the ultimate size it will be when carved it is always best to break a large stone to the proper size. This is better than attempting to chop, by slow stages, a small figure from the large piece.

To split a stone, score a groove into the stone all around the area to be broken away. The groove should be about one inch in depth. It may be made with your print chisel. Then, at intervals of perhaps five inches, drive a heavy chisel deeper into the groove, working around the stone. It will split evenly after a few of these are driven.

One can have a stone cut by a stone saw at any builder's workshop or at a tombstone cutter's place. They, of course, can cut exactly the shape you wish and their cut will be even, whereas, a split stone may be quite irregular in its break.

COMPOSITION Three dimensional organization of structural planes and emphasis on what is important to the vitality of the piece are sculptural characteristics most to be desired in composing.

In order to achieve such sculptural quality, it is sometimes necessary to abandon realistic proportions and details in favor of arbitrary forms which are perhaps distortions, but contribute more to the composition than would the natural.

In carving, the material to be used is always of the same hardness from the beginning, in the rough block, all the way to the final stage of finish.

It is inevitably more laborious than the modeling process, but the labor has its own compensating pleasure and, to me, at least, it is a more exhilarating, satisfying process of achieving a concept.

Direct carving allows for few mistakes. Greater concentration is required, for corrections are impossible without a modification of one's original plan.

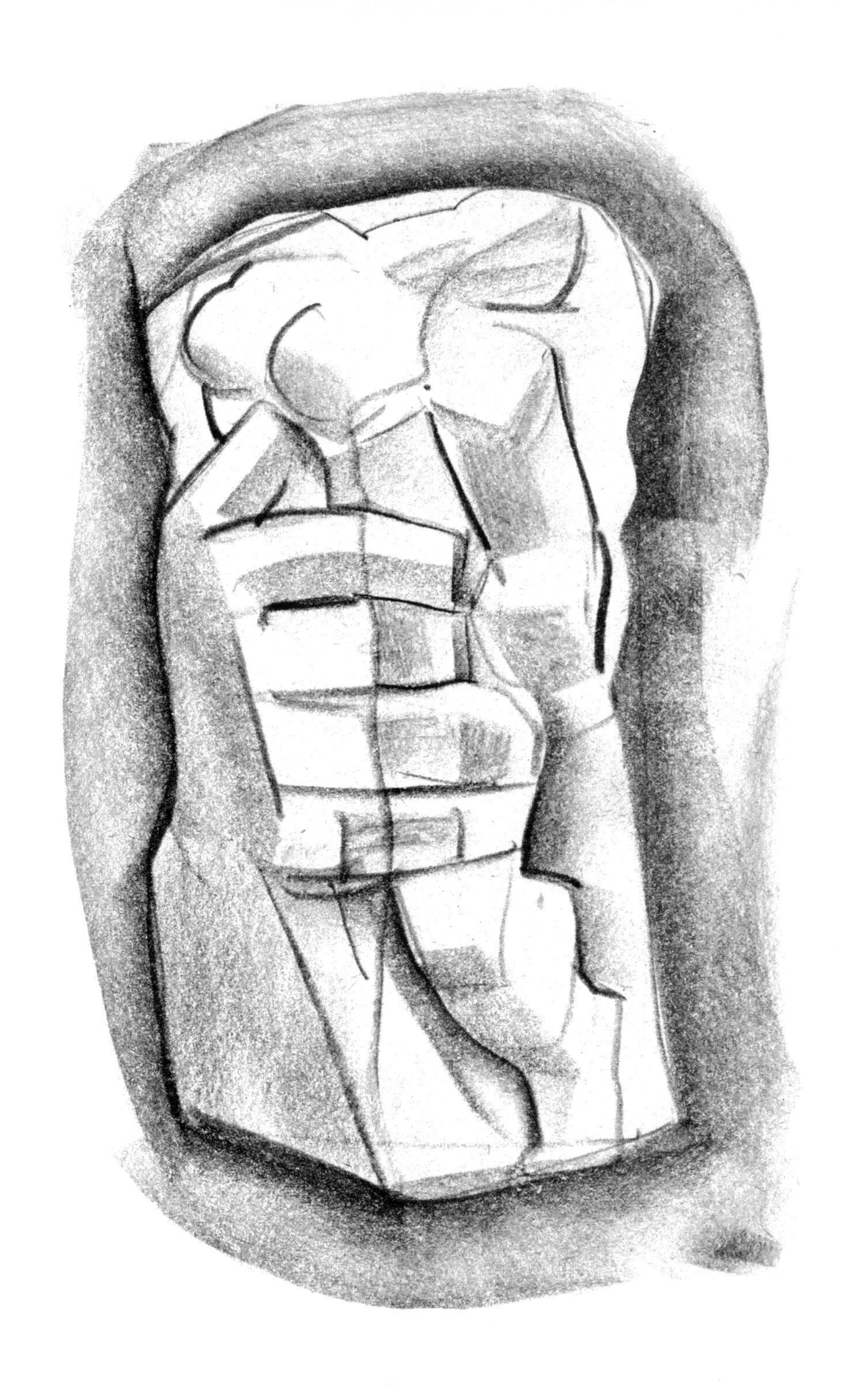

LIMESTONE COMPOSITION Every successful piece of sculpture is a composition in that it has a planned relationship of form to form, a purposeful direction to one movement in contrast to another and a general allover pattern of planes, masses, and line which give it unity.

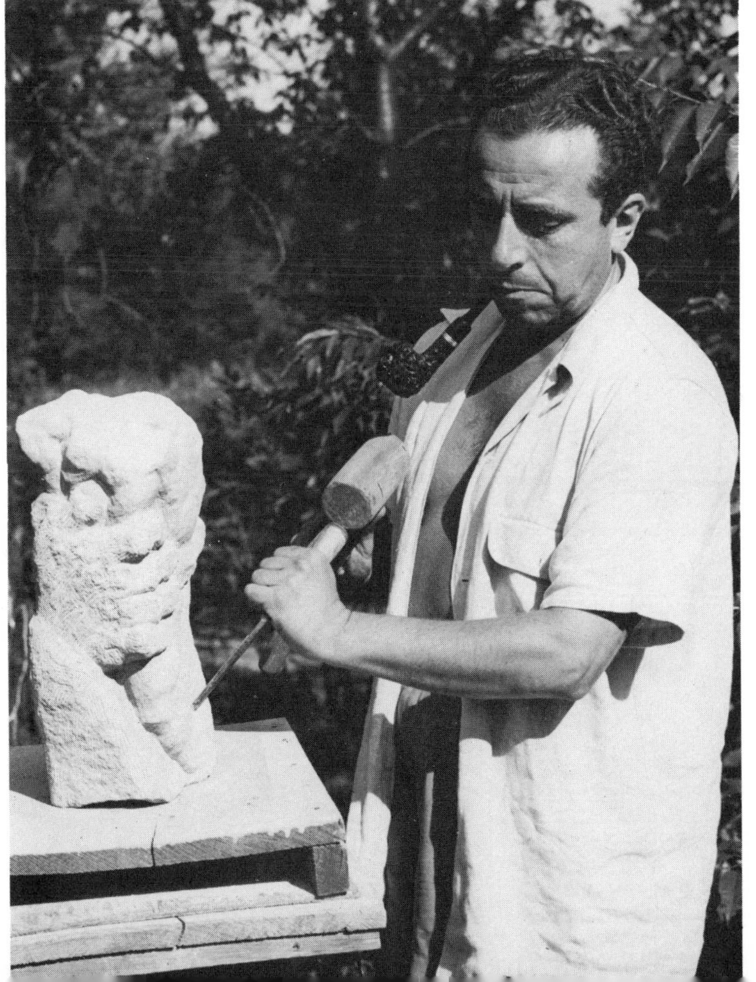

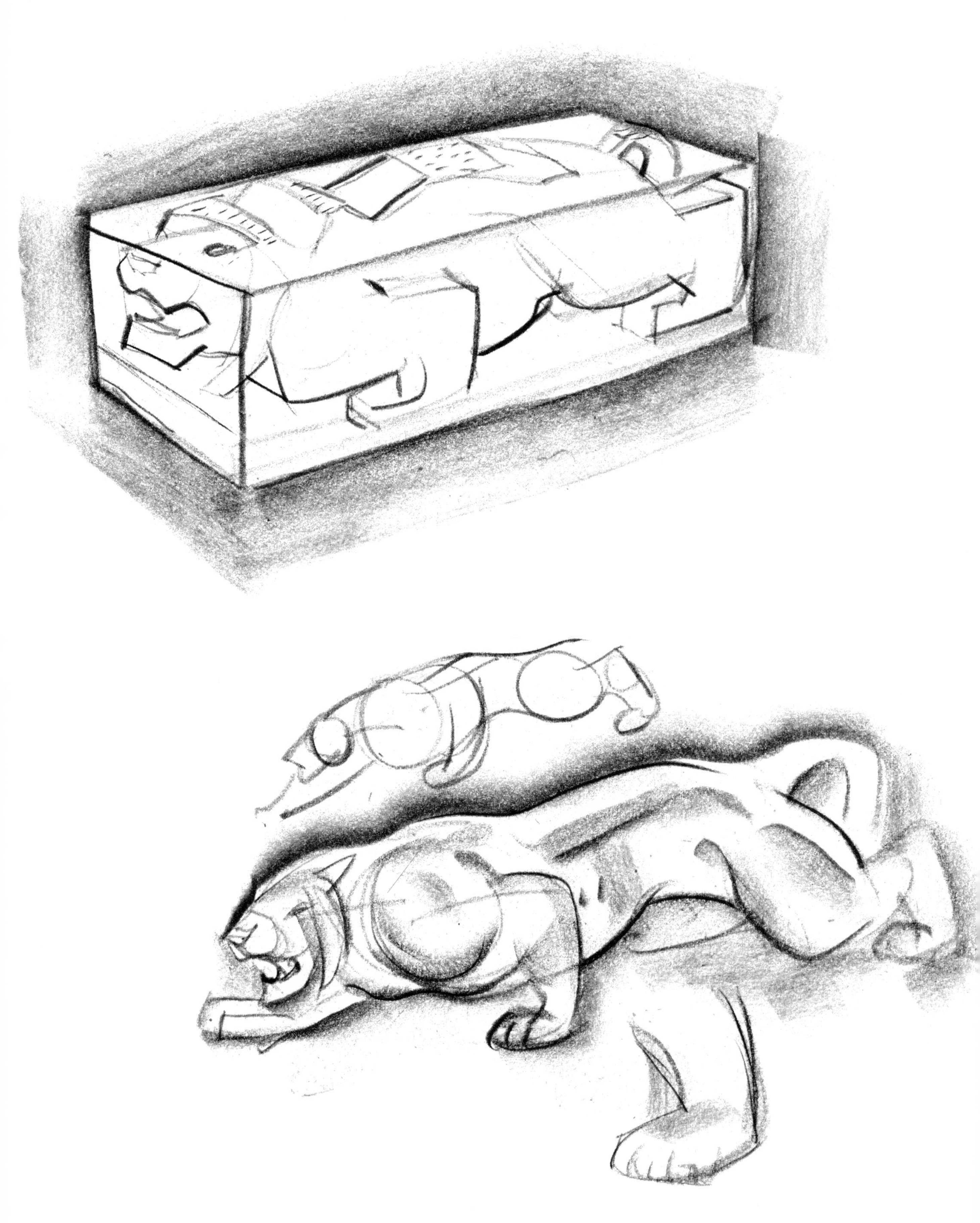

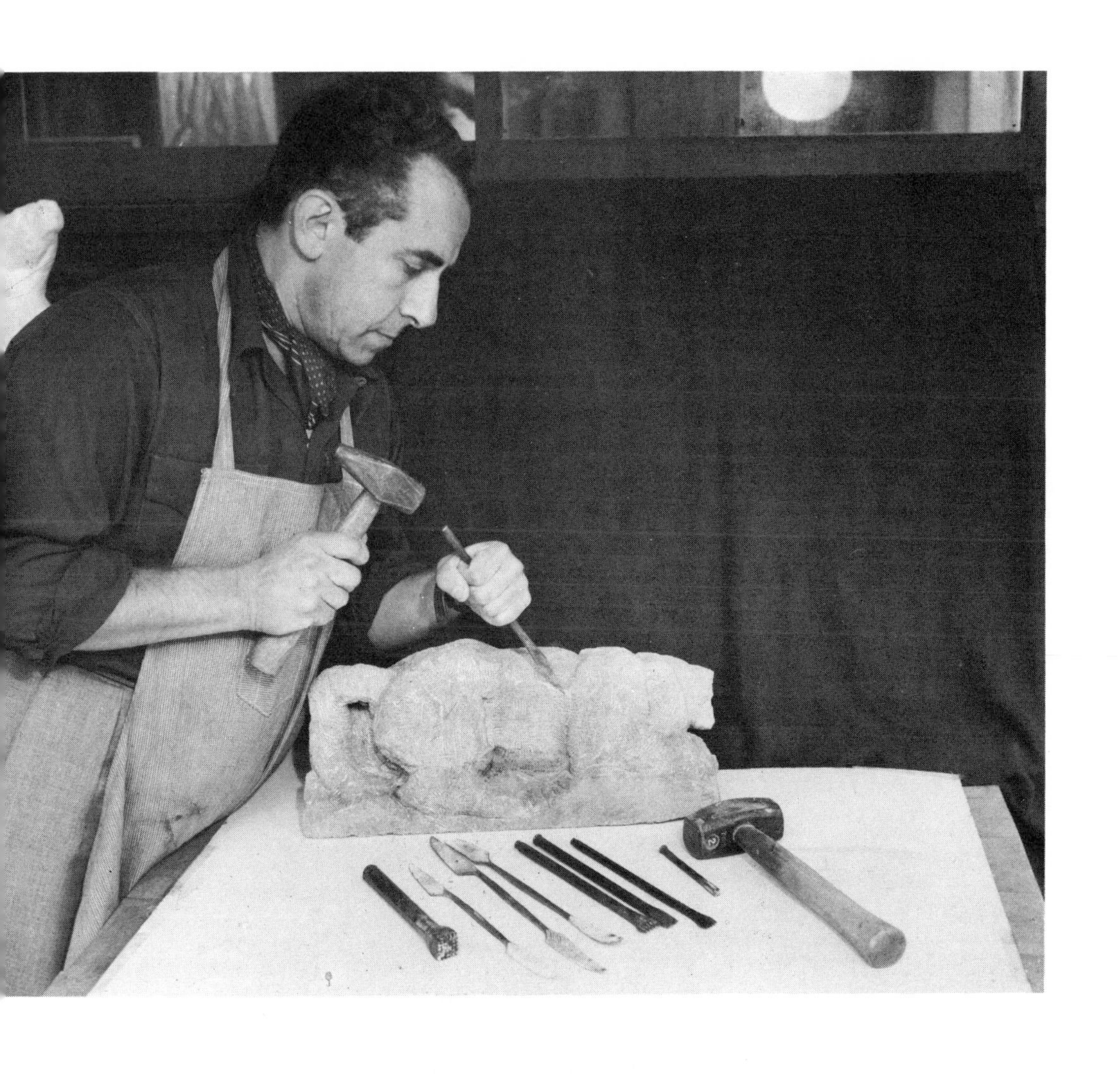

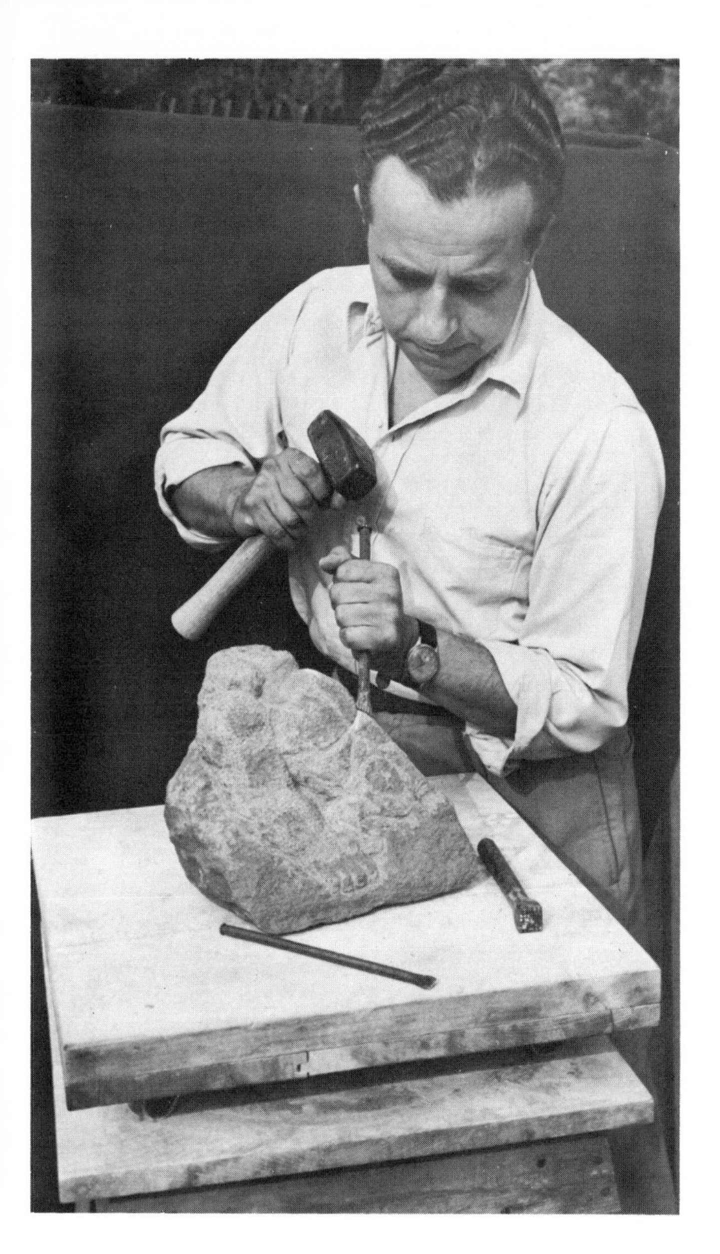

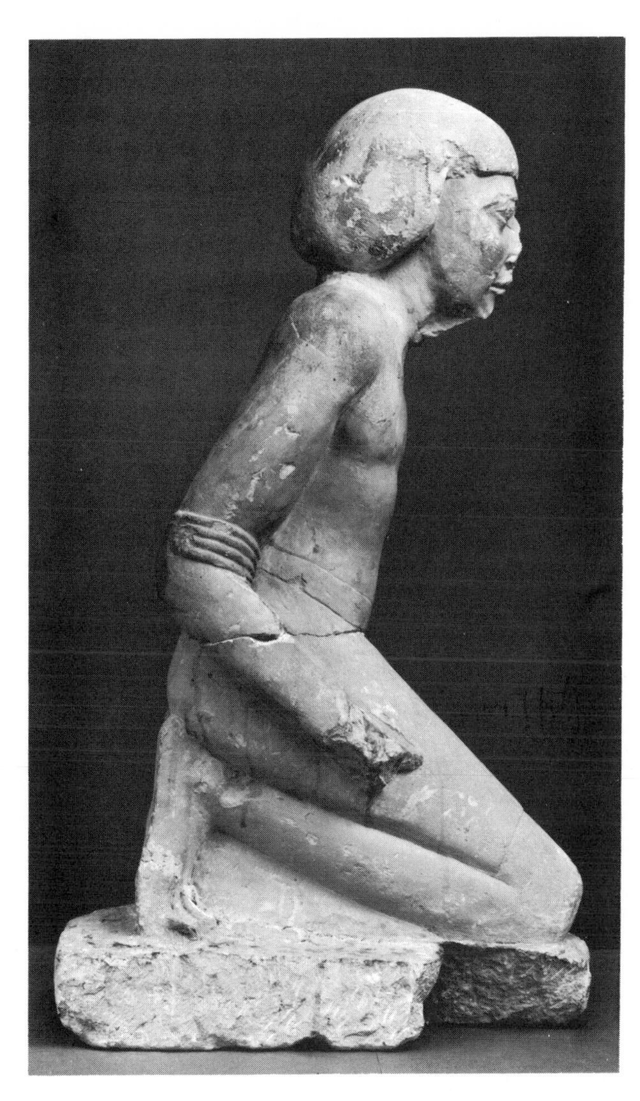

"Statue of a Captive." Egyptian, Sixth Dynasty, about 2400 B.C. Limestone.

Red granite statuette of granary official. Egyptian, Fifth Dynasty, about 2500 B.C.

MARBLE

Marble has always been a most popular stone for sculpture for many reasons.

Durable, relatively soft, it exists in many varieties of color, grain, and texture. It may be given a high polish, or its original rough surfaces may be allowed to remain. In either case, it is a stone of distinction.

It is indigenous to many places—virtually every state has some variety of marble. It is relatively easy to procure because in our cities where demolition of fine old buildings is constantly taking place, good pieces of marble are often found and cheaply bought.

It is important to test the stone for flaws before you begin an ambitious carving project. A flaw can ruin many days of work. Pour water over the stone. Dark streaks of suspicious difference from the normal grain marks imply flaws. Such a piece must be avoided, but sometimes a flaw may not be detectable by surface manifestations when wet. You must take your chances and when a flaw is encountered during the working, use your ingenuity in working around it or through it carefully. It is not always fatal to the carving and sometimes its discolorations may add to the interest of the patina.

Marble which is grease or oil streaked should be avoided because the streaks are probably quite deep, marble being very porous and absorbent.

Another test for flaws is by the "ring." A metal hammer should give a clear even ring against the stone except where flaws of any great depth appear. These areas give a dull "off" sound which are clues to the size of the flaws.

When you have found a stone of a size and color to your liking turn it about until it stands securely. When it is most comfortable, it is in its natural balance and ready for working.

TORSO IN MARBLE A decision as to what to carve is often dictated by the shape of the stone on hand at the time. Every sculptor has lying about in his studio odd-shaped stones, some broken off a larger block, others picked up at various times because they were good stone though he had nothing in mind suitable for that particular shape at the time of purchase.

When finally he approaches that stone, a concept must be tailored to some extent by the given space involved. On the other hand, the accidents of shape often suggest the subject, for the story to be told lies close to the original shape.

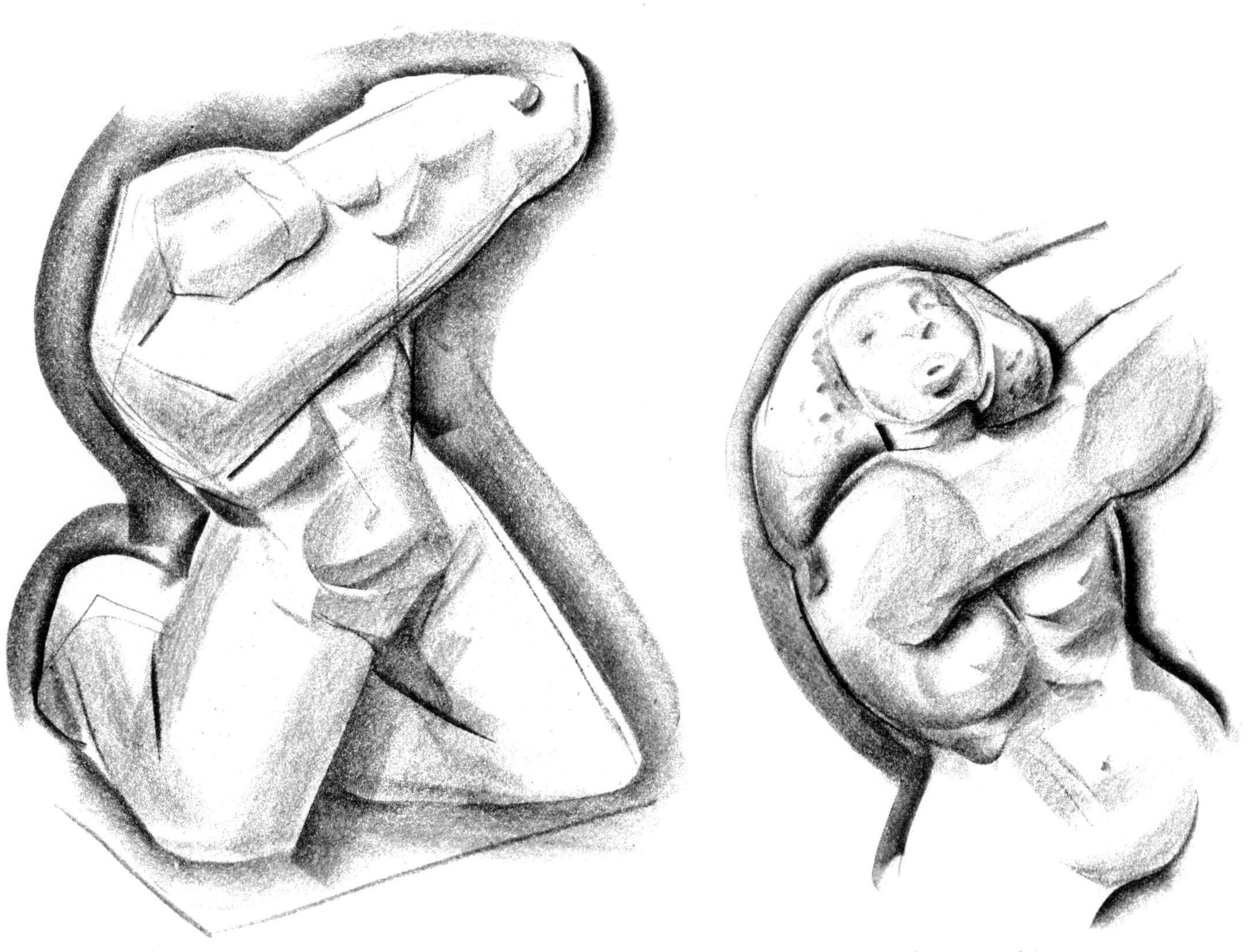

This was the case in the carving of the following torso in white marble. The odd-shaped piece, a sort of a squared-off dumbbell shape, called for some imagining in order to utilize its areas effectually. While the stone's shape must not solely rule your decision as to what to do, there must be a certain give and take involved. The stone says certain things to you and you make your reply in relation to it.

After turning the stone on all sides, seeking its natural base and balance, there followed the mental process of "seeing" the theme in the shape. The dynamic theme of the symbolic mother and child evolved in my mind's eye out of the shape of the stone.

A rough diagram of the movement and its possible scope within the shape followed. The next sketch blocked out the planes and masses and acted as a guide to the cutting.

Other sketches, like the shoulder, torso, and head-detail sketch, gave additional sources to which to return during the carving process.

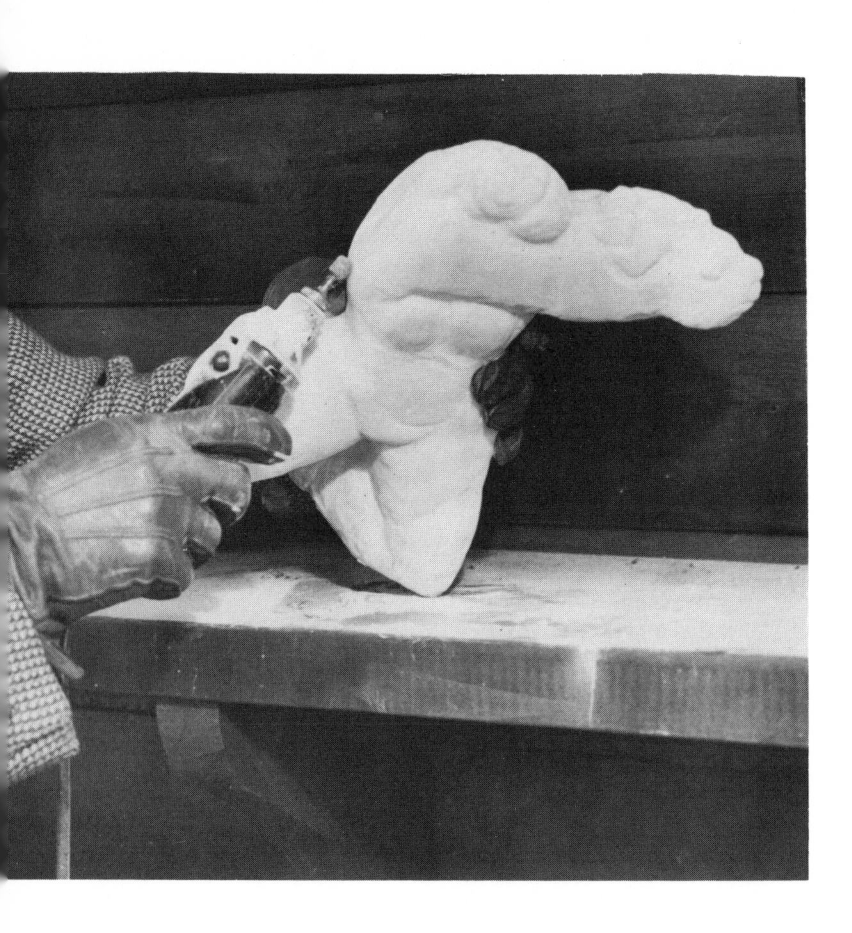

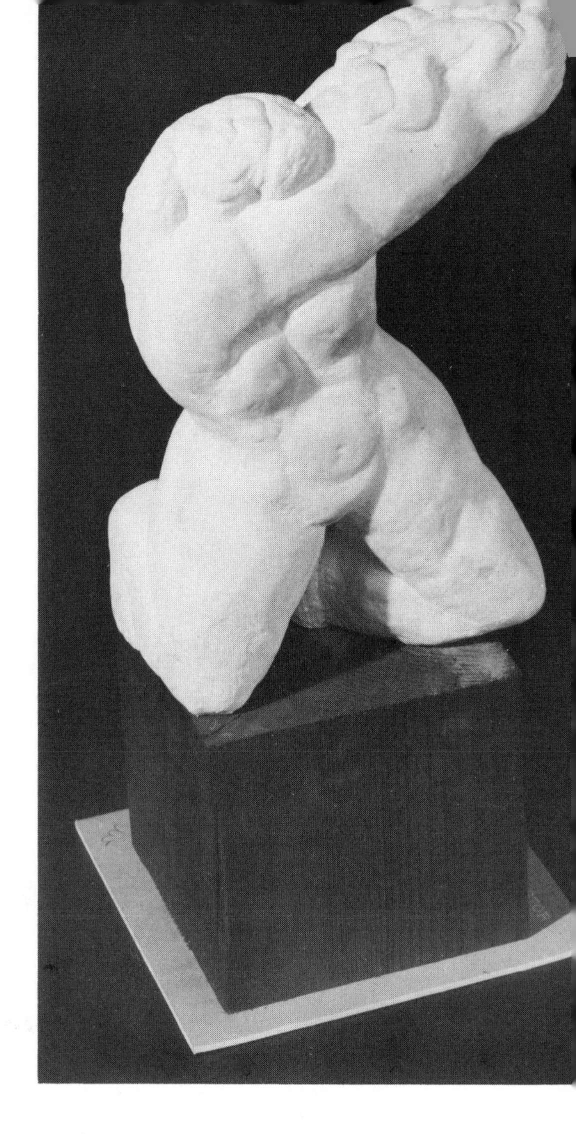

The next step was the roughing out on the stone after drawing a few lines of direction directly on the surface.

Since the final figure was to be quite close to the original shape there was no question of chopping away huge chunks. The parts to be cut were relatively small, the tools were necessarily the lighter, finer ones, and the mallet blows short and light.

The projecting arms called for strength and the decision not to make them slim was partly guided by this material reason and partly by the nature of the theme, the concept being that of elemental motherhood, and, as I saw it, it was to be a powerful symbol in monolithic strength.

While the arm forms were strong, there is always danger when chopping on a projecting ledge of stone. An inner flow or too hard a blow can easily break off such a ledge. Gentle, short, strokes of the mallet on a shallow angle cut of the tool minimizes such risks.

The only cutting in any real depth involved was that of the area between the thighs, although this, too, was suggested by the original shape.

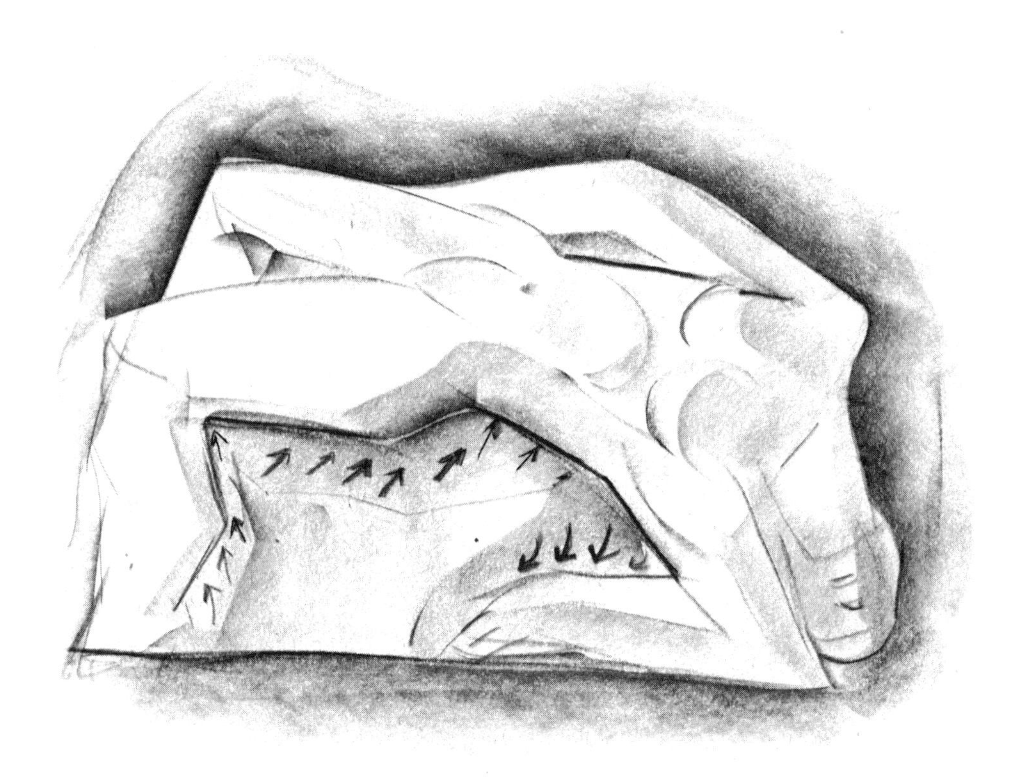

Marble block in which the figure conforms to the original shape of the block.

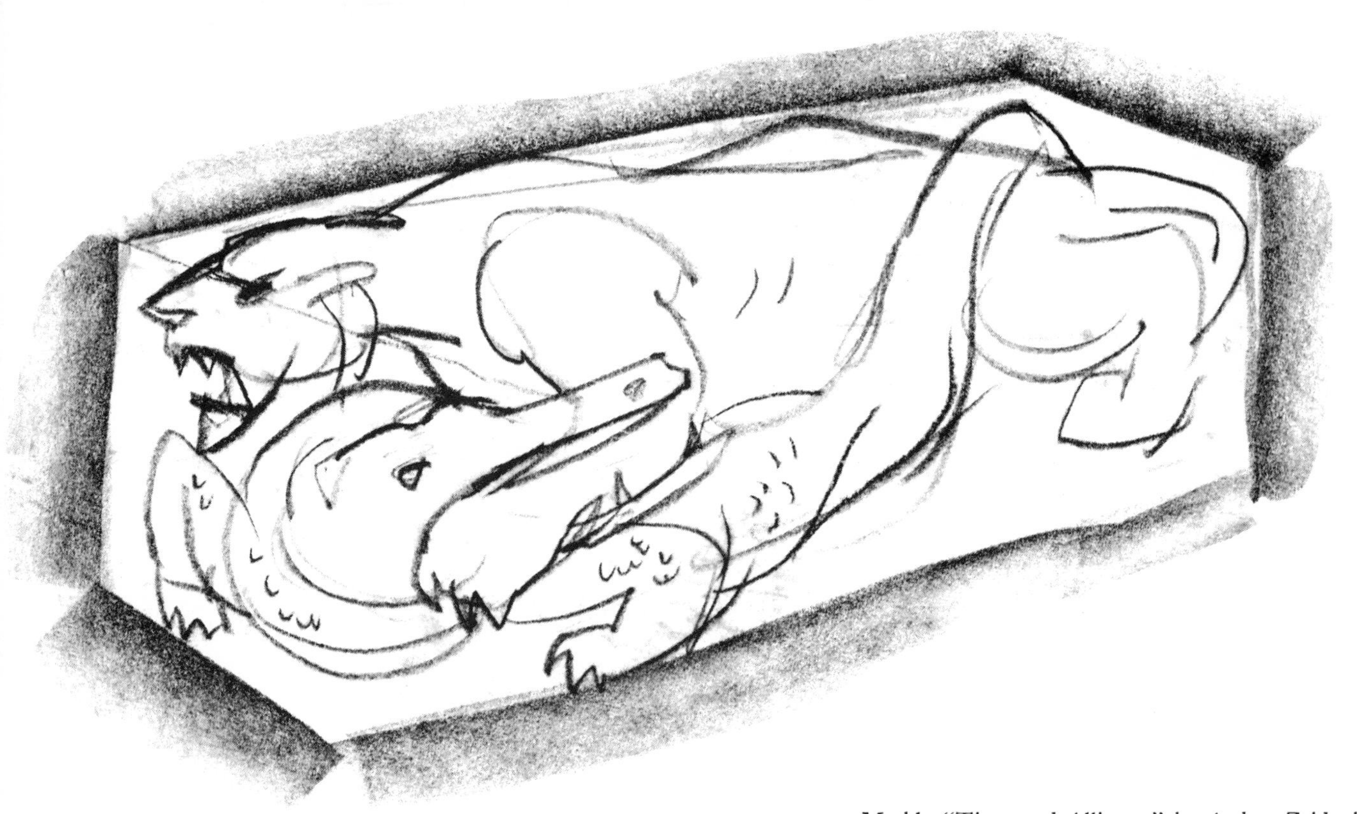

Marble "Tiger and Alligator" by Arthur Zaidenberg.

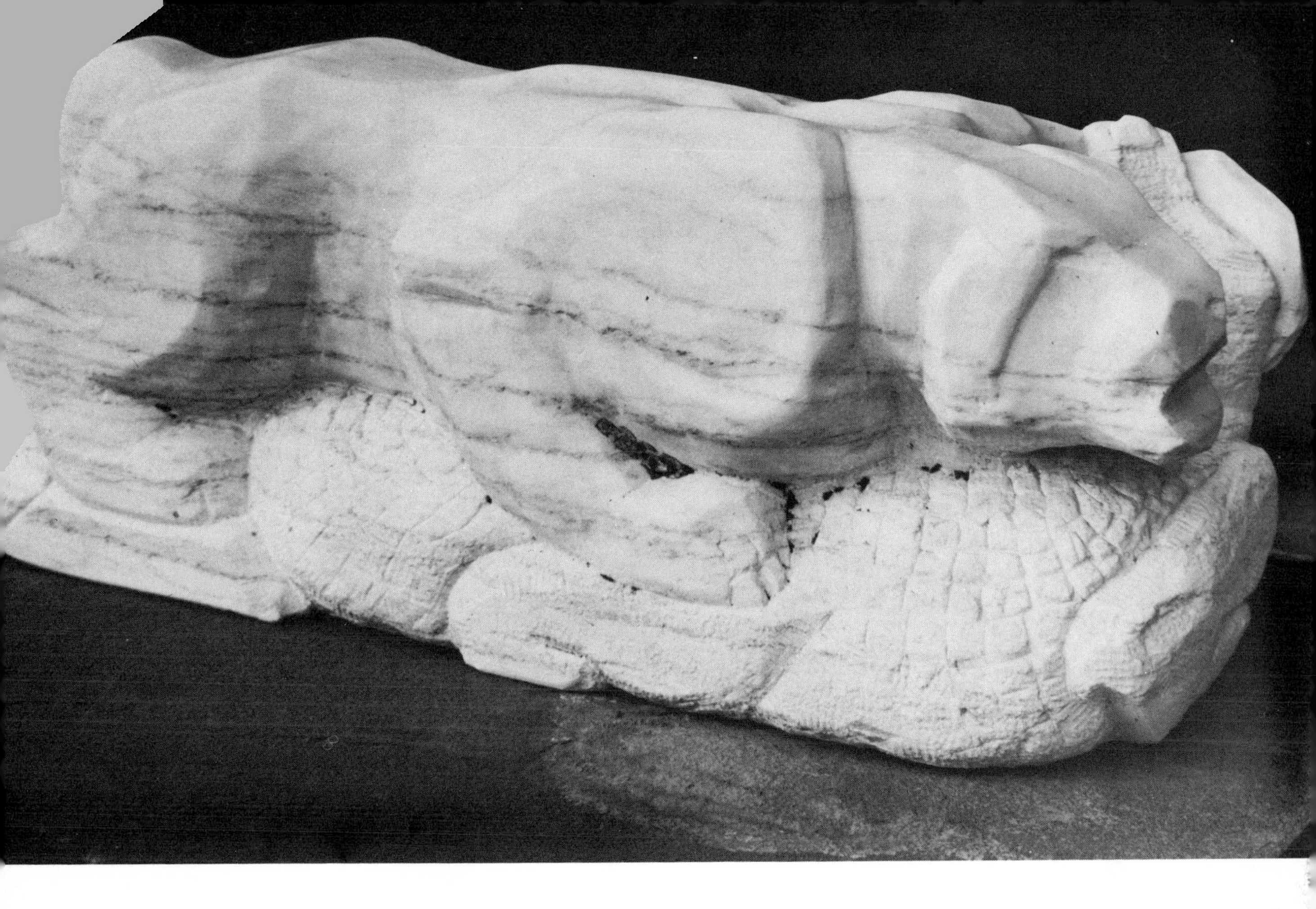

These three views of an animal composition done in Vermont marble exemplify the rugged simplicity in which a stone should be carved.

Avoid deep holes or slender protruding forms both for practical reasons and for aesthetic ones.

This marble was relatively soft. It pulverizes rather than chips under the blows of the mallet and powders easily under the rasp.

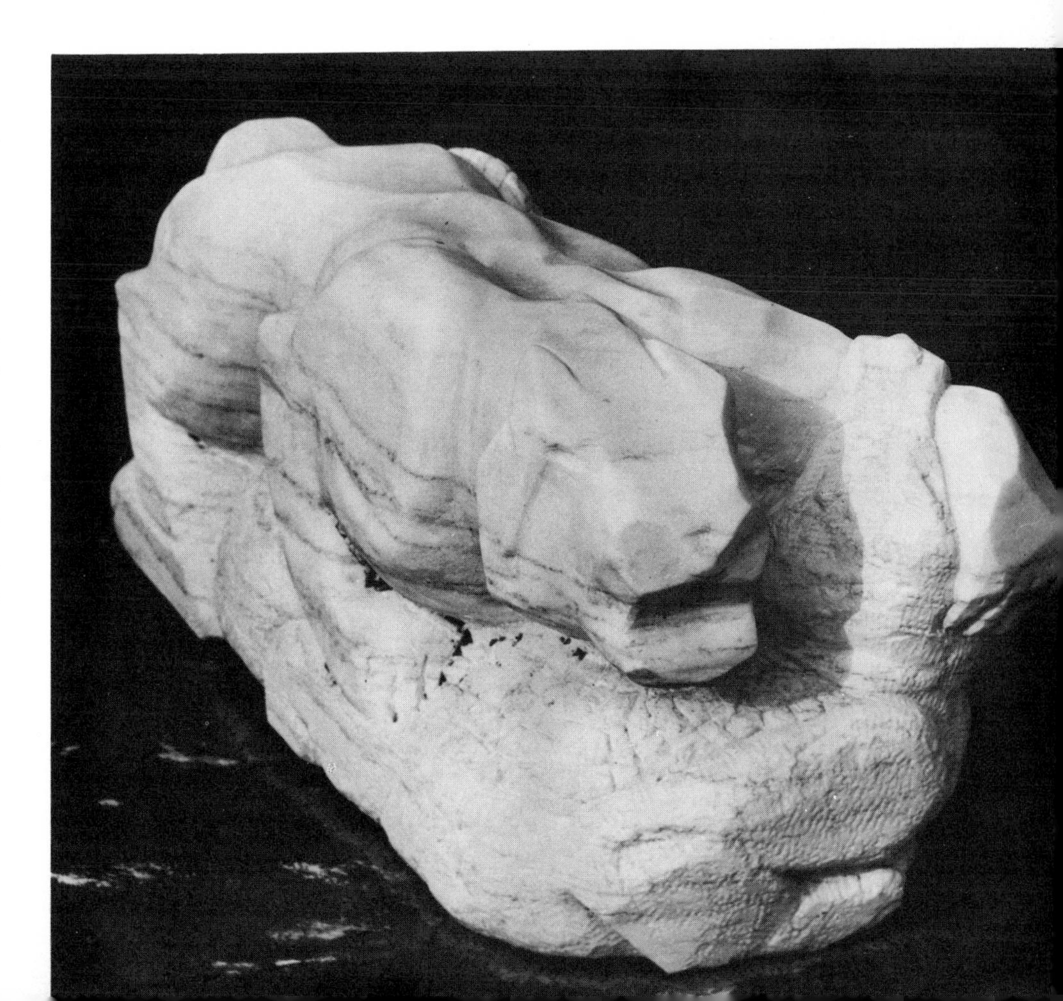

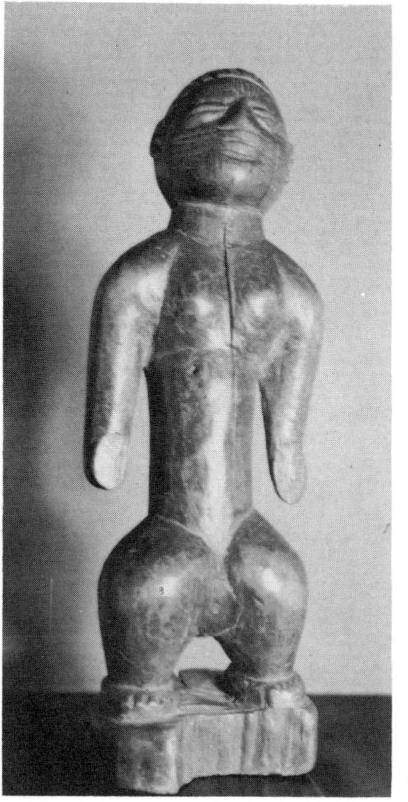

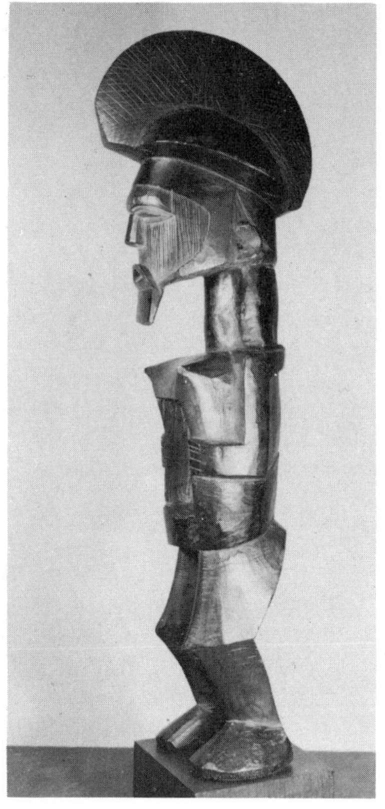

WOOD CARVING

Most of the sculpture we have inherited from the past is carved sculpture. This is not due to the fact that carving was more popular than modeling, but rather that the durability of a substance which must be carved is greater than that of the modeling materials.

Most of the work which remained is in stone, the most durable of sculpture material. A considerable amount is in wood, a substance which, though quite vulnerable to worms and rot, is not so easily shattered by a blow and, therefore, has survived many vicissitudes of time and maltreatment.

This is a very complete set of wood carving tools, including sharpening stone and oil. Such a set of tools is only necessary for quite ambitious projects in hard woods.

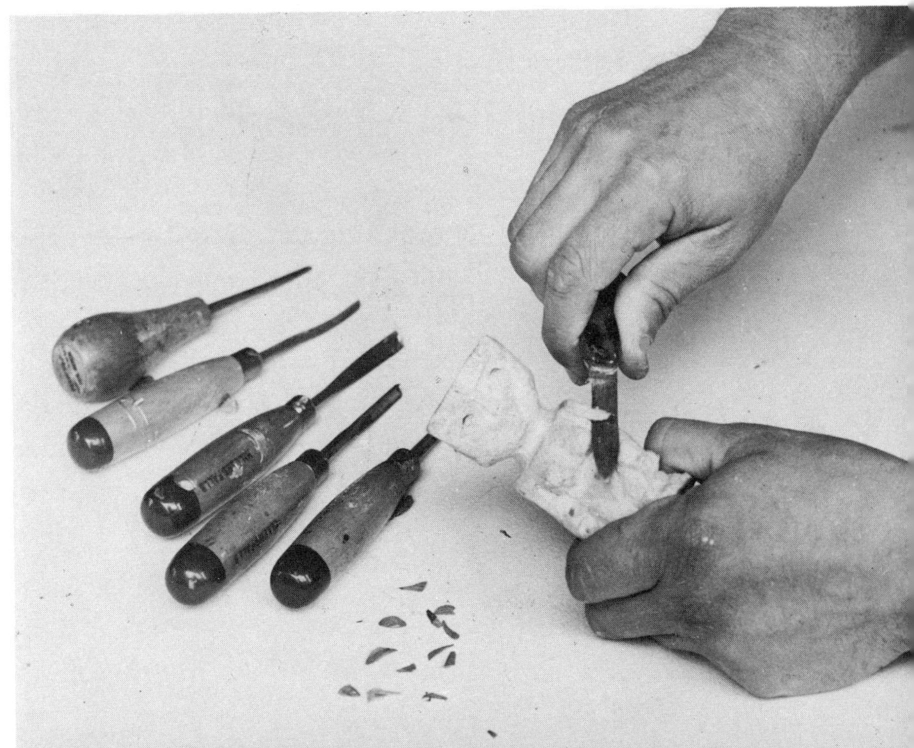

Wood is ubiquitous, cheap, and relatively easy to carve. The approach to carving wood is essentially the same as to carving in stone. The tools employed are different.

The visualization of your figure in wood is guided by several considerations not present in stone. The direction of the grain, a more serious issue in wood than in stone, helps decide your forms, for you must cut with the grain and not against it. Wood lends itself to freer play in the matter of gesture and action, being by its nature softer and less heavy in appearance. That which can be carved becomingly in wood appears forced in stone.

A good, smooth wood to carve is mahogany. It cuts evenly and freely and is most pleasant to work.

When in search of wood at your local lumberyard see to it that you ask for seasoned pieces, well dried. Try to get a block which sits firmly on its own base and then shore it up solidly with other blocks as indicated in the sketch. If you have a work bench with a strong rise, set up your block on that.

Walk around the block, study its grain directions. See what they have to tell you. Properly exploited, the flow of the grain in a block of wood can contribute enormously to the beauty of the finished piece. Sometimes in this preliminary study you will find your theme in the grain, a flowing suggestion waiting to be released by your chisel.

Draw your concept roughly on the four sides of your block. They will naturally not jibe completely. You have much cutting and rounding to do before your sides will co-ordinate. But, you can begin to visualize the ultimate figure if you have indications of the road you are to travel to reach it.

It is, of course, best to make a plasteline model of your projected figure, but your paper sketches are a great help also (and the two are not mutually exclusive).

Begin gouging out the shape roughly, following the grain of the wood and using a deep gouge and a wooden mallet. Try to cut with long even gouges, holding the chisel at an angle to the wood which will allow free easy strokes to drive it.

Work your roughing out procedure evenly all around the figure. Do not try for detail until the whole concept stands in simple, monolithic strength, ready for detail.

Now approach your wood with smaller gouges, well sharpened. Good sharp tools aid in giving crispness to your work and pleasure in the doing of it.

Most of the details and finish can be achieved with small gouges and wood chisels. If a smooth finish is required, use various qualities of sandpaper and finally a coat of floor wax.

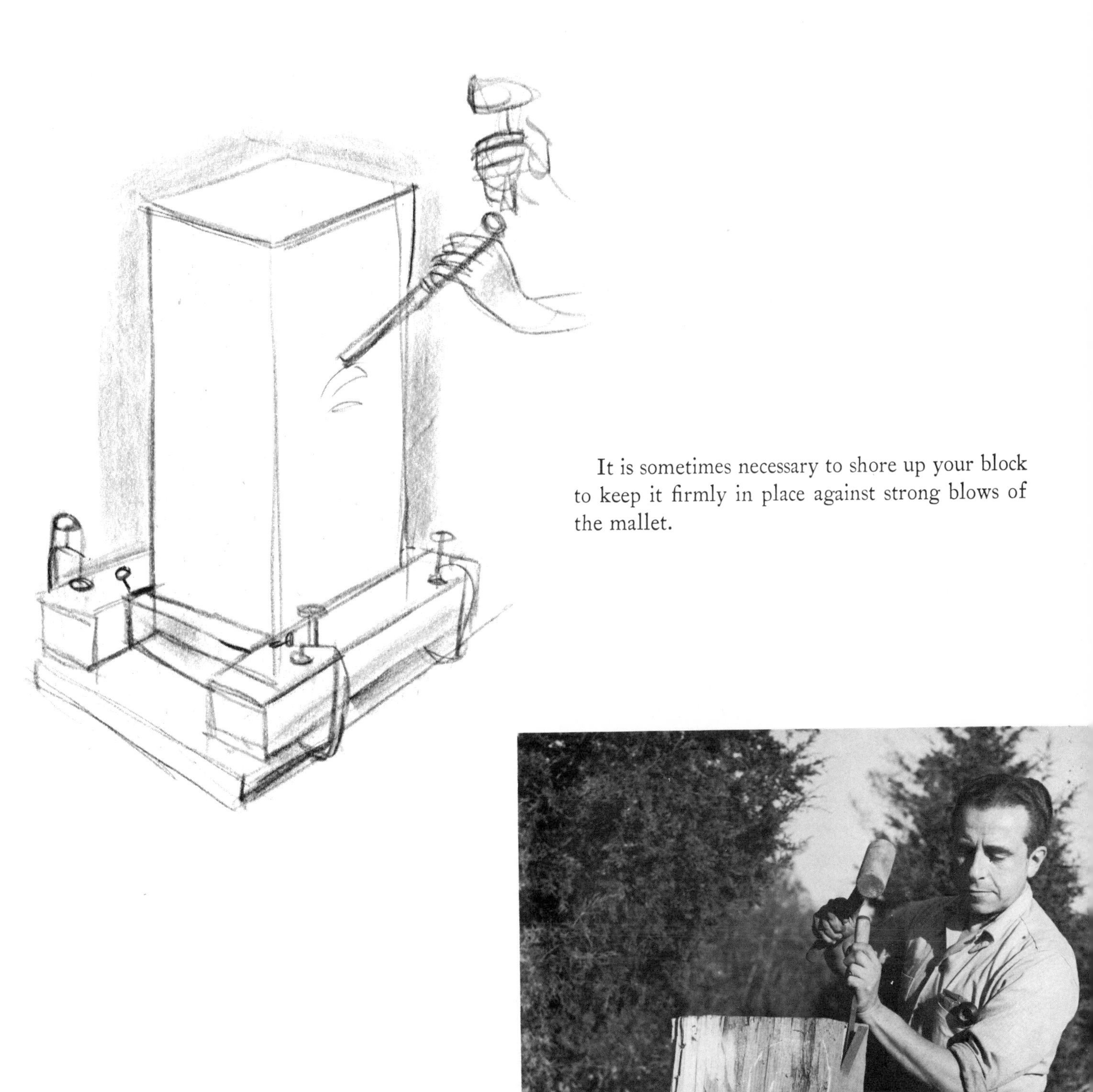

It is sometimes necessary to shore up your block to keep it firmly in place against strong blows of the mallet.

WOODS

The great variety of woods adds much to the variety of sculpture. Different materials cause different types of work. The commonplace pine wood and various soft woods plentiful in certain areas makes for ease in cutting and therefore causes a tendency to add detail and elaborations which would be difficult in hard woods. Areas where hard woods are the most prevalent produce sculptors of greater austerity in their concepts.

It is important to choose the right wood for the character of the work you plan. Balsa, the lightest of woods, would not be a suitable medium for monumental simplicity. Ebony would not be right for cute little figurines, undertaken in a light wood.

The discipline imposed by a hard wood is a good one, but one should be careful that the physical struggle does not dull the concept with evidence of laborious effort. On the other hand, the ease with which a piece of pine or balsa may be whittled should not tend to lead you too much to littleness and overstatement.

You must be in control of your medium; its intrinsic virtues may be utilized to advantage, if the wood is a partial influence and not your master.

Here are some woods you may use:

Ebony—a dark wood almost black; when varnished or polished, very black. The blackest natural ebony comes from Madagascar. The texture is very compact and hard. Its fine pores and its great durability makes it a most esteemed wood for sculpture.

Mahogany—a hard, fine porous wood, very durable, and almost insect proof. Mostly dark.

Boxwood—hard, heavy, and durable, yellow in color. Because it is to be had only in small pieces, it is used for pieces of small proportion.

Pine—there are innumerable species of pine wood which may be carved. A relatively soft wood, it offers a grain problem, and only certain species are durable.

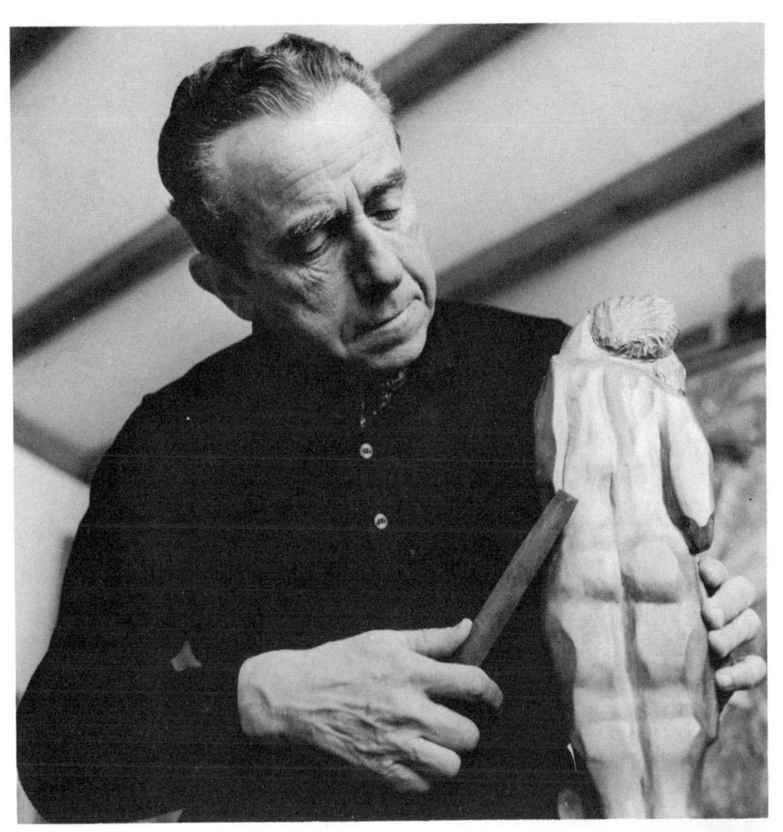

RELIEF

When a sculptured piece is raised in volume against a flat plaque, it is called a relief.

One may work in bas-relief (low relief) or haut-relief (high relief). Sometimes a relief is a full-bodied figure projected from the plaque, but in most cases, the front and two sides of a figure are shown raised from the flat plane.

The raised figure or figures are intended to convey the impression of full bodied roundness even though the rear view is not possible. This, in a sense, eliminated one of the special virtues of sculpture, that of being able to "walk around" a piece. It places the relief sculptor in somewhat the same category as the painter—it is more of a pictorial art. It may, however, be a medium of unusual distinction and many great sculptors have used it magnificently, particularly for architectural decoration.

Methods of working in relief as in all sculpture vary with the medium used.

The modeling process is, as in three dimensional work, a building-up procedure, the carved relief is the whittling away of areas, leaving the untouched surface in relief.

RELIEFS

Here is the general approach to modeling a panel in relief.

A base plaque must first be made of your working material for modeling either clay or plasteline. This flat plaque should be regarded as the canvas upon which you will execute your raised design.

Make your plaque about 1 inch thick. This will allow for a firm foundation for your relief forms and also give sufficient depth for intaglio or engraved aids to your sculpture. A perfectly flat surface for your plaque, such as a large drawing board or any level surface (wallboard or fiberboard), should first be prepared. Shellac it, and then tack two parallel strips of wood on the outer edges of your proposed plaque size. Now fill the area in solidly, between these two "curb" strips, with well-rolled sausages of clay.

When you have built a solid area of clay, shave the surface evenly by run-

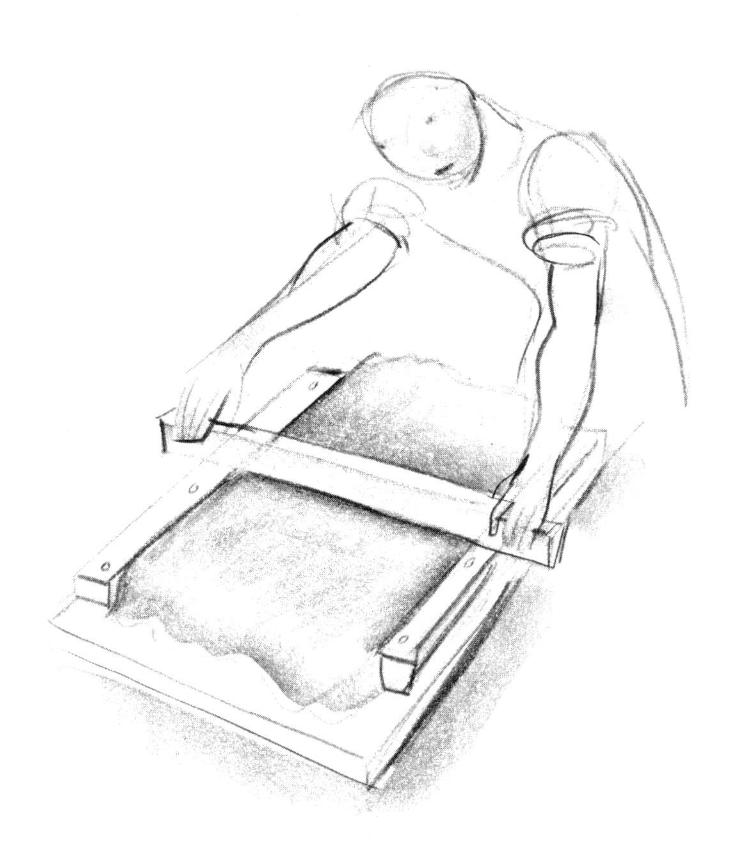

ning a wooden ruler edge or a long even strip of wood up and down over the clay, the strip's edges resting on the curb strips. You now have a working surface about 1 inch thick evenly distributed throughout the square (or oblong) plaque. You now proceed to scratch your design in this smooth surface.

When you have drawn your scratch outline you have a choice of procedures. You may scoop out to a depth of perhaps ½ inch all around the outlines of your drawn design, thereby throwing the drawing into relief against a lowered background. Or you may simply regard the base as a platform upon which you add clay to build the figures of your design, raising them above the surface of the plaque. Your raised figures will, of course, be three sided rather than four, the fourth being suggested within the flat plaque area.

You may also combine the two methods described here, using both the cut around and the build up. The choice of methods depends entirely on the needs of your concept.

Sculptors have worked in such high relief as to make their plaque a vertical background for virtually four-sided figures.

CARVED BAS-RELIEF

The most common method of relief is that by which the figures are thrown into raised contrast by lowering the bed of stone around them. Sometimes the bed is hollowed somewhat more in the neighborhood of the contours of the figures.

The Egyptians sometimes hollowed deeply immediately around the figures leaving the figures flat in relief against the hollow, but on an even plane with the remainder of the stone "bed." This method, aside from being decorative and different, also served to protect the figures, the high bed guarding it from accidental injury and effects of time and weather. This method may also be considered as valuable in saving the time and effort needed in sinking the entire surrounding bed.

Another system of relief carving is for the bed and the surface of the figures to be on the same level with just the contours sunk by grooved lines. Of course, this allows for very little modeling of the figures. The result is actually silhouette.

MOBILES

ALEXANDER CALDER, a splendid artist of great inventiveness, gave us the first fine mobiles and thereby added a new dimension to the concept of sculpture.

When the balanced shapes were suspended by a slim wire affixed to the ceiling, the sculptures began to move and dance with the slightest breeze, and the balanced forms turned and swayed, changing the relationship of the forms to one another and varying the color, lighting, and position of those forms to the viewer's eye.

The fact is that *never* in a mobile is exactly the same aspect repeated, and to all intents and purposes endless numbers of different sculptural forms are evoked by one well-planned work.

The most successful mobiles are abstract in design. Abstraction seems to lend itself best to the ever-changing character of the moving forms. However, figures have been used successfully on occasion when the kinetic play is used thoughtfully.

Mobiles may be made of almost any materials. Cardboard, plywood, and even heavy metals, if properly balanced, will float gracefully in the air.

These mobiles are cut from one piece of plywood and bent into rhythmic patterns of design which turn in the breeze.

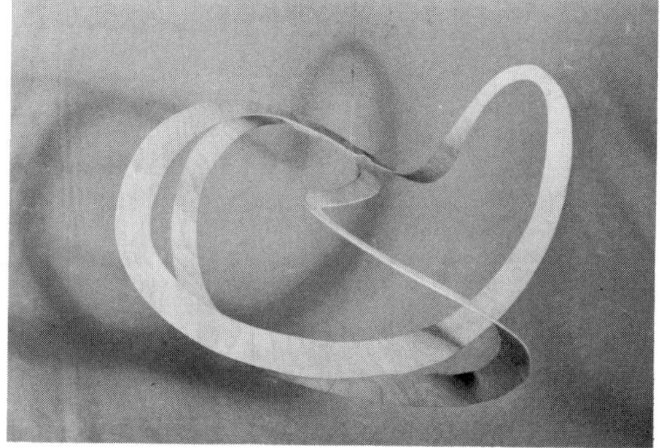

Two mobiles of plywood by John McClellan.

HOW TO PRACTICE MAKING MOBILES

1. Suspend a horizontal length of lightweight rod from a hook in a ceiling beam or from the top of a doorway by a nylon string (fishing line is excellent) or by lightweight wire, so that the rod may be slipped easily along the knot and balance adjustments can be made easily.

2. Suspend, by short nylon string, wires or forms from each end of the original rod. When the added objects are unequal in weight and balance must be restored move the rod to the right or left and thus compensate for imbalances.

3. Continue adding structural forms suspended from either end (or both), always readjusting weights and balances for both good design and even suspension.

Here are a few suggested first-principle mobile designs.

Once you have acquired a feeling for balance of your structural forms, you may become as complex as your sense of engineering and design allow.

Mobile of origami-folded birds suspended from a branch. By Valerie Beere, age ten.

Plywood mobile turned by small motor affixed to ceiling. By John McClellan.

CONSTRUCTIONS

ANOTHER medium of expression which is currently popular among sculptors of imagination who seek to depart from the classic and traditional is that of "constructing."

Under no compulsion to be restricted to the anatomy of figures or the utilitarian limitations imposed upon the architect, the constructionist sculptor builds flights of fancy answerable only to his own good taste. The rules imposed are his own. The materials for construction are as wide in range as there are objects in the world which are available for his creative urge.

Bone or glass, paper or steel, plastics or rocks, feathers or fibers—the constructionist may combine any or all of these.

Glue and epoxy, cement or nails, wire or rope, nylon thread or rubber bands all may serve as means of attaching parts to one another.

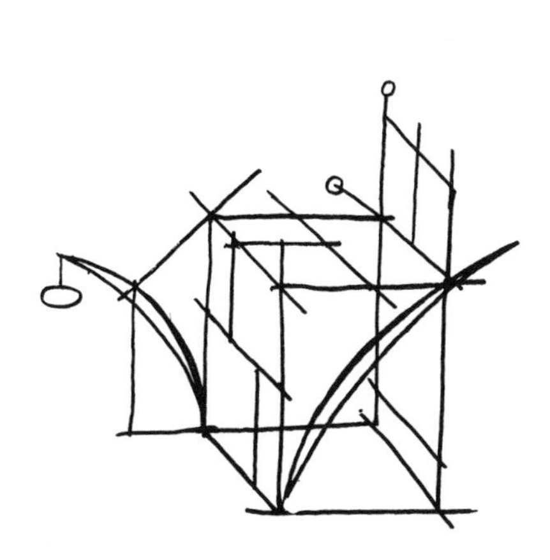

THE NEW AND THE DARING

ALTHOUGH all the traditional methods of sculpting are still used by many artists all over the world, a huge variety of daring techniques and uses of new materials, as well as the use of the classic materials in utterly new ways, have gained the attention of the art world.

Synthetics, plastics and plexiglass, electricity for kinetics, mobiles, and even self-destructive sculptures, magnets and changes in air pressure have all been employed by serious sculptors to contrive vital sculpture in which movement and physical change in the structures are part of the sculptural statement.

The freedom resulting from the release from traditional materials for sculpture has certainly produced many ludicrous excesses, though often not without interesting qualities.

The world has watched as "sculptors" wrapped entire buildings in thousands of cubic feet of plastic *empaquetage* or scraped swathes of sand over acres of beach and called these sculpture. Others have produced showers of resin or filled whole rooms from floor to ceiling with thousands of phallic symbols. Still others have utilized the tactile "feel of things" rather than their appearance as a form of sculptural expression.

And why not? These and the countless other vagaries of inventive and creative minds amuse and stimulate the beholder, and the student is advised to go to see them whenever possible or examine them in photographs reproduced in books on contemporary sculpture.

These highly individual sculptural forms, however, are not within the province of this book's teaching range. It would be entirely improper, as a matter of fact, to presume to teach the use of expressive forms so uniquely personal as those described above.

However, the vast range of new materials and the current trend to combine in multimedia structures several or many materials are rewarding sources of inspiration to the young sculptor and should not be discouraged by this author's preference for more conventional materials and themes.

APPENDIX

Where to Get Sculpture Tools and Materials

Sculpture House, Inc.—Tools and materials, also casting—38 East 30 Street, New York, N.Y. 10016

Ettl Studios, Inc.—Tools and materials—Ettl Lane, Glenville, Conn.

J. H. Monteath—Wood for sculptors—2500 Park Avenue, Bronx, N.Y. 10451

Alexander's Sculptural Service—Casting—117 East 39 Street, New York, N.Y. 10016

Sculpture Associates—Tools, wood, alabaster—114 East 25 Street, New York, N.Y. 10010

Stewart Clay Company—133 Mulberry Street, New York, N.Y. 10002

(Most of these houses furnish catalogues on request.)

A letter to Sculpture House will get you information as to where sculpture tools and materials are obtainable in your locality in the U.S. or Canada.

BIBLIOGRAPHY

Barr, Alfred H., Jr. *Picasso, Fifty Years of His Art.* New York: Arno Press, 1968.

———. *Cubism and Abstract Art.* New York: Arno Press, 1968.

Hale, Nathan Cabot. *Welded Sculpture.* New York: Watson-Guptill, 1968.

Kultermann, Udo. *The New Sculpture: Environment and Assemblages.* New York: Praeger, 1968.

Licht, F. S. *Sculpture: The Nineteenth and Twentieth Centuries.* History of Western Sculpture. Greenwich, Conn.: New York Graphic Society, 1967.

Meilach, Dona, and Seiden, Donald. *Direct Metal Sculpture: Creative Techniques and Appreciation.* New York: Crown Publishers, 1966.

Read, Herbert. *Art Now: An Introduction to the Theory of Modern Painting and Sculpture.* 2d ed. New York: Pitman Publishing Corp., 1960.

———. *A Concise History of Modern Sculpture.* World of Art Series. New York: Praeger, 1964.

Rood, John. *Sculpture with a Torch.* Minneapolis: University of Minnesota Press, 1968.

Wilenski, Reginald H. *The Meaning of Modern Sculpture.* Boston: Beacon Press, 1961.

THE AUTHOR

ARTHUR ZAIDENBERG says of himself:

"I have always painted. Sculpture came to me relatively late in life and it now consumes virtually all of my time.

"I studied at the Art Students League and the National Academy in New York, then went to Paris on a scholarship and attended the Beaux Arts and worked with André Lhote. I also studied in Rome, Munich and London.

"I believe I have painted more murals in public buildings than any other painter in the United States. I have traveled around the world seven times, and executed murals for many hotels and for the S.S. *Rotterdam*. My work is in the Metropolitan Museum of Art and the Brooklyn Museum, and I have had many one-man shows in New York City and other places.

"My wife and I now live six months of the year in Woodstock, New York, and the other six in Mexico, where we have built our own house."

Born in Brooklyn, Mr. Zaidenberg has written many successful books in the field of art, and has illustrated handsome editions of *The Plays of William Shakespeare, Thaïs* and *Against the Grain.*